PROLIFERS
a novel

PROLIFERS

a novel

Revised Second Edition

Michael William O'Malley

Title: Prolifers a novel
Author: Michael William O'Malley
Publication Date: January 2011 by IngramSpark
Publisher: Gospel of Life Publications

Published in the Philippines by Sanctity of Life Publications
PO Box 8060
Paranaque Central Post Office
Paranaque City
Philippines 1700

Website: www.prolifersanovel.com
Email: feastofinnocents@yahoo.com

Copyright @ Canada 2011 Prolifers a novel
ISBN 9780986692208

Library and Archives Canada Cataloguing in Publication
O'Malley, Michael William, 1948
Prolifers a novel / Michael William O'Malley

ISBN 9780986692222

1. Title
PS8629   M315P76 2011   C815'.6   C2011-900067-9

Revised Second Edition
Copyright @ Canada Prolifers a novel Revised Second Edition 2021
published by IngramSpark

ISBN Print Book Prolifers a novel Revised Second Edition 9780986692222
ISBN Ebook Prolifers a novel Revised Second Edition 9780986692239

All rights copyrighted and reserved.

"The greatest destroyer of peace today is abortion."

—Mother Teresa of Calcutta

AUTHOR'S NOTE

What is it like to be a pro-lifer in a pro-abortion society? What is it like to be an aborted woman? Is there a connection between the sexual revolution of the nineteen sixties and legalized abortion? Do pro-lifers have any hope to end abortion and restore legal protection for the right to life of unborn children? Or is the neighborhood abortion center now a permanent new institution in our society?

This novel explores those story questions among others. **The book has a harder, more detailed, concrete edge than the usual Christian pro-life novel, including explicit even graphic scenes of sex, rape and violence.** This is a realistic novel. Conventional wisdom in the publishing industry is that it is impossible to write a good novel from the pro-life point of view. Such a book they say would be moralizing and preaching rather than good story telling. Publishers also consider that books about abortion won't sell, that no one wants to read about it.

Yet the passionate struggle over abortion is an important story, with huge stakes involved, frequently commanding news media attention, and playing a prominent part in contemporary politics. So why is the subject a problem in writing and publishing creative fiction that finds a readership?

There is nothing like a good story to read for a while. That was my goal as a novelist, to express the high drama of the pro-life opposition to legal abortion. It is a story of ordinary people in their daily activities up against powerful forces and beset by their own human limitations, but they are not going away.

1

When Sadie Summers arrived at the crisis pregnancy center she pushed the door of her boyfriend's dented Mustang open with her shoulder, stepped out the passenger side onto the sidewalk, and stopped to turn around, leaning half over to look back at Rick sitting behind the steering wheel.

'You coming?'

'I'll wait here.'

'You'd better.'

Rick shrugged. Sadie took one last dig. 'You don't need any more. You still stink. I can smell it from here. I can practically taste it.' He closed his eyes.

'Animal.' She said.

'Just go.'

'The car is freezing by the way. As bad as out here.'

'What do you expect? It's a convertible in winter, and the roof is ripped.'

'You promised to fix it.'

'What do you expect?' The patch was glued but didn't hold. I'll have to try again.'

'Before next summer I hope'

Sadie swung the damaged car door hard so it would close, hearing the dull thud of metal on twisted metal. She turned and looked at the house, which she had expected to be an office building. She hesitated for a moment, wondering if she was in the right place, but then saw the small sign on the side of the house: **CRISIS PREGNANCY CENTER**. She strode down the walkway to the front door, the high heels of her winter leather boots clicking on the cold cement, grabbed the doorknob, and blasted through the entrance like a bomb exploding, slamming the door behind her with a crack as loud as a gunshot.

Julie, the receptionist in the outer office, swiveled her chair to look at the new client, her skin shivering at the chilly air blowing in with Sadie through the doorway. The new client's disruptive entrance startled her. Julie's baby Jeffrey sat on the floor, banging his rattle on the vinyl tiles, fascinated by the sound and the sight of the changing colors inside his toy. He lifted his eyes to look at Sadie's noisy arrival. Sadie looked down at him, and said, 'I don't want a baby.'

'Please come with me,' Julie said, not wanting to talk to her. A single mother, Julie wanted to help women in a crisis pregnancy, but she was young, and was nervous every time the telephone rang, or someone walked through the door. She wished Mickey was in his office at the back, but he was in court, dragged in front of Judge Dockendorff once again. Julie led Sadie into the counseling room with her baby Jeffrey crawling on the floor behind them, and introduced her to the woman sitting behind the old desk: 'This is Dolores.'

Sadie sat on the very edge of the chair facing the desk, ready to talk to Dolores in the inner office room. Julie picked up Jeffrey and left them together, closing the door behind her as she withdrew. Sadie said it again: 'I'm not having this baby.'

But your baby is a baby, Dolores thought, looking across at

Sadie seated so close in front of her, only the desk between them. Now was not the time to reveal the Center was pro-life. She needed some time to talk to Sadie first.

'We can help you here.'

'I want it done fast.'

'You seem upset. What happened?'

'My stupid boyfriend.'

'What did he do?'

'I caught him smiling at my sister.'

'Just smiling?'

'It was that kind of a smile. She was smiling back. They did it right in front of me.'

'Did what? Do you think they're having an affair?'

'I don't know if anything happened, but the smile's enough. He likes her. I saw right through them. He saw me watching him, and then looked away. He was guilty.'

'You don't trust him?'

'He's cheated on me before. There's no way I want him or his baby. He's an animal.'

Dolores felt for the miraculous medal she kept on a silver chain hidden beneath the high neckline of her dress, the medallion with the engraving of the Virgin Mary standing on a snake beneath her feet. She found comfort there when she touched her necklace. She said a silent prayer in her mind: Mother Mary, help me. Help me keep Sadie and her baby away from that terrible place across the street. She focused her attention on what Sadie said.

'Do you blame your sister?'

Sadie waved the suggestion away. 'I like my sister. She can

have him if she wants. I can't wait to get away from him. Smiling at another woman when I'm pregnant, flirting with my own sister, I'm not going to stand for it.'

'Did you talk to him about it?'

'He denied it, said it was nothing. He said I was imagining things.'

'Maybe it wasn't serious.'

'I know what I saw. When can I get it done? The sooner the better.'

* * *

'All stand. The Court of Queen's Bench, Judicial District of Calgary, is now in session, the Honorable Judge Lester A. Dockendorff presiding.'

Mickey rose to his feet at the court clerk's command, and Judge Dockendorff, wearing his black judicial robe, entered the courtroom through the door in the back wall behind the elevated judge's desk. Jessica Sterne, the lawyer for the Craigenback Abortion Clinic, also stood to honor the entrance of the judge. Her co-counsel stood beside her. Jessica Sterne always brought another lawyer with her to the hearings. The second lawyer never spoke, but it looked impressive to have a team of lawyers opposing Mickey. The Craigenback Abortion Clinic had arranged the emergency court hearing for an order to disconnect the Crisis Pregnancy Center's telephone, claiming false advertising in the phone book. Judge Dockendorff walked a few steps forward, paused for a moment standing in front of a prominent chair, upholstered in purple velvet for the judge, and made a courteous half bow towards Jessica Sterne. He did not look at Mickey Finnegan.

The only other people present were the court clerk, the court reporter, and the two extra security guards Judge Dockendorff always requested whenever the case involved pro-lifers. The guards stood by the opposite walls of the courtroom, their guns visible holstered on their belts, readily available. The judge took his seat of judgment, only four days before Christmas in this emergency hearing.

Judge Dockendorff enjoyed his jousts with the religious fanatics in the pro-life cases, besting them and putting them in their place. Most judges did not allow any mention of Christianity in their courtrooms; religion belonged in private life, outside the courthouse door, but Judge Lester Dockendorff indulged his peculiar taste for religious debate, among his other eccentricities. He lost no time either winning the religious argument, or cutting it off with his authority. Mickey Finnegan was always an interesting opponent, and Dockendorff alternated between almost liking him and despising him. Sometimes Mickey amused him playing lawyer, but when the legal issues were contentious and the debates heated Judge Dockendorff was firmly in control. A suave, well-groomed man, he was a member of the board of directors of several community associations in the city, and he could not have been more the opposite of Mickey Finnegan, who was regarded by the best people as at least faintly disreputable. Judge Dockendorff nodded towards Jessica Sterne: 'Counsel, you may begin.'

* * *

The Christmas wreath hanging in the window of the inner office of the Crisis Pregnancy Center glowed from real candle burning inside its circle of green holly leaves, enlivening the artificial light bulbs in the room. The wreath and candle smelled fresh, spreading warmth and cheer after the gray and cold winter day outside. The soft music of the Christmas carol Silent Night played on the radio placed on the bookshelf behind the counselor's desk. Sadie looked across at Dolores; the woman was old enough to be her mother. She seemed odd, with a plain shapeless tent of a brown dress covering her whole body up to her neck, her bobbed black hair, dark brown eyes and light brown skin, yet bright red patent leather shoes on her feet showing under the desk. The shoes were flats but flashy. Sadie saw Dolores looked like a sensible, middle-aged matron, but coupled with the suggestion of a wild exuberance. Sadie felt puzzled with her impressions of Dolores, not used to the way Filipinas were conservative yet liked bright colors.

'Strange seeing the baby crawling on the floor.'

'We let Julie bring her baby to work. Does seeing him bother you?'

'She's no older than me.'

'Julie's a young volunteer.'

'The baby's cute, it just seemed different. Like your office in a house.'

'Many people have their offices in a house. If you can find the right layout, it's a good way to go.'

Sadie noticed the large reference books in the bookcase, the covers displaying color photographs of unborn children in their mothers' wombs, the pictures taken with the latest fiber optic technology. Her doubts grew.

'Are you professional counsellors? Will you help me here?'

All is calm, all is bright-

Dolores swiveled her ample body in the office chair, reaching behind her to turn off the radio. She turned back to face Sadie. 'Our director trains us. We are volunteer counsellors.'

Sadie still looked suspicious of the strange new surroundings. 'Who's your boss? Who run's this place?'

'Mickey Finnegan.'

***

Mickey sat down and glanced behind him while Jessica Sterne took the podium to speak, Mickey looking beyond the wooden railing separating the judge and lawyers from the public spectators sitting in the wooden pews. No one was there, the benches empty except for a bored looking reporter from the Daily Record, and another reporter from one of the radio stations. Mickey was dressed in his best clothes for court, wearing a black blazer and gray pants, with a white shirt, a burgundy tie, and polished black leather shoes. Jessica Sterne matched him in her black pantsuit, with a white, open collared blouse, and high-heeled black pumps. They had faced each other before in other abortion cases, and both were well practiced in presenting their arguments, taking their turns standing at the centrally placed lectern between the two tables separating the plaintiff from the defendant. Jessica Sterne was a high priced lawyer, a senior partner in one of Calgary's largest law firms Fitch, Fitch, & Watson,

LLP, with nationwide offices across Canada.

Mickey's shaking hands almost betrayed him when he reached for a glass of water to ease his dry throat. He did not want Judge Dockendorff or Jessica Sterne to see his tremor. A trickle of sweat at the collar of his shirt dripped down his neck. The dark wooden panels lining the walls and the solid oak furniture spread their authority over him. The only other places he had to stand were in Sacred Heart Church with its soaring gray stone walls, just before the priest entered the central aisle to begin the procession at the beginning of mass, or at public events when the crowd rose to sing O Canada. In those places he was not trembling and sweating. Here in the courtroom he found himself deep inside Dockendorff's lair, a pro-life activist up against a judge who always ruled against him.

'Your Honor,' Jessica Sterne began, 'this case is a claim by the Plaintiff Craigenback Abortion Clinic against the Defendants Mickey Finnegan, Dolores Cruz, the Crisis Pregnancy Center, and others, for their false advertising in the new telephone directory-'

Mickey stood up. 'I object-'

'Sit down Mr. Finnegan, and wait your turn to speak. Please keep these proceedings civil.'

'Your Honor, I am making an objection. I am entitled to make objections in court.'

Judge Dockendorff was still not looking at Mickey, but spoke to him while reading some papers on his desk: 'Mr. Finnegan, I find you playing at lawyer offensive. I find you arguing with me offensive. If you insist on representing yourself, you are bound by the rules of court.'

'Your Honor, I am making my submissions and objections to the court as a lawyer should.'

'Overruled. Sit down Mr. Finnegan. Don't interrupt again. I want to hear what Ms. Sterne has to say.'

* * *

'Finnegan?' Sadie questioned. 'Wasn't he the man on TV arrested at an abortion clinic?'

'No relation.'

'Are you pro-life?'

'We are pro-woman.'

'But are you qualified?'

'We are here to help women in a crisis pregnancy. That can mean a lot of things.'

'Tell me about it.'

'Are you in a crisis?'

'Every day.'

'Pregnancy can be hard on a woman's feelings.'

'It's not pregnancy hormones, what Rick says. It's him.'

'What makes you think you might be pregnant?'

'I'm late. Very late. Something's wrong.'

Far better to turn the discussion around, to get Sadie talking about herself than answer questions about Mickey. How explain he lived and worked in the back part of the house as a full-time volunteer for pro-life, while the front of the house served as the Crisis Pregnancy Center? A single man who had never married, he made the sacrifice of working for pro-life with no salary. The pro-life center received no funding from the government or the churches, and did not charge clients for their counselling. Only a small band of faithful financial supporters donated money to the Center. Mickey used some of the donations for food to keep body and soul together, and lived in the house, with his bedroom in the back.

The location of the Center was ideal, just across the street from the Craigenback Abortion Clinic, also operating in a converted house on the same residential street. Dr. Craigenback wanted to keep a low profile, and displayed no signs advertising his abortion business. Sadie never noticed Craigenback's clinic when she arrived at the Center, intent on finding the address she found in the phone book. The house for the Crisis Pregnancy Center looked run down to her when she first saw it. The house was old, built a hundred years ago, but the pro-lifers were glad to have it. A generous benefactor gave them the house to provide an alternative to the abortion clinic. The elderly owner, a widow who lived in the house for sixty years ever since she was a young bride, said she could not bear to live in the neighborhood anymore after Craigenback moved in. She said it was time she accepted moving into the nursing home. Watching her beloved street become home to an abortion mill ruined it all for her. A recent newcomer to Calgary, Sadie did not know any of the public history of the two opposing offices.

***

Mickey continued arguing even after Judge Dockendorff admonished him to be silent. He had learned before he must fight in court to make himself heard. 'Your Honor, the

Craigenback Abortion Clinic is in court today because our advertising in the new telephone book is better than their advertising. They were not expecting the Crisis Pregnancy Center to have large, full color displays in the Family Planning, Birth Control and Abortion sections of the Yellow Pages. I submit it is an abuse to allow competitors to come to court to undo the effects of a rival's better advertising. Other companies who are in business can't seek court enforcement on their competition, and undo the effects of free enterprise. And this is about more than business, something more important. This is about social justice, so our rights to exist and operate a Crisis Pregnancy Center should have even greater protection.'

'This is about business rights Your Honor,' Jessica Sterne said. 'Everyone is now going to the Crisis Pregnancy Center. The Craigenback Abortion Clinic is empty, ever since the new phone book came out. It is obvious fraud for the anti-abortionists to pretend they are providing abortion services in the Abortion section of the Yellow Pages.'

'Your Honor, this is not about business. This is about abortion, about freedom of religion and freedom of speech, about our democratic constitutional rights.'

Judge Dockendorff finally looked down at Mickey from his high bench. 'Mr. Finnegan, I can already see we have a problem here. Your actions in the phone book are causing a disturbance to the system. We cannot have problems and disturbances disrupting the system. The role of the courts, my role as a judge, is to control any unforeseen problems, and maintain the smooth functioning of society. The written laws cannot foresee all the events arising in human situations. I wish you understood why I am here.'

'I think I understand Judge. Is it your view from the outset I constitute a problem and disturbance merely because someone complains? The hearing today has hardly begun.'

'Mr. Finnegan, I will overlook your inappropriate insinuations of bias on my part. Please sit down and be quiet, and yes, let us begin this hearing. The problem must be corrected. Troublemakers must be dealt with, and order restored.'

'A false order is a disorder.'

Judge Dockendorff shook his head. 'Please spare me your vague philosophy. This is a court of law.'

'I also object to Ms. Sterne always calling us 'anti-abortionists'. We are pro-lifers, which is our self-designation, our name if you will, Pro-lifers. Calling us 'anti-abortionists' is a neat semantic trick to make the people who oppose abortion wear the two negative words 'anti' and 'abortion' both around our necks, like some double scarlet letter A stigmatizing us. I most strenuously object. Everyone is entitled to be called by the proper name. I might point out I never stoop to calling Ms. Sterne and her colleagues and client Dr. Craigenback 'anti-life."

'Mr. Finnegan, it would seem this case is about more important names than what you are complaining about now. I refer to the disputed names you placed in the phone book. Please sit down. I won't tell you again.'

* * *

It was true, Dolores thought. She was not related to Mickey; he was not part of her family. The pro-lifers really did care about women. The abortion war was fought on a battleground of words, and she had to fight fire with fire, use words cleverly herself. She never lied to a client; she could always offer a true interpretation to justify what she said. Didn't the Lord himself counsel the disciples to be as wise as serpents and harmless as doves? If she was hiding a Jewish refugee in the basement, and a storm trooper came to the door and asked her about it, should she tell him the truth? Give the Jew to the soldier to be deported to a concentration camp and killed? Or should she lie? Definitely, hiding the man in the basement and lying about it would be the right thing to do. The storm trooper had no right to know the truth. If she hid all the facts about herself and the Center from Sadie at the start of their conversation, she would soon bring her to the fullness of truth by the end.

Didn't everyone only gradually reveal the truth, if they ever revealed the whole truth about themselves to anyone, even those closest to them? Didn't everyone have secrets? What did she know about Mickey really, even though they worked closely together? And liked each other? She could tell he liked her. But he never talked about himself, all business, all pro-life. No, she wanted to have a chance to talk to Sadie first, before losing her right from the start with all the confusion and stereotypes, all the misinformation and propaganda floating around about abortion and pro-life. Dolores felt as always her main task was to help Sadie respect the life of her baby. She liked to keep things simple.

***

Mickey continued standing, caught up in the heat of the courtroom exchanges.

'Sit down Mr. Finnegan. I won't tell you again,' Judge Dockendorff repeated.

Mickey sat in his chair, and Jessica Sterne resumed her speech. A strong feminist, she believed in freedom of choice and abortion rights for women, and argued at length with passion and sincerity for her client the Craigenback Abortion Clinic. Dr. Craigenback was a well-paying client, but she was also happy to represent him and all he stood for on principle. 'Your Honor, as I was saying before I was so rudely interrupted, the Defendant Crisis Pregnancy Center which Mr. Finnegan directs, has placed several new listings, new names, in this year's telephone directory recently distributed throughout Calgary. Those names are false and misleading, meant to confuse the public and draw people seeking abortion counselling to end up at the anti-abortion so-called Crisis Pregnancy Center, instead of going to my client where they really intended to go. Once they arrive at the anti-abortion Center, the women are subjected to harassment and intimidation by the pro-lifers, as they like to call themselves. These people invade the most personal and private decisions of women. We ask the Court to intervene with an emergency injunction to disconnect the telephone of the Crisis Pregnancy Center, and the related names.'

'These are very serious allegations. What proof do you have?'

'The affidavit evidence of the Plaintiff sets out the pages

of the new telephone directory. If I may refer you to Exhibit A, the new names listed in the phone book all list the same phone number and the same address as the Crisis Pregnancy Center. Those names are:

Aid to Women
Crisis Pregnancy Center
Woman's Reproductive Health Center
Abortion Accurate Information
Pregnancy Problem Center
Abortion Trauma Counselling Center
Family Planning Center
Birth Control Center.

And just above my client's telephone listing, Craigenback Abortion Clinic, he has placed the name Counselling Abortion Center, trying to lure people to call him first. You see how the letters CO in Counselling come just before and above the letters CR in Craigenback in the phone book?'

Judge Dockendorff shook his head from side to side as he read the affidavit evidence of Mickey's new listings in the telephone directory. Finally, his eyes looked over his glasses at Mickey silent below him.

'Mr. Finnegan, as I am sure you know from the other injunctions against you, the test for such immediate relief before a trial is irreparable harm to the plaintiff. We can continue with this hearing and you can say the things you always say, but is there any question on the face of it you are intending irreparable harm to the Craigenback Clinic?'

'Your Honor, I am intending to prevent irreparable harm to the mothers and children damaged and killed in the abortion mill. Or you could call it an abortuary. It's certainly not a medical clinic. No diseases are treated there.'

'Abortuary? There is no such word.'

'The world does not want to see it for what it really is. Semantics and euphemisms are preferred to reality. I am challenging the deceptive use of words. I am not the dishonest one.'

'We shall see about that.'

2

Dolores continued answering Sadie's questions about the Crisis Pregnancy Center with a question, redirecting her attention and keeping control of the interview, the way Mickey taught her.

'You came alone today?'
'My boyfriend drove me.'
'Is he in the waiting room?'
'He's outside, in the car.'
'He's waiting outside?'
'I asked him but he wouldn't come in.'
'He just dropped you off?'
'He can make himself invisible when he wants to. He just disappears.'
'Isn't he supporting you?'
'We live together, but we pay our own way.'
'I meant supporting you in what you're facing.'
'He said it's women stuff, and I should take care of it.'
'It's his baby too.'
'He doesn't want it. And now I don't neither, not after seeing him with my sister.'

* * *

Judge Dockendorff examined the pages cut from the phone book in Exhibit A. 'All these names go to the telephone number and the address of the Defendants?'

Jessica Sterne nodded her head. 'That's right Your Honor. You see what he's done? He has blanketed the phone book in all the different sections someone might turn to looking for abortion information.'

'I'm stunned. Never in my entire career on the bench have I seen such an egregious fraud, an anti-choice center masquerading as a health clinic.'

'Yes, Your Honor, the Defendants are deliberately misleading and confusing vulnerable women at a critical time in their lives, and hindering them from accessing the legitimate and legal abortion services they have every right and freedom to seek.'

Sterne looked at her papers, and raised her head to press her point.

'Mr. Finnegan's center operates in a house just across the street from my client's medical clinic. Not only does he use the same approximate address to confuse people and direct them to his center, but now he confuses people by setting up just above my client's listing in the phone book. Dr. Craigenback performs legal, useful and wanted services in the community for women's health, and he us now under siege by the anti-choice fanatics.'

Mickey stood again. 'I must object to the intemperate language of my friend. And I'm afraid I must object to your own language calling us 'anti-choice'. That is pro-abortion rhetoric.'

'She can say anything she wants to in court Mr. Finnegan. Here all speech is absolutely privileged to get at the truth.'

'What is the truth is that abortion takes a human life of a growing child.'

'That is not before me today in this hearing.'

'I also object to the characterization the Craigenback Abortion Clinic as 'under siege'. It's pro-lifers who are besieged. Why can't we be allowed to exist in our freedom to operate? Why must they, the so-called 'freedom of choice' people, interfere with our freedom, and the public's freedom? Even seeking court restrictions on our freedoms in this hearing today?'

'All we are asking for is the freedom to operate the abortion clinic without the pro-lifers' interference. Mr. Finnegan twists it all backwards, confusing the issues, just like his confusing phone advertising.'

'Abortion twists the truth with its lies.'

Dockendorff ignored Mickey. Sitting high up on his judge's bench, he spoke to Jessica Sterne with a quick glance in an aside about Mickey. 'I have never seen anything like it.'

* * *

Dolores leaned forward, folding her hands together on the desk. In church she clasped her hands as a gesture of prayer, but here in the counselling room she wanted to show a sign of her interest in what Sadie said to her.

'Rick should have come in with you.'

'He does what he wants. He knows I'm mad at him.'

'How did you hear about us?'

'In the Yellow Pages of the phone book. I saw your ad so I came.'

'Good. You're in the right place.'
'Do you do the abortions right here?'

***

Judge Dockendorff perched high on his bench above them; his head sticking out of his black robe with his carefully groomed hair like some great feathered bird of prey, ready to swoop down on the defenseless field mice scurrying far beneath him. The pro-lifers had nicknamed him Judge Death. Now he glared at Mickey. 'Mr. Finnegan, you have engaged in many questionable actions in your single minded obsession with abortion over the years, but this latest stunt of yours in the public phone book is beyond…I don't know how to describe it. What made you think you could get away with it? What do you think you are doing?'

Mickey was ready to answer the accusations. He already made the same defense to the interrogations of the news reporters the last two weeks, ever since the new phone book came out, and his listings were discovered, creating a public stir in Calgary. Judge Dockendorff had found him guilty and ruled in Craigenback's favor before the hearing even began, before he had a chance to say anything, but Mickey still tried to mount his defense and make his submissions of fact and law to the court. Dockendorff was right about one thing–the public court was a forum for speaking the truth.

***

Sadie's direct questions were adding to her tension. First the scene with Dora earlier in the morning when Mickey fired her, and then Mickey going to court again to try and save the Center. Now dealing with this tough drop-in. Dolores didn't want to see the Crisis Pregnancy Center closed down, lose her chance to help the women. She knew the abortion system did not want their interference, and it seemed the people did not want their help. Hardly anyone came to the Center before, but things changed this year when Mickey put the new advertising in the phone book. Seeing all the women who came now was draining, but worth it.

'You don't need an appointment here. We're glad to help you.'

'I really want to get this done fast.'

'First, we'll get some information from you, then give you a free pregnancy test, and then show you some video information while we do the test.'

Sadie looked at the television in the corner of the counselling room. 'On the TV there?'

Dolores nodded.

'What's the video about?'

'It's a brief presentation about abortion techniques, possible complications, alternatives.'

'I know what I want.'

* * *

'Your Honor, with all due respect, what Ms. Sterne said is false. Let me-'

'False? Judge Dockendorff interrupted. 'You have the nerve to accuse her of being false?'

Mickey ignored Dockendorff's insult and continued his

legal arguments. 'Please let me explain. It's all about the women confused and harmed by the abortion clinic.'

The judge now looked at Mickey directly. 'You made the same accusations before. Are you one of them?'

'Pardon?'

'Mr. Finnegan, this may surprise you, but abortion is not before me in this case. The constitution is not before me. Freedom of religion and freedom of speech is not before me. This is a case of business rights, and alleged fraud interfering with a private business. You cannot pass off your pro-life center as an abortion clinic to the public. According to our laws, an abortion clinic has as much right to protection of its business as a barbershop or an automobile mechanic. Only business rights are before the court in this case.'

'An abortion clinic is not a business. The counselling we provide shows women the truth about dangerous abortion procedures, and gives them alternatives and support. We are not doing anything wrong. There should even be laws making the kind of counselling we give legally mandatory to women seeking abortions. It's a good thing we do. If the Craigenback Abortion Clinic is a business, it is in the business of selling abortions on false pretenses.'

'Do you have any evidence of your accusations?'

'They don't make any money on childbirth or adoptions. They make money on abortions. The clinic is in a conflict of interest. They don't counsel on the dangers of abortion, both physical and emotional dangers, and the alternatives of childbirth and adoption. There's no money in it for them. We don't charge at all. Pro-life is not in it for the money.

Instead of giving full and accurate medical information to their clients, the Plaintiff misleads and manipulates women.'

'Your Honor,' Jessica Sterne said, 'you are absolutely correct my client the Craigenback Abortion Clinic is just another normal service carrying on its business. There is nothing contentious about birth control and abortion, despite the strident shouting of a religious fringe minority to turn back the clock. I respectfully submit the Court must intervene to put a stop to this irrational harassment we constantly endure, now even turning the phone book into a battleground. And I point out Dr. Craigenback is a doctor who employs nurses. It is Mr. Finnegan and his amateur volunteers who are spreading false medical information about termination of pregnancy.'

* * *

Dolores straightened her back, sitting more upright in the chair from her hunched position with her hands folded. 'You have to watch the video. You need information to give informed consent for a medical procedure.'

Sadie saw she must go through the system to get what she wanted. It was all a bureaucracy, even abortion. 'I'll watch it, but my mind's made up.'

* * *

Mickey continued to rebut Sterne's attack. 'Your Honor, the Crisis Pregnancy Center helps women in a crisis pregnancy. The abortion clinic doesn't. They help themselves to their money. They hurt the women, and the children all die of course. I can make the same argument the Plaintiff is making. The Craigenback Abortion Clinic is an egregious and disingenuous fraud on the public.'

Judge Dockendorff was amused at Mickey using the legal vocabulary. 'Egregious? Disingenuous? Mr. Finnegan, what have you been reading? You cannot steal the abortion clinic's patients, you cannot steal their business name, and you cannot steal their clients.'

Mickey silently endured the mockery. They always called him Mr. Finnegan in court, setting him apart as either the accused, or an ordinary citizen who was not a professional lawyer, not one of the fraternity. But he was determined to defend the Crisis Pregnancy Center, even though he was not respected by the court.

***

Dolores noticed Sadie's rigid posture, sitting upright on the edge of the chair. 'You seem tense.'

'I'm not happy the way things are going.'

'The problems with Rick?'

'Lots of problems. I can't be pregnant. It's too much on top of everything else.

Dolores smiled. 'You can tell me all about it. Start by telling me your name.'

'Sadie.' She exhaled her breath in a long sigh. 'I'm sorry if I seemed rude at first.'

'I understand.'

'It's just I refuse to be a victim. I'm not going to take it.'

Dolores saw Sadie kept her winter coat buttoned up in the warm office. 'Why don't you take your coat off dear, and stay awhile?'

Sadie smiled at the old-fashioned invitation, but declined. 'I'm okay.'

'Might as well be comfortable,' Dolores said, but Sadie still remained completely enclosed in her bulky winter coat, her right hand closed in a fist in her lap, her thumb tucked inside the fist, her fingers clenched so tight her knuckles were white.

Dolores wanted to be reassuring. 'Dolores-' she said, blushed at her mistake, recovered, and got back on track. 'Sadie we can help you here. You came to the right place.'

* * *

'Your Honor, we are not stealing the abortion clinic's name or clients. We have every right to exist and counsel women from a pro-life perspective. The abortionists cannot copyright or trademark the common words family planning and birth control. They cannot even lay claim to the common word abortion. They do not own the public. It's the law, nobody owns common words, and certainly no one owns the people.'

'Your Honor,' Jessica Sterne responded, 'I believe you have heard enough. Can you please give us your decision?'

'Your Honor, I'm entitled to finish my argument,' Mickey said, 'without being rushed to judgment.'

'This is an informal hearing for a temporary injunction Mr. Finnegan. You will have ample scope for sworn legal evidence and argument at the full trial for the permanent injunction the Plaintiff is seeking.'

Mickey was experienced with injunctions, knew how the system really worked. 'I'm afraid a temporary injunction often becomes permanent without a full trial. It just sits there forever. The case is really decided at this stage. So I have to make my arguments now. Please bear with me a moment longer.'

Judge Dockendorff looked at his watch.

'Proceed, but if you get too long-winded I will cut you off.'

'Thank you, Your Honor. What I want to say is this. All of our company names are true and describe our counselling services. We provide birth control information, and family planning counselling, teaching natural family planning as opposed to artificial contraception. We provide true information about abortion. We help women suffering from post-abortion trauma. We help women reproduce which is healthy for them. There is a good explanation for all the different names advertised in the phone book. It is not illegal for a corporation to have several subsidiaries, operating through them and their different names. At the Crisis Pregnancy Center we are what you might call a pro-life conglomerate. So you see, even the business argument favors us.'

Judge Dockendorff's head tilted backwards as he laughed. He was not buying it. 'Mr. Finnegan, what you have done is a public nuisance. You have made a mockery of everything, and aggressively attacked the entire family planning system in Calgary. It did not take long to find you out as soon as the new phone book was distributed. I'm afraid Ms. Sterne is right in her characterizations. You anti-abortionists know no restraint.'

Jessica Sterne did not have to do much arguing in front

of Judge Dockendorff to win, but she thought she should say something. 'If you look into our affidavit evidence Your Honor, all of Mr. Finnegan's 'corporations' are empty shell companies, just names in the phone book. He and his associates do not possess the financial resources to be a 'pro-life conglomerate'. The Crisis Pregnancy Center is only a handful of anti-abortion extremists operating out of a rundown house. My client, the Craigenback Abortion Clinic, is an established and substantial medical clinic providing real medical services in Calgary. There is simply no comparison.'

* * *

I must not judge this woman, Dolores reminded herself. Her very first client Linda had taught her that, Linda surprising her with honest, insightful admissions in the talk after the video, despite all her initial pretenses. Sadie might not be living the right way, but Dolores had learned from experience there was always more to people than she could ever fully know. Why did I have to make that slip of the tongue? Calling Sadie by my name? She thought of how the other pro-lifers called her Brave Soul for doing this stressful counselling work with women expecting abortions. If they only knew how nervous I get. But we're in it now.

'I'll just ask you a few more questions Sadie, to get you started on the intake process. It won't take long.'

* * *

'Objection, Your Honor. Medical clinic? Services? As I said before, pregnancy is not a disease. Abortion is the killing of babies-'

'Your Honor, I object to Mr. Finnegan's terminology. I ask you order him to refrain from the use of the words baby, infant, child, or victim. In law, the fetus is not a human being until after birth. His language is prejudicial, inflammatory, and legally imprecise.'

'I am using common sense words to express what everyone really knows-'

'No, Mr. Finnegan. Ms. Sterne is correct. You do not understand the precise ways lawyers think and express themselves as they are trained to do in law school. You have not had the benefit of higher education. I agree those words baby, infant and child have no standing in law on the issues before this court.'

'But you just defended her right to speak her opinions about pro-lifers in court. This is all simply denial of reality. Denial is a primitive defense mechanism. It has nothing to do with sophisticated higher understanding.'

'Mr. Finnegan, I have heard enough. I know what you are going to say before you say it. You will say abortion is not medicine, and not a service. You and I have been over this ground before. I am not here to wrangle over words-'

'But this case is all about words, the ads in the phone book.'

'Whether you like it or not, approve of it or not, abortion is legal. You cannot interfere with other people's legal rights. I have already ruled arguments about abortion are not before this court. Your latest actions are an offensive scandal. I am making my ruling. I am ordering an emergency injunction that the telephone company disconnect your telephone line immediately. Your latest shenanigans with this 'counselling center' are a serious matter. This court takes its responsibilities very seriously. Your audacity in trying to take over the phonebook and interfere with people is embarrassing. You are acting like an immature child, and like a child limits and controls must be set for you. Court is adjourned.'

* * *

Dolores hoped against hope the video might change Sadie's mind about abortion. So many times the women did change, stunned by the presentation of the truth. She could sense the change of hearts the moment she walked back into the counselling room after the client watched the video in privacy. Other times she could sense rejection of the video information from the hard look in the woman's eyes, and the blank and silent television screen, Dolores feeling the emptiness in the room. She wanted Sadie to see the video first before they talked, the visual information on the video the only hope to reach her.

* * *

This pompous judge takes himself very seriously, Mickey thought, sitting down after Judge Dockendorff left the courtroom, and gathering his legal papers, stuffing them into his briefcase. He felt even more nervous than usual today, so much was at stake. Firing Dora earlier in the morning for harassing Julie was stressful, and now the unfair court hearing. At least he did not allow his shyness to silence him from speaking out. He was glad his voice did not quaver. He would hate them to see how nervous he was in front of them. They did not intimidate him, he told himself, he was high strung, always had been. It was something about himself he could not change and must accept.

* * *

Dolores touched the miraculous medal of Mary again hidden beneath her dress. Hail Mary, full of grace, pray for us sinners. The silent prayer said in the privacy of her mind gave her the courage she needed to counsel all the women day after day. This morning she especially needed to pray. If Mickey lost again in court, which seemed likely, this young woman Sadie might be the last client she would ever see at the Crisis Pregnancy Center. Pray for us now and at the hour of our death. Amen.

* * *

Mickey walked home from the Courthouse in the fresh winter air, walking up the Center street hill back to his office where he both lived and worked. One of his throbbing headaches began, and he thought the cold air might help. Walking always helped him think. He needed some time to think. Dolores would be so disappointed at the news. He was disappointed in himself for referring more than once in the hearing to Craigenback's abortion mill as a clinic. He had spoken out against the use of the word clinic in association with abortion, but it was so easy to fall into that use of words, conventional reality accepted by everyone. He began talking to himself, as was his habit, only a little whisper as he walked and thought in his intensity. 'What can we do now to stop abortion?' he said to himself. 'What can we do now?'

3

Dolores heard the front door of the house open, and Mickey's voice saying hello to Julie. She stood and said to Sadie: 'Excuse me a moment, I'll be right back.'

She walked into the waiting room and shushed Mickey with her finger on her lips. Mickey indicated with a nod of his head towards the back part of the house, and he and Dolores walked down the hallway to his office and bedroom.

'I didn't want the new client to see or hear you Mickey. She has seen you before on the news, and I told her you weren't connected to me.'

'How is she?'

'Uptight. Wants an abortion, but I sense there may be a chance to change her mind. She doesn't hold things back. Maybe God can touch her if she stays open. What happened in court?'

Mickey slumped into the chair behind his desk, running fingers of his right hand through his brown curly hair, turning slightly gray, his eyes looking tired as he rubbed them. Dolores stood in front of the desk, looking down at him. She saw at 42 he still kept his youthful boyish face and trim body, although he recently needed eyeglasses, the words getting too blurry to make out anymore. He did a lot of reading in his law researches. Mickey was a dedicated pro-lifer, but Dolores wished he knew how to relax, and maybe notice her. Charlie Kelly made fun of Mickey's intensity: 'His hair's on too tight,' Charlie said, 'even his curly hair is clenched.'

Mickey drew a deep breath. He looked at her, preparing himself for the explosion. 'We lost. Judge Dockendorff ruled in Craigenback's favor. He ordered the telephone company to disconnect our phone line as soon as possible. There's supposed to be a trial about it later, but often in these cases they just sit on the temporary emergency injunction forever.'

'How can the abortion clinic go to court and cut off the telephone of a crisis pregnancy center? If they have freedom of choice, why can't we have our freedom to operate?'

'It has nothing to do with freedom. It's about abortion.'

'How does Dockendorff get to judge all of our cases? He's biased against us. The man's nothing but a powerful pervert.'

'It doesn't matter. If not him then another. All the judges rule the same way in favor of abortion and against pro-life. What can I do?'

'I've got to get back to Sadie.'

'Julie and I will pray for you while you talk.'

'I'm going to need it.'

Mickey brightened. 'All is not lost. Maybe we can force a trial over the injunction and put abortion on trial. The courts are great public platforms.'

'Not if Dockendorff is the judge again. The Daily Record will either ignore the trial, or slant the news to make us look bad. I don't like the courts and lawyers and judges. You're a fool to believe in law and justice. Dockendorff has an iron fist in a velvet glove, and someday he will hammer you down.

All we can do is take it.'

'I don't have to take it. I can fight back.'

'We do, we have to take it.'

Mickey could not help smiling at her. They were very different but they were close. 'Dolores, you're so fierce. You tell us all off.'

Dolores didn't smile: 'I got to get back.'

'She might be our last client.'

'I don't know if I completely agree with our approach Mickey. It's so tense, leading the clients on at first. I still feel dishonest about it sometimes. Now the whole world has come down on us. This client, I have a feeling she's going to get mad when she doesn't get an abortion here. She asked me a lot of direct questions, and I had to talk around things.'

'It's not deception. It's mental reservation. It's morally permissible in Catholic theology. We've gone over this before.'

'But in my conscience I don't feel right about it. I still get twinges.'

'We owe it to the people to withhold the truth from them at the start. It's a noble lie, meant to help them. We have to lie to people at first to have a chance to tell them the truth at the end. The Craigenback Abortion Clinic lies to the people from beginning to end, and never tells them the truth.'

'But still-'

'All warfare is based on deception. So says Sun-Tzu. Let's talk about it later, you've got to get back.'

'Are we just con artists here?'

'One of the first principles of a good con man is to look the part, dress and talk and act the part, and most people will accept the part. It seems to work with our pro-life abortion center.'

'Until now. With our phone disconnected. It doesn't look we have any principles anymore, in the eyes of the world.'

'Google mental reservation in Catholic theology, about lies of necessity to protect victims from aggressors. It is a permissible moral option to withhold the truth in some grave situations, or use ambiguous words in difficult circumstances. Legal abortion has invaded and conquered our country, and we are the pro-life underground resistance fighting on. In a war a soldier has to do things he would not do in peacetime. It's hard to explain mental reservation. Judge Dockendorff would never understand it. Even other pro-lifers like Dora and Sara take the simplistic view we are lying to people.'

'Dora and Sara are Evangelicals. They see things differently from Catholics.'

'They are baptized Christians, and they know abortion is wrong.'

'You take such risks Mickey. In every way. I worry about you.'

'I'll be okay.'

'Be careful Mickey. So many things going on now. You've got enemies. I've got to get back to Sadie.'

'Don't worry,' he said, as Dolores turned to leave, 'I'll be careful.' His headache was still hammering his temples. When she was gone he opened a desk drawer and took out his bottle of pills, shook four of the painkillers into his hand, and went into the kitchen for a glass of water.

4

Dolores re-entered the counselling room and sat behind her desk again. 'Sorry I had to leave you for a moment. I was thinking, are you sure your boyfriend won't come in and join us?'

'He said he didn't want to.'

'It seems a waste with him so close, sitting out in the car.'

'When he doesn't want to do something he's just stubborn.'

'I'd like to invite him to come in, if you don't mind. It would be good for him to see the video too.'

'You can try. I want to have him here with me.'

'I'll be right back. No harm in trying.'

'I'll wait here.'

Dolores left the counselling room again, got her coat from the rack by the front door, and walked outside to talk to Rick. She saw him sitting behind the wheel of the car parked in front of the house, the motor still running to keep the heater going. Cigarette smoke filled the car, and he looked half-asleep, as if he had a headache, his eyes closed and his forehead pressed against the cold glass of the driver's side window. Dolores stepped into the road and around the car and knocked on the window where his head leaned. She was shivering in the cold winter air, a few snowflakes falling gently on her. Rick was startled by the noise of her knock, and rolled the car window halfway down. His bloodshot eyes looked at her, long stringy hair obscuring his young face, a scraggly growth of beard on his cheeks. He was skinny, and looked pale to Dolores. What's a pretty woman like Sadie doing with a loser like this, what did she see in him? Dolores crossed her arms in front of her chest to warm herself. 'Hello Rick, my name is Dolores. Sadie told me your name. Will you come in and join us?'

'No, I'm okay.' He waved his cigarette hand in the direction of the house, his voice sounding hoarse. 'How long is this going to take?'

'We have to ask some questions, do the pregnancy test, give Sadie some information. It can take a while, maybe one or two hours.'

'Too long. I can't wait.'

'It depends how long she needs to talk.'

'I'll come back in an hour.'

A woman who lived on the street came walking by in an orange parka. She waved to Dolores as she passed, walked to the corner, turned around and walked back. She turned around at the other corner and walked by again, then walked back and forth all during the talk with Rick, waving in silence at Dolores every time she passed them.

'Are you sure you won't come in? It's important.'

'I stay out of this woman's stuff. I know Sadie will complain about me, but when she's on the rag it's temporary insanity. She's dissatisfied with everything.'

'She has missed her period.'

'Same difference, same emotional crisis.'

'A woman's cycle can be hard on her.'

'I don't go for all the woman's feelings stuff. Why do I want to have long talks about women's feelings? Why do I have to hear about her period? Who needs it? Who cares? Feelings, feelings, feelings.'

'What else is there?'

'Oh no, you're one too.'

'When Sadie wants to talk to you about her period, she wants to create intimacy with you. Get closer.'

'We're intimate. We have sex. That other thing is women's stuff. She can talk to her girlfriends about it. Not to me.'

'Intimacy to you only means sex with her?'

'What else does it mean?'

'Intimacy means a lot of things living together. Women are more logical than men. We seem to understand more of things. With our hearts.'

'Are you kidding?'

'It's true.'

Rick laughed. 'With all those mixed up feelings? All those hormones when her period comes? That makes her logical and sensible?'

Dolores looked into Rick's bleary eyes, wrapped her arms tighter around her to ward off the cold. 'A lot of things can get in the way of straight thinking.'

'What do you mean?'

'Feelings, hormones, alcohol, drugs, many things can cloud our judgment.'

'I don't have a drinking problem. We had a big party last night.'

She wasn't going to stand in the cold street and argue about denial. 'If you love her-'

'I always tell her if she wants to have a long talk about her feelings she can call one of her girlfriends, and have a great time complaining about me. She's a world champion complainer, never appreciates what she has. Now she can talk about me to you.'

'But Rick-'

'So you see it's best I'm not there.' He took a drag on his cigarette, looked at her again. 'I guess you think I'm insensitive too.'

'A woman needs to know she is loved, appreciated, her feelings heard and understood, acknowledged and respected.'

'That's a mouthful.'

Dolores did not like this young man's attitude. 'You should be more diplomatic with Sadie. And with me.'

'I'm diplomatic. I fake an interest in what she's saying sometimes. But I can't do it all the time.' Rick noticed the woman in the orange coat walking back and forth on the sidewalk, waving her hand at them. 'This place is nuts. What's the kooky woman doing? Is she picketing you?'

'She is not a kook. Her name is Ethel, one of our neighbors. She is bipolar, and she spends hours walking every day to burn off her manic energy.'

'She's crazy. Just walking back and forth on the sidewalk. A trip to nowhere when it's cold outside.'

'I think she's brave. She is doing the best she can, fighting for her sanity every day. It might look foolish to us, but she has a serious purpose.'

'Yeah, yeah.'

Dolores wanted to keep Rick engaged in the growing conversation, keep him talking. 'Ethel wants to be pregnant, but she's 50 now. Keeps hoping she can get pregnant with her husband anyway, and have a baby. She wants to be a mother very much. Her husband thinks it's unlikely if not impossible at their ages, but she keeps hoping. It's very sad.'

'Not very realistic on her part.'

'You don't know how much having children can mean to some people who can't. How much it hurts. Ethel dreams about babies. You and Sadie are lucky, to be young and healthy, to be having a baby.'

'We're lucky? That manic woman's disturbed. She has enough problems without getting pregnant. How can she ever look after a child? Why does her husband put up with her empty dreams?'

'He loves her. She bitterly complains sometimes, accuses him of being an old man with low sperm count, things she read about, and says she is not the problem because she is still having her periods, but she doesn't understand a woman is born with all of her eggs, and her eggs are also 50 years old now.'

'Sadie isn't crazy like her. We're normal people. She shouldn't be dreaming of a baby, and blaming her husband. Someone should tell her the truth.'

'I had a talk with her husband once, George. He said why take away her hope. He said if he tries to say there is no hope she gets even angrier at him, accuses him of not wanting a child. Ethel's psychiatrist is against it, he doesn't think she can handle a pregnancy with her mental illness. It seems everyone is against babies these days. She says she is in a pregnancy crisis in a different way.'

'Her husband was right to try and tell her the truth. Why string her along with false hopes?'

'He can't bear her sadness. She says she has dreams of babies abandoned and floating dying in a swamp, the lost children. Nobody claims them. She picks the babies up from drowning in the swamp and tries to breathe life back into them, all the babies dressed in white swaddling clothes, blue and pink ribbons in their hair wet and dirty from the swamp, the babies crying in their distress.'

'What a depressing nightmare. I don't like dreams, all jumbled and crazy with so many bad feelings. I wake up exhausted from dreams, like I've been working all night instead of resting. I feel relieved when I wake up to the real world again, crazy as the real world is. Sometimes my heart is pounding, and I'm panting when I wake up from dreams. I never remember them. I'm glad they're quickly forgotten in the normal daylight.'

'George understands Ethel's nighttime dreams are reflections of her positive daytime dream of having children. He doesn't want to trample on her dreams. Maybe your bad dreams come from the alcohol. Sleeping off a drunk isn't restful for the body.'

Rick's face twisted away at the repeated references to drinking. 'So no one can talk to Ethel. She wants what she wants.' He looked at his watch. 'Just get on with it with Sadie.'

'We can tell you some truths here Rick. You should come in. Hear what we have to say. Give Sadie a chance to tell you how she feels. You should at least listen to her.'

'Oh, I have to listen to her, don't worry. Sadie's high maintenance. She has so many emotional needs I get tired of it.'

'You make your girlfriend sound like a burden.'

Rick rubbed his head, the pain behind his eyes still throbbing. 'She's a demanding bitch with a lot of issues. No guarantee we will be together much longer.'

'Does she know that, how you really feel?'

'Sometimes I wish I never got involved with her. When she's in one of her bad moods, it's like being stuck in a closet with a bobcat. She's no victim.'

'She?'

'Yeah, you know, Sadie.'

'So you don't care about her feelings? Are you telling me things you want me to pass on to her?'

'I don't need your lectures.'

'Abortion is serious. If you love her, you should come in, and learn about it. We show a good video, with lots of information.'

'Lady, I get it. A baby is as real as it gets. We just don't want it.'

'You know? Then–'

'Who cares? I got something I have to do.'

Rick put the car into gear, the engine already running for the heater, preparing to drive away.

'Just let me ask you one question Rick. Sadie seems upset about you and her sister.'

'She imagined the whole thing,' Rick said, turning his head

away. 'You can't imagine how many moods she goes through in a day.' He rolled up the window with his free left hand, some ash falling onto the floor mats of the car as his right hand grabbed the steering wheel, took his foot off the brake, and drove away, leaving Dolores standing alone, shivering in the street.

While she was outside talking to Rick baby Jeffrey crawled through the open doorway of the counselling room to visit Sadie still sitting in her chair, pulling himself up and tugging at her coat, whimpering to be lifted onto her lap. Sadie called out. 'Your baby's in here,' but did not pick him up. She did touch him, trying to quiet him. 'Hi little guy,' she said, patting his head. 'Don't cry.' Where is everyone, she wondered? She didn't want to be left alone in this place with this kid. Dolores came back in the counselling office, and Julie rushed in and picked up Jeffrey.

'I'm sorry. I hope he wasn't annoying you.'

'It's okay. He's a cute baby.'

'Thank you.'

Julie left the counselling room again carrying Jeffrey. Dolores closed the door behind her, and went back to her seat behind the desk. 'Rick didn't want to come in.'

'I told you.'

'It seems I keep walking out on you before we can get started.'

'I'm used to it.'

'Rick said he had something to do, and would be back in an hour.'

'He left?'

'Yes.'

'He left me here alone?'

'I'm afraid so dear. I saw him drive off.'

'That–' Sadie stifled the curse. 'He probably went for a beer to cure his hangover.'

5

The telephone call came on Mickey's private line in the backroom. Jeffrey was playing at his feet underneath the desk. Dolores and Sadie were talking in the counselling room at the front of the house, and Julie was answering the public telephone in the reception area. Craigenback's lawyers and the telephone company needed a little more time to disconnect the Crisis Pregnancy Center telephone line Julie was still using.

'We heard what happened in court today on the radio news. Don't worry about Craigenback. We'll deal with him.'

'Who is this? How did you get this number?'

'You're wasting your time. A pro-lifer who goes to court is a fool.'

'Who are you?'

'The Warriors of God. We'll take care of things. The system is useless.'

'Don't do anything violent here.'

'Whoever takes the blood of man, by man shall his blood be shed.'

'Please, no violence. It's wrong, and counter-productive. We'll lose our demonstration rights, get moved even farther away from the abortion clinic behind wider buffer zones.'

'It scares the hell out of them. They have to live with the fear they might have to face dying too. Just like the babies.'

'Violence on our side is not the answer. We're talking about protecting women and children in pro-life, not killing people.'

'The Warriors are protecting women and children from the killers. No one else is doing anything.'

'Pro-life has to be non-violent, respecting all human life.'

'Yeah, yeah, that's the line for the evening news. Reassure everyone you are nice guys.

'We mean it, I understand you want to kill killers, but was want to be consistent on the worth of all human life.'

'Don't be a hypocrite about us and our methods.'

'Methods? You take the law into your own hands. Pro-life vigilantes.'

'So do you.'

'Civil disobedience is different. Your violence lets the pro-aborts say we are the problem.'

'They also say your actions are a form of violence towards abortion clinics. They lie all the time. You know that. We save babies. A dead abortionist can't kill anymore. They reap what they sow. When a bunch of you are invading and occupying their building and won't leave you call it non-violent civil disobedience and they call it a violent office invasion. And it sure looks aggressive.'

'More babies die in the long run because pro-life violence turns people against us.'

'People are conformist sheep, born to be caught and killed, sheared while they bleat. They will believe anything fed to them. Look how easily they swallow freedom of choice and abortion rights.'

'Who are you people? Have we ever met?'

'No, but I've seen you. We're around.'

'Are you at the Craigenback demonstrations?'

'Let's just say we can be part of many groups.'

Julie came to the door of his office with an important message, but Mickey waved her away. He wanted to keep the caller talking, find out more. This was the first time he ever made contact with the Warriors of God, only hearing about them before.

'I don't believe you have members in the pro-life groups. You're completely different from us.'

'You might be surprised.'

'Have you been making bomb threats at Craigenback's? They call the police now when we protest, and the cops come and investigate for bombs while we picket. I thought they were making it up.'

'Everything will be taken care of.'

Mickey's hand gripped the phone receiver tighter. 'You're making me more worried. Have you actually been there watching when the police come?'

'Maybe, maybe not.'

'This isn't something to play cagey games about. Let's meet and talk.'

The caller laughed. 'No, I don't think so.'

'You don't trust me?'

'You're better than most, but you're still working within the system. It's war Finnegan. Abortion is a war on women and children. The Warriors of God are fighting back, not like the pro-life pacifists.'

This person sounded more serious than the usual crank call meant to upset him. Was the cold voice an act trying to scare him, making such deadly threats so calmly, not seeming to care anymore? He needed to keep the conversation going, get a feel for what was happening. 'It's a war of ideas, and truth and love, not a shooting war throwing bombs.'

'You're the same as us. You use methods everyone says are unethical, lying to draw people into your counselling center.'

'We are completely different. We harm no one. We just talk to people. Civilization will be lost if we all descend into open violent warfare.'

'Civilization was lost when they first started killing unwanted children, and said it was legal. I've heard you say the same thing.'

'But I never said we should cross the line and start killing back.'

'We just took your own position to its logical conclusion.'

'Can't we talk about this some more, face to face?'

'Can I trust you not to turn me in?'

Mickey didn't know what to say. He didn't want to be an accomplice shielding the Warriors. He was silent for a moment. The caller laughed again. 'I thought so.'

'Who are you?'

'You have to take us seriously.'

'I take you very seriously.'

'No, you don't take abortion seriously enough. We do.'

'Because I don't believe in violence I don't take abortion seriously?'

'I have to go now. Your phones may be tapped. The

government is probably watching and listening to you. You ever think of that?'

'We're not criminals. We're just a pregnancy center.'

'Maybe they don't tap your phones. They just cut them off.'

Mickey made a last effort to reach the caller. 'So you're willing to kill in the name of life?'

'Goodbye Mickey Finnegan. See you around.'

'You people are out of your minds,' Mickey said into the dead phone, hearing the click at the other end hanging up. He still did not know if people really were making bomb threats at Craigenback's, or whether the abortionist and his staff were behind the phony complaints. He did not know if it was true the Warriors of God had come to Calgary. But who would make such a sick telephone call? Was there any cause to worry about a dangerous new development in pro-life in his city? Something else concerned him—the caller was a woman. Another headache struck him. He needed some more of his little white pills.

6

Dolores looked at Sadie sitting in front of her, this young woman so determined to get an abortion. How much stress could she take in one day? Mickey going to court to fight the injunction on their phone line, and losing, and earlier in the day the tension when he fired Dora. The firing was a long time coming, and Mickey really did not have a choice. The problems first started over Julie, and her baby Jeffrey.

Julie used to be a virgin, an adolescent Catholic who believed sex belonged in marriage. Christian moral teaching was so strong in her she became a chastity teacher for other teenagers, giving talks to student groups as she wore her T-shirt proclaiming the slogan TRUE LOVE WAITS. Many of the other teens were impressed by Julie's sincerity, and changed their sexually active lives. They started to abstain from sex, taking a pledge to remain abstinent until they were married. They had a name for it: Secondary Virginity. The once sexually active teenagers were not physical virgins anymore, but with their new commitment to chastity they were secondary virgins, re-virginized spiritually.

When Julie was 19, she met James Roberts. He also came to volunteer at the Crisis Pregnancy Center, a handsome Catholic man ten years older. At 29 James was a single father, his son staying with him after the divorce. Whenever James spoke of his 'ex-wife' Julie felt uncomfortable. The contradiction in the phrase 'ex-wife' was foreign to her, as a Catholic who did not believe in divorce. It made no sense to speak of an ex-wife. James seemed sincere in his love of the Lord and of his son, and active in pro-life work. A relationship of friendship developed between Julie and James, which deepened as they shared in pro-life activities. He rarely spoke of his wife, except to say some things implying she was an unstable woman with emotional problems. Julie saw James was a good man taking care of a motherless son, a man wronged by a bad woman.

The first time Julie and James made love was on a warm summer night, after drinking some dandelion wine, lying on a blanket on a deserted beach under the stars. The shining full moon made the nighttime bright, a warm campfire blazed beside them, and the fresh, clean smelling breeze from Sikome Lake in Fish Creek park caressed the skin of their naked bodies. The night was beautiful, and Julie became fully aroused as soon as he started kissing her, his tongue penetrating deep into her mouth, his strong legs spreading hers apart. They lay locked in close embrace afterwards, but Julie started crying as James held her, feeling both the pleasure and the pain of her loss of virginity. But James savored taking a virgin for her first time.

'We shouldn't have done this James. It's a sin. We have to go to Confession, and not do it again.'

'Did you enjoy it?'

'Yes. I love you, and I felt the pleasure of sex, of making love, but I feel ashamed too. I wanted to save my virginity for my husband, to walk down the aisle in white, and really deserve it, a virgin bride. Now I feel tarnished-what is that over there?'

'What's wrong?'

She pointed at the sand, 'there's a black snake crawling by the fire.'

James threw a stick at the snake, its sinuous body undulating away across the dunes. 'It's gone now.'

'Creepy. It could have crawled over us when we were-'

'Calm down.' His hand stroked her hair. 'Your body and sex are natural Julie. Don't be a puritan. God created sex to be enjoyed. God is for sex.' James licked her neck, and put his tongue inside her ear.

Julie was breathing hard as he aroused her again.

'Sex belongs in marriage. I'm not a puritan, but I feel like such a hypocrite, after what I always preached to others.'

'I love you Julie. Don't feel bad.'

His hand moved down, caressing her thighs.

'We can't do this again.'

'Are you saying you want to get married?' He kissed her earlobe, his lips and teeth nibbling, his warm breath blowing inside her ear.

Julie's body stretched in languid pleasure. 'I don't know. I mean, only married people should have sex.'

'I can't marry you in the Church unless I get an annulment. It takes a long time.'

'I'm not angling for you to marry me. I'm just saying we have no right to do this.'

'We love each other.' James fondled her breast.

'Are you sure? Maybe you love yourself, and want me.'

'I love you and want you, again and again.' His tongue

continued licking her neck.

'We have to obey God to really know love,' Julie said, moaning.

What a charming hypocrite she is, James thought, the little ways she let him know how much she enjoyed the sex despite her protests. She's a horny broad for a virgin. She twisted away. 'Don't force me,' she said, lying under him on the blanket, moving her groin against him. He smiled to himself, his head buried in her neck so she could not see him. James started kissing her again, His hands cupped and caressed her breasts, and his head bent down to kiss each hard and erect nipple. He went down farther on her, sliding his head between her legs and licking her, concentrating on making the figure 8 on her clitoris with the tip of his tongue. Julie became aroused enough for James to push her head down to his groin. Julie apologized, 'I don't know what to do.'

'I'll guide you. First, kiss it all over. Take your time kissing it. Then take me in your mouth and suck it up and down, slow at first and then faster and faster. Then use your teeth lightly, biting my cock, up and down the shaft and the head, biting me all over, but softly. Don't bite too hard. Use your tongue too, so I can see it, licking around the head of my cock and up and down the shaft. Don't be shy about it, dropping your eyes. Look me right in the eye with a bold stare. It's the direct eye contact while you're sucking a cock that really makes it hot.'

Julie followed his instructions, and James Roberts began to moan, especially when she used her teeth to bite him. He didn't want to come in her mouth this time, as he much as he enjoyed seeing a woman's mouth full of his semen and the satisfaction he felt when she swallowed it. But he had other plans for Julie.

'Turn over,' he said, shifting her with his hand on her hip.

'What are you doing?' Julie asked.

'Pull your knees up under you so your bum is in the air. Doggy style.'

'Like that?'

'Yeah I love the view, the cheeks of your rounded ass, your hips flaring out. You have a beautiful body.'

Then he fingered her anus, going deeper and deeper, slowly relaxing her tight sphincter muscles while he licked and kissed and covered her behind with his own biting.

'I'm relaxing you,' James said. 'You're so tight.'

Julie began to relax and it felt good as she writhed on the bed beneath him as he fingered her back door. James bent over her and focused on kissing her anus, licking the soft tissues all around it and even in the center of it.

'O' Julie said, 'that could be dirty. Aren't you worried about infection?'

'I'm sure you keep yourself clean.'

'I do.'

'I know. You're that kind of a girl just looking at you.'

He began kissing and licking her anus and taking small bites. He gathered his saliva and spit on her anus.

'O, O What are you doing?'

'I'm eating your ass. It's called rimming. It's delicious. And I'm lubricating you. The asshole is dry.'

'Why are you lubricating me?'

James shifted higher to place his penis just in front of her anus.

'Don't worry,' James said, 'now its time to lose your ass virginity.'

'No! I don't want to do that.'

'Get ready for an exquisite pleasure.' He maneuvered his body to enter her from behind. He found her opening and penetrated.

'Booty sex is my favorite.'

Julie couldn't believe it was happening.

'It's sodomy. It's against God. A mortal sin.'

James pushed his erect penis harder against her anus, and it slipped in deeper. Julie wriggled under him, trying to stop it. But James found her resistance exciting.

'It's sodomy!' She said. 'Please stop.'

'This is the age of sodomy,' James said. 'And forcible sodomy, that's the best'

Julie moaned despite herself, her breathing deepening.

'See?" James said. 'You like it. It feels good. There's nothing like it. They call it the glory hole. Your ass muscles relax for entry, but they still grab on tight to my cock. I love it. Your body loves it too, even if your religious scruples don't.'

Julie moaned again. James began growling, and wrapped her hair around his hand and pulled her head back straining her neck. Julie yelled 'Ow' and said, 'I can't breathe.' James felt his total domination and control of her so instinctively right he could no longer contain himself as he pumped inside her and came, ejaculating and he shouted too, his semen dripping out of her while she cried on the blanket on the beach. James placed his hand under her dripping anus and caught the semen, and smeared it on the cheeks of her ass.

Julie said. 'O'.

'I'm marking you, 'James said. 'Your ass is mine.'

'Smearing your hand on my behind seems weird.'

'But you felt it. You seem sensitive to everything I do.'

She didn't know what to think anymore. Her feelings were so conflicted at the shame, and yet she felt the pleasure.

'I feel dirty,' she said.

'Don't beat yourself up about it. If it felt good, you might come to love it too. All we did tonight was, you just fucked me.'

'O God,' Julie said.

'Next time you will enjoy it too.'

'No, I don't want to do sodomy again. Why are you obsessed with that?'

'When I see your sweet little ass twitching under your tight jeans when you walk I can't help getting turned on.'

'I don't mean to do that. I'm just walking.'

'You can't help it either. You're just naturally sexy. And you do wear the tight jeans. With the high heel pumps.'

'So it's my fault for not dressing modestly? Is that what you're telling me?

'Now don't get all huffy. I ;m just saying you are lovely young woman and a total turn on for someone like me.'

'Someone like you? Like What?'

'A red blooded man who likes attractive women. Anything wrong with that?'

'I mean it. I don't want to do it again. I'm sore now.'

'Someday you will come up to me and you will say Fuck me James, Fuck me in ass.'
'O God.'
'You'll get used to it. You will want it.'
'No.'
'Okay,' he lied, 'next time we have sex we'll just finish the blowjob. Did you like that?'
'You do taste good,'
'Even better when I come in your mouth.'
'I tasted some of your semen. Yuck.'
'And this time lick and suck my balls, take them right into your mouth, one at a time. You can do it.' James guided her hand to start stroking his penis again.
'We can do lots of positions. You can sit on top of me and ride me like a cowgirl while I fondle your hanging breasts. Or you can sit on me facing the other way, the reverse cowgirl, and get some more stimulation. And of course we can always do a 69, you laying on top of me reversed while we both do oral sex at the same time. You might like that too.'
'I am curious.'
'But right now, give me a hand job, while you kiss my nipples. Kiss and suck and bite them.'
'You're insatiable.'
'You do it to me.'
'Do you have the energy?'
'Let's try it and see.'
Julie stroked him up and down with her hand while she sucked his nipples. James moaned audibly at the pleasure she was giving him.

'Don't stop.'

She became aroused again herself and kept stroking his penis and kissing and licking and biting his nipples. He grew erect.

'Talk to me about my cock.'

'Mmm. Your cock is so long and hard.'

'That's it. Hold me tighter, and pump me up and down faster and faster. Spit on my cock first to lubricate my cock with your saliva. The skin on skin friction from your dry had is a bit painful.'

'This is making me wet too.'

Julie's right hand went down to her vagina and she rubbed her clitoris while her left hand squeezed her fingers around his penis. Then she rolled her body over his, and lay on top of him, and brushed the swollen nipples of her breasts lightly over his chest from side to side. James was surprised and delighted with her new found sexual aggression. He came again, this time in her hand, the sticky semen lubricating him as her hand kept pumping him up and down.

'Stop,' he said, 'it's too sensitive now.'

'Had enough? Julie asked, with a sly smile, enjoying her power making him climax. 'Are you okay?'

'God, that's as good as sucking me off.'

'Glad you liked it,' she said, feeling more confident in her sexuality. She was learning fast how to enjoy both their bodies in the many variations of sex.

'We are intimate now,' James said. 'We have shared sexual intimacy.'

Julie snuggled herself against him.

'I do feel close to you.'

James reached his hand down and lightly caressed the skin of the cheeks of her bum.'

'You feel so good. The pleasures of the flesh. The sweets of sin.'

'Sin? Do you think we did something wrong too'

'All I know is it feels so good.'

'God made if feel good so we would marry and procreate and keep the survival of the human race.'

'There you go preaching again.'

'What do you want me to do?'

'I'd like it if you talked dirty to me. That's exciting.'

'Like what?'

James was still caressing the cheeks of her ass.

'When we're doing it, you can say, 'O Shit,' and 'O Fuck.'

'You like hearing that?'

'Yeah, It turns me on to hear you turned on, not quiet and repressed, holding it all in.'

Julie lightly held his sticky wet penis in her hand.

'Why do you have to be so crude?'

'On the contrary, talking dirty is a refinement of the sexual experience, it enhances it, a world of privacy just between us beyond polite society.'

'I tell you what, I'll fuck you, and I'll suck your cock, and let you rim my ass, but I don't want you poking in my ass. There have to be limits. Is that open enough talk for you?'

'Now you're talking babe. I knew you had it in you.'

'But no more poking in my behind. Leave that alone.'

'You can poke me there, you know. Put a finger up inside

me while I'm on top of you in the missionary position. Then you massage my prostate, that feels good during sex. Or you can massage my prostate with your finger while you are kneeling in front of me sucking me.'

'I don't want to put my fingers in you. It's not sanitary.'

'Is it okay if I bury my face in your beautiful sweet ass? I love that.'

'Are you trying to turn me into a wanton woman?'

'I just want a woman who likes sex. Sex is very important to me.'

She didn't answer. She was falling asleep.

He wasn't concerned she refused his desire for anal sex, because he believed when she was aroused she would get carried away and not be able to help herself. He could force her again. She had already accepted it, despite her protests. She was still here.

'Let's get some sleep now, Julie said. 'Sleeping on the beach under the stars, with the waves of the lake lapping on the shore.'

'I know what you mean. Afterwards, everything seems so silent and still, yet all the sounds are so clear and enhanced. The afterglow of lovemaking. It's so peaceful. All your senses are relaxed and yet heightened. '

'Yeah Peaceful. Is what they mean about the fulfillment of making love, the orgasm of two in one, the intimacy, the oneness, the transcendence, and something known only to those two people involved in their shared experience?'

'I guess.'

'But when we are old and sick, and our bodies racked with

pain and dying, will the pleasures of sex mean anything to us then? Or will it all be forgotten?'

'You're still religious, thinking as you always have before.'

'I'm glad, but I feel like I'm changed now too.'

'Do we have any food?' He asked.

7

Julie was swept away by James's passion and her own awakened desire. Despite her firm resolution to abstain from sex after their first night together, she always gave in to him again, even when they worked together late at night at the Crisis Pregnancy Center, preparing the monthly newsletter to their supporters. James and Julie tried to be quiet when they made love in the Center's office, but sometimes James would throw Julie down on the rug on the floor, and take her there. Sex at the pregnancy center was dangerous, with Mickey sleeping in the back part of the house, just down the hallway, but Julie found the rough sex with James thrilling, something she never expected of herself. The dark allure of the forbidden pleasures on the floor of the Crisis Pregnancy Center at night was so intense she forgot it was the same room where she counselled clients in the daytime on the need for chastity. But now she was burning in the flames of sex, and her only brief relief was even more sex with James.

One night when she and James lay in each other's arms afterwards on the floor of the counselling room, Julie saw the locked door handle turn, and heard Mickey knock on the door, and heard his puzzled voice ask: 'Is anyone there?' Julie remained perfectly still, signaling James to be quiet too. 'How can this door be locked?' She heard Mickey say, and heard and saw the doorknob turning when Mickey tried it again, Julie not daring to move or even breathe. To her relief Mickey went back to his end of the house, and nothing more happened. Julie was never questioned about the locked door at night in the counselling room, but she wondered uneasily what Mickey and Dolores might know.

Whenever James would sodomize Julie she would protest but soon give way to her deep breathing and moaning enjoying it. The complaining and then the acquiescence and surrender became part of their foreplay, very satisfying to James. Sometimes she would wiggle her bum trying to make it hard for him to penetrate her but James liked that too and was strong enough to pin her down and do it. Once she even sat up beside him on her bum so he could not sodomize her, but she was smiling. James put it the contradictions down to the mysteries of a woman's nature. When he wanted to lick her anus he would ask her to position herself so he could reach her bum, and she willingly cooperated, shifting around so his mouth could reach her. James found her participation as thrilling as her resistance, and liked to hear her little moans of pleasure as he licked her. During the sodomy he especially liked it when she said 'O Fuck, O Shit.' He knew she was enjoying it and encouraging him, but she would deny that.

Finally, Julie knew she had to break off with James, her conflicted guilt between her beliefs and her feelings was so great. Fr. MacIntyre at Sacred Heart warned her in confession if she answered his calls to come to the Crisis Pregnancy Center at night again she would be committing mortal sin. She could lose her soul and salvation. Julie respected Fr. MacIntyre as a wise old priest, and as a Christian believer she was afraid of going to Hell.

Her confession was frank and honest, Julie kneeling on the purple cushion in the dim confessional, her hands clasped in front of her. She was embarrassed to start, but the anonymity of the dark helped her open up, even though she knew Fr. MacIntyre knew her and would recognize her voice. Beginning was the hard part. Once she began her confession Julie knew the reality of the truth being discussed would carry her through. Confession always got easier as she went along saying everything, even if she was reluctant.

'Father, I'm sexually active. I do a lot of things I never believed in before, but I got to like them.'

'What have you done my child?'

'Everything. Sexual intercourse. My boyfriend introduced me to oral and anal sex. I resisted at first, but I wanted to please him, and he kept coaxing me. When I gave in I liked the pleasure, but I always felt bad about it afterwards. He even licks my anus, but I could never do it to him when he asked me to. It's a dirty part of the body. I just can't do that. He calls it rimming. Sometimes we masturbate each other, and do the 69 position, or I just go down on him.'

'You have been corrupted by the deadly sin of lust, lower than the beasts in the fields. Sodomy is a mortal sin. It destroys sanctifying grace in the soul, and leads to eternal damnation. The Church teaches sexual acts should be in marriage and always open to life.'

'I'm confused. I don't understand anymore. James says it's just an exquisite pleasure, and how could a little thing like anal sex lead to Hell, and what does it matter during the infertile time in my cycle when I can't conceive a baby anyway? He's very persuasive.'

'It matters. The Church, and Scripture both condemn sodomy. So do the Fathers of the Church. Always the same teaching. St Thomas Aquinas calls it the sin against nature. The Catholic Church teaches sodomy is one of the four sins crying to heaven for vengeance. Do you want to risk your eternal salvation for a few moments of transitory sexual pleasure?'

'I don't know what to think. James says everyone is doing it. Is everyone going to Hell?'

'Why are you confessing if it's all okay?'

'I feel bad about it.'

'You must obey even if you don't understand. Believe in God and the Church, trust the Bible and centuries of Christian tradition. Chasten the body to heal the soul. Deny yourself these forbidden pleasures. Use the missionary position, and only after you are married. Your confusion shows the blindness of mind following indulgence in the filth of sexual sin. The Devil loves to tempt the pure into this sin more than anything else. The fiend is ecstatic at sexual corruption, when the best become the worst.'

'My boyfriend says our bodies are good, and if something feels good we can do it.'

'Our bodies are good in their proper place. Your body is the temple of the Holy Spirit, a living sacrifice to God. Keep yourself clean and pure. Your seductive boyfriend is leading you down the primrose path to Hell. He is quite mistaken in what he thinks is right and wrong. He is preaching the sexual revolution, not Christianity, even if he is a Catholic. St. Thomas called what you are doing luxuria, the pursuit of pleasure beyond the proper purpose of things.'

'To tell you the truth, he scares me now. He wants us to choke each other at the time of climax. He says it intensifies the pleasure of the orgasm. What if he goes too far, or I go too far, and someone dies?'

'You have to end this relationship.'

Julie sighed, her tension draining away in the darkness through the release of words. 'Yes Father, I will obey the teaching of the Church. If I get confused again, I will hold on to what you say.'

'How did you fall into such sin with your background, with all that you know?'

'There was something in me, drawing me to him. I wanted to try everything. Not miss out.'

'Just like Eve. The apple looked good, and tasted good, but it cost her paradise in the end. Sin always promises to give us the world, but gives us nothing, and takes everything away.'

Julie listened to Fr. MacIntyre, and steeled herself to resist her temptations in her weakened state. The next time James called, she told him she was not meeting him at the Crisis Pregnancy Center in the nighttime anymore. 'I can't see you James. I hate and detest what we do. It's dirty.'

'But you enjoy it, I can tell, you can't deny you enjoy it, with the little sounds you make, the way you call my name. You're a very sexy woman.'

'Yes, I enjoy it, but it makes me sick, to tell you the truth. I feel horrible afterward.'

'You're not making sense.'

'I might like it, but I don't want to like it. Our relationship is not pleasing to God.'

'If it feels good, God made it feel good.'

'You always say that. Why won't you get an annulment and marry me, if you're a Catholic man?'

James was silent. Then he said: 'I'm not really divorced. We're just separated.'

'What? You told me you were divorced.'

"Same thing.'

'It's not the same at all. I never would have gone out with you if I knew you were separated. You're still married, not even divorced.'

'A technicality.'

'You're a liar. You've lied to me all along.'

'I just didn't tell you everything. Did you tell me everything?'

'Is this what you want, is it over?'

'I don't know, the way you're talking.'

Julie had meant to break up with him, but now it seemed he was leaving her and she tried to hang on to him as it was all slipping away.

'Wait–Don't you want to rape me?'

'Is that what you want?'

'Sometimes I think about it.'

'Julie,' he said, 'I already did."

Then he hung up.

This religious broad is kinkier than me, James thought. After the telephone call, Julie never saw him again. She heard he left a letter of resignation addressed to Mickey, and moved out of Calgary. She was too embarrassed to show much interest in his departure, and did not ask Mickey to see the letter. Julie hoped Mickey would never learn what happened between her and James.

8

A month later when her period was late Julie used one of the Center's tests to confirm she was pregnant. She admitted to everyone she was going to have a baby. She would not say who the father was. Julie told James' mother she was pregnant, and asked her how she could get in touch with him. James' mother suggested Julie should visit the Craigenback Abortion Clinic, and hung up on her too. Mickey and Dolores accepted Julie as they accepted any of the single mothers who came to the Crisis Pregnancy Center, treating her with respect and dignity, assuring her she was a welcome and valued member of their pro-life group.

Some of the other women who volunteered at the Center, especially the older ones Dora and Sara, were more affected by the scandal. They never looked at Julie the same way again. Dora's husband was a pastor in the evangelical church. In her late thirties she was an attractive woman with penetrating blue eyes and auburn hair. A woman of strong Christian morality and missionary zeal, she was not afraid to be an evangelizing soul for the conversion of sinners. Her inseparable friend Sara was an elderly woman, a widow and a grandmother, but she was not sweet. The tensions between the proper older women and Julie the young single mother went on for months during her advancing pregnancy, and the dissension was even worse when baby Jeffrey was born, and Julie started bringing him with her to the Center.

Dolores and Mickey enjoyed seeing a baby crawling around the Crisis Pregnancy Center's floor, and later balancing himself on the walls of the office with his tiny hands as his body developed and he began to learn to walk. Jeffrey was a good counselor, the greatest example possible to the doubtful women coming to the Center as clients having their own baby would not ruin their lives. He was such a happy, smiling, good-natured and loving baby no one could deny he was beautiful. He invented his own game of opening and closing all the doors to every room in the house, again and again swinging the doors closed from his perch sitting on the floor, laughing delightedly. His infectious joy at the great game playing with the giant toys of the doors added a charm to the Crisis Pregnancy Center far beyond any social work agency.

Mickey's interventions with Dora and Sara and their friends at the Center became more numerous as the women constantly put Julie down in their desire to distance themselves from her and her sin. The group of women at the Center banded together in a pecking order, with Julie at the bottom. They complained that having Julie in the Center, especially with her baby, was unprofessional. Mickey defended Julie and Jeffrey. Dora and Sara began to insinuate Mickey must be attracted to her. They started insulting Julie more and more. The beginning of the end came just last week. As soon as Mickey came through the front door of the Center after returning from one of his court hearings, he walked into Dora fighting with Julie. Mickey had lost in court again, and he was tired of Dora and Sara and the other women picking on Julie. He asked Dora to apologize to her: 'You have to apologize. She deserves to be well treated here. She had her baby, that's pro-life. The fact she fell into sexual temptation is less of a sin than covering up a pregnancy with abortion, the real hypocrisy. Some people do have abortions, and then come out to the pro-life rally.'

'I'm not going to apologize to a child-woman. She shouldn't be here.'

'If you won't apologize to Julie, I'm afraid you'll have to leave. We can't have this fighting among the volunteers. And I hope it will be a sincere apology, from the heart.'

'Why do you favor her? Are you after her yourself?'

'All this negativity is not healthy. It's not Christian. It's not pro-life.'

'I'm not going to have a Catholic preach to me what it means to be a Christian.'

'Can't we leave religious differences out of our pro-life work? Most do.'

'You're naïve Mickey. Don't you know Julie is in love with you? She's using Jeffrey to get to you. She wants you to marry her, be a father to her baby.'

'I'm way too old for her. I'm not personally interested in Julie. This is about pro-life and single mothers.'

'You're a blind man if you can't see the little slut for what she is.'

Mickey tried to ignore all the insults. 'You're the older woman Dora. Show some mature leadership for the other women. Julie is young, and doing the best she can. She has a tough road as a single mother.'

'I'm willing to talk to her, but she has to approach me first, and she should be the one apologizing for trying to get me in trouble. That wasn't nice.'

'Good grief,' Mickey exploded, 'and what if Julie says you have to approach her first, and apologize to her? Where does it end?' He walked away from her.

'Don't be so petty about it,' Dora said to his retreating back.

Dora thought about it overnight, and the next day decided she would apologize to Julie, as much as she hated the idea, just to keep her program alive of reforming the Crisis Pregnancy Center. She intended to show leadership all right, more than Mickey knew. He was present for the apology in the front office of the Center. Dora said she was sorry if she said anything to hurt Julie's feelings. Julie said she accepted Dora's apology, and hoped they could get along in the future and do some good work for the mothers and the babies. When Dora left the meeting after her forced apology to Julie she silently vowed Mickey would have to pay for this latest outrage, even though she walked out of the office smiling and hugging Julie.

Mickey finally had to remove her. Dora could not hid her true feelings of animosity towards Julie any longer, despite her apology the week before. The friction between the women continued, and Dora began listing all of her complaints against Mickey and the way he ran the Center. She admitted she never felt right working as a counselor from the beginning. The Center was dishonest, she said. She didn't like it when the clients got angry when they discovered they were not going to get abortions. She didn't think it was Christian to deceive people. She objected to mixing in information against birth control with pregnancy counselling. She thought contraception was a separate issue, and women had a right to it. She said Julie was an unmarried woman, and a bad example to the clients. She lectured Mickey that when he used the bathroom he should put the toilet seat down again for the women. When Mickey fired her, he had to take her by the arm and escort her out of the house, and shut the door in her face when she kept arguing back.

Dora stood on the sidewalk outside the house, looking back at Mickey standing in the doorway.

'You will pay for this.'

Mickey had enough of her.

'Don't go away mad. Just go away.'

Dolores was worried. Dora knew everything about their operation, knew all of the people. Some of them were still her friends on the inside. She could do a lot of damage, and Dolores thought Dora would want to get even, and feel morally justified about her revenge. Mickey didn't realize the fury Dora was capable of as a woman scorned. After he fired Dora Mickey said he was glad she was gone, she was so difficult and disruptive. He hoped the pregnancy center would be peaceful now. Dolores was not so sure. She had known trouble was coming the day Mickey wondered out loud in front of the volunteers how Dora's husband could have married her. She warned him afterwards: 'Don't you know what you said will get back to Dora, and she will crucify you for it? You just made an enemy.'

'It's her voice I can't stand, harsh and grating. It hurts my ears. Nothing soft and feminine or lovely about it. How can her husband bear listening to Dora's loud voice all day long? She never shuts up. As soon as she enters a room she takes over. She reminds me of the old joke of the man who never spoke to his wife for three weeks, because he didn't want to interrupt her. Why do women need to talk so much?'

'Mickey, why ask for trouble, when we have so much as it is?'

'The problem is so few people volunteer for pro-life we have to take who we can get. I should never have allowed her in here.'

The scene earlier in the morning firing Dora was ugly, but though she was worried what might happen next, Dolores admitted to herself she too was glad Dora was gone.

9

'Why not take your coat off dear? Dolores asked Sadie again. 'It's so warm in here.'

Sadie unzipped her winter coat but did not remove it, revealing a slim figure, sitting in her tight fitting jeans, and wearing a simple white blouse. Sunglasses rested in her brown hair. Her complexion was smooth and unblemished, her teeth even and white. Manicured fingernails, with a light pink polish, set off her subdued but alluring femininity. Sadie was a young woman who would have been beautiful, except for the anxious furrows Dolores saw were pinching her mouth. For all the regularity of her features, her face was set in a hard expression diminishing her attractiveness. Dolores checked, glancing quickly. Sadie was not wearing any rings. She still balanced on the front edge of the chair, her right hand lying in her lap, the hand clenched tight in a fist wrapped around her thumb, her knuckles white.

Dolores explained the Crisis Pregnancy Center's procedure. 'I will ask you a few questions on this form. Then we can do the pregnancy test for you.'

Rick would be back soon. 'Will this take very long?'

'Maybe an hour for everything. What is your last name?'

He should be gone at least an hour. 'Summers. Sadie Summers.'

'How old are you?'

'Twenty-one.'
'Birth date?'
'May 19, 1997.'
'What is your address?'
'36 Brentwood Terrace, Apartment 4.'
'Telephone number?'
'547, 4442.'
'Religion?'
'What does it matter?'
'Sometimes religious beliefs can play a part in someone's decisions. Pregnancy is a matter of conscience.'
'Catholic.'
'When was the date of your last period, the day it began?'
'How quick can I get this done.'
'I need some information Sadie. First things first.'
'I'm in a hurry. Rick gets impatient.'
'What will he do?'
'Get angry. Tell me off for making him wait.'
This was worth exploring. Dolores leaned towards Sadie. 'Does he hit you.'
'He's come close. Two weeks ago he was so mad he punched the wall. His hand was sore for days. I was frightened. It was me he wanted to hit, and punch hard.'
'Did he take responsibility for his violence?'
'He said he couldn't stand my voice digging at him.'
'So he blamed you for provoking him.'
'Yeah, but he was nice to me afterwards. Brought me some flowers.'
'Abuse and forgiveness, is it a pattern?'

'We fight and make up, like everyone. I do dig at him sometimes.'

'Do you know how to protect yourself?'

'I called the woman's shelter the last time, to see what my rights were, just in case. I was scared.'

'Why do you stay with him?'

'He has his good points. I keep hoping he will change.'

'Are you willing to stay with him despite the smile at your sister?'

'I feel a little calmer now. Maybe we can work it out.' Sadie noticed the plastic models of unborn children at different stages of development sitting on the bookshelf behind Dolores. Her eyes widened. 'What kind of place is this? There seems to be a lot of baby stuff around. And a real live baby. Are you sure you're going to help me here?'

Dolores wanted to keep the conversation going, get Sadie to stay and watch the video. The video information was the heart of the counselling, cutting through all the misinformation floating around. 'Of course we're here to help you dear.'

This choice about abortion was the most important decision possible in the life of this young woman. These moments of private decision were what the public struggle was all about. It was all happening here inside the Crisis Pregnancy Center, but what went on in their talk would never be on the evening news. She was privileged during the brief time she spent with another woman, a stranger, to share in her deepest concerns at a critical turning point in her life. She was even more blessed when she witnessed a change of mind away from death to life.

So many of the women just needed some information, some support. Needed some caring, woman to woman, heart to heart. Sometimes the women were difficult to reach, hardened in their selfish resolve to kill their own son or daughter, threatened by child's interference with their own lives. But most of the clients were ordinary women, confused and scared, without encouragement in their pregnancy. After all the shouting of all the slogans, all the false rationalizations and twisted semantics, abortion came down to this: a mother and a baby, and the terrible choice.

Sadie was fidgeting in her chair. Dolores re-directed her attention back to the interview questions. 'When was the date of your last period, the day you first began bleeding?'

Sadie wanted to talk when heard the question. She needed to talk about her periods, and this woman seemed interested. Her periods were always a problem for her. Talking helped, but Rick never wanted to listen to her about her periods. 'October 1st. It lasted five days, heavy bleeding and cramping, my back and legs were very sore. I felt so weak I had to lie down and rest on the couch. I couldn't do much. I was irritated with my boyfriend, he didn't seem to care at all what I was going through.'

Dolores let Sadie talk, not sharing yet what Rick said about her outside, his dislike of women's feelings. 'He didn't show any sympathy?'

'None. He doesn't understand what it is for a woman to lose blood every month.'

'A woman's period is something many men find hard to deal with. Only women bleed.'

'He's just not interested. He won't hear about it, blocks me out.'

'When were you expecting your next period.'

'About every four weeks.'

'Do you have late periods.'

'Not this late. Sometimes I can be hard to predict.'

'Today is December 21st. A week late is enough time for the test to show if you're pregnant. You've missed two periods since October 1st, November 1st and December 1st, assuming you have a four week cycle, maybe eleven weeks now. Why have you waited so long?'

'I was hoping it would come again in December, even if I missed the whole month of November. But it never did.'

'Are you so irregular sometimes you miss two periods?'

'Yeah, it happens. I don't understand it myself.'

I bet she's on the Pill, Dolores thought, and no one ever explained it to her, how the Pill really works, how disruptive it can be to a woman's true cycle. 'Did you have any discussions with Rick about the possibility of being pregnant?'

'No, we both just kind of ignored it. Like I said, he doesn't pay much attention to my periods.'

'Stress and tension, or ill heath, can be other reasons delaying a period. Have you been sick?'

'No, I'm fine.'

'Any unusual stress or tension lately?'

Sadie's face reddened, the blood rising to her skin. 'My boyfriend and me have been fighting about a lot of things. My sister wasn't the only one.'

The boyfriend seemed to be a dominant issue with Sadie.

Now was not the time to get sidetracked about him too much. Dolores needed to get the information about her reproductive history first. But maybe letting her talk about him would get them somewhere. She would play it by ear. 'You're not getting along with him?'

Sadie picked up a wrapped Christmas candy from the bowl on the desk. 'May I?'

'Yes, of course.'

Sadie focused her attention on opening the candy wrapper, not answering the question at first. Then she let it all out. 'He's a real jerk, he keeps saying 'You take care of it.' He's out there somewhere doing what he likes to do, which is usually drink.' Sadie was so upset with Rick she was repeating her complaints about him, his lack of presence. The coward, she thought. Sadie kept a record of wrongs, and when she and Rick had fights she would bring up everything she resented back to the beginning of their relationship. She continued her list of grievances. 'He's always like this. When my period is coming, and I don't feel well, he just tells me 'Don't be so cranky.' He tells me to leave him alone with my bad moods. 'Don't take it out on me,' he says. He says it's not his business, and goes out and leaves me alone all day when I'm resting on the couch and don't feel like doing anything, the cramps killing me, and he's out there somewhere avoiding me. Driving away leaving me here is the kind of thing he does.'

Dolores continued with the more specific, closed questions after her initial open questions, building on the response of the client as Mickey had trained her. 'Did he say why he didn't want to come in today? Outside of wanting you to take care of it?'

Sadie crossed one of her legs over the other, her top leg swinging back and forth. 'He said just get rid of it, we can't afford a baby, we aren't married and he isn't ready to be tied down. He said it wasn't part of the deal when we moved in to live together. He's angry the Pill didn't work. He's suspicious maybe I didn't take it on purpose. He thinks I deliberately got pregnant to trap him into marriage. He used a condom too for double protection, but the condom broke. I wasn't trying to trap him into marriage. I sometimes forget to take the Pill. I don't like all the effects of it. I don't want to lose him. I love him. But he just won't talk about his feelings and pulls away from me. He gets distant when I try to get him to talk. I never know what he's thinking.'

'Sounds like this time he told you a lot of what he thinks.'

'But it's all negative. It's not really him, or all of him. He's just scared of commitment and fatherhood. I know him. Some things he won't admit.'

Dolores was glad to see Sadie engaging in the conversation. The client was drawn into the well-designed process of the pro-life counselling session, meant to change her mind about abortion, with the goal of saving both mother and child. The most important thing was to get Sadie to stay and watch the video. The information on the video changed many minds. The women didn't know the truth about abortion. They didn't know the facts of the child's amazing and speedy development in the mother's womb. They didn't know what really went on in the abortion procedures, what they did to the baby. The women didn't know the dangers to themselves from abortion.

The Center had saved many lives with their new yellow pages phone book advertising. The receptionist volunteers like Julie were carefully trained to be non-committal on the telephone. The important thing was to get the clients to come in, and see the pro-life video, and talk to the pro-life counselor. The offer of a free pregnancy test in the telephone book ads was only a hook to get the women to come in. They could buy the same pregnancy test themselves at any drug store, and do the test at home. Dolores wanted to keep Sadie talking: 'It's very common with the men, the problem of talking about their feelings. They can be such children.'

Sadie laughed, nodding her head in agreement. 'I know. Rick is so immature. I don't know why I stay with him sometimes.'

'Rick said the same things to me outside. He wouldn't talk about his own feelings, and he said he doesn't like to talk about women's feelings. He seemed to almost have contempt for them.'

'When he talks to me that way I feel broken into pieces.'

'You're very hurt.'

'I go to him with my heart wide open, and he turns away. He stabs me right in the heart.'

'Relationships are tough.'

'It's unfair.'

She is really talking to me, Dolores thought, developing a relationship with me. Maybe she can be reached. 'Do you have any children Sadie?'

Sadie blushed and looked away. 'Outside of Rick, no, I'm

too young.'
　But she wasn't telling the whole truth to her counsellor.

10

Even before Mickey fired Dora, she plotted with her friend Sara to remove him from pro-life. They hoped the authorities would arrest him soon, and charge him with fraud. They went around to several government departments telling everyone who would listen what they knew about the Crisis Pregnancy Center.

'What can we do now you're no longer on the inside? Sara asked Dora.

'We still have friends in the Center, and we can get some of our other friends to watch the house, see who comes in and out. And we can keep trying to get someone to act.'

'They don't want to do anything. The last man, he said he had to be careful with Mickey, because he knew all the loopholes.'

'We'll get him. We'll get him down.'

'He's so smart.'

'He'll slip up.'

Dora planned to get her friends to start watching the Crisis Pregnancy Center right away. She and her friends also started making silent telephone calls to the Center, just listening without saying anything, keeping the pressure on Mickey and his volunteers, letting them know they were being watched.

'The naive fool Mickey Finnegan,' Dora said, 'he's forgotten he put me on the Crisis Pregnancy Center's bank account as a signing officer, in case anything happened to him. I could clean him out at any time.'

'He should be wiped out,' Dora said. 'He gets his money from donations, and people don't know how crooked the Center is. He gets money out of government grants too, and they don't even know they are giving it to pro-life. The government thinks it is supporting Family Planning, with all his phony names. Pro-life doesn't need dirty government money. We can trust in God.'

'I heard he gets welfare too, pretending he's sick and can't work.'

'He is sick. We should go to every single place he gets money, and turn him in.'

'It's only right. He's a crook.'

'We should do what's right. We can't stand by and let something wrong go on without reporting it.'

'Pro-life is moral. He's not.'

'He should go out to work like other men.'

'I'll talk to Sergeant Ryan about it.'

'What a great idea. Let's do it. We'll totally surprise him. Blindside him. If we have a policeman like Dave Ryan back us up, we can take the money from the Center's bank account. Give it to the police, or one of the other government people.'

'Yeah,' Dora said, liking the plan more and more. 'With no money to operate the Center he'll be finished. Maybe charged too.'

'Without money he can't do anything. The Center will collapse.'

Dora could not refrain from voicing her grudging respect

for Mickey, much as she wanted to oust and replace him. 'Mickey is strong willed. He should have been brought down a long time ago. But he keeps popping back up.'

Her cool blue eyes glittered with satisfaction at her recurrent thought of seeing Mickey led away from a courtroom in handcuffs, convicted of fraud. He was an embarrassment to pro-life, and yet many people accepted him as the spokesman, the public face of pro-life in Calgary. He had to be discredited. It was the only way to get rid of him for good.

Then someone respectable could speak for pro-life, someone like herself. She deserved the leadership. With Mickey gone she could take over the house, operate the Crisis Pregnancy Center the honest way it should be run. Mickey did more harm than good. None of the pro-lifers ever elected him as their leader and spokesman. The pro-abortion news media elected him the pro-life leader, and they all went to him for interviews just because of all his grandstanding stunts. He had made a name for himself, that was how the system worked, but he was not the only pro-lifer in Calgary. The others like her and Sara deserved some attention too. They were not supporting players in the Mickey Finnegan Show. They were stars in their own right. The news media labeled Mickey the Abortion Fighter, and it went to his head. No one wanted Mickey really, not the pro-aborts, and not the pro-lifers. They all wanted to get rid of him. He wasn't needed. The public should know the truth. The pro-life movement could get along very well without Mickey Finnegan.

Dora was glad she had an ally like Sara. She kept thinking and talking, scheming against Mickey with her good friend, as they walked away from the house of the Crisis Pregnancy Center the same morning after Mickey had shown her the door, practically shoved her out the door. Who was he lecture them? Who was he to teach them anything? Who was Julie to still be on the inside, the little slut who had Mickey wrapped around her finger?

There would be a judgment coming, Dora vowed, *she would see to it personally.*

11

'Have you had an abortion before?' Dolores wanted to keep Sadie on track during the intake interview, guiding her through the questions on the form. They could talk more about her boyfriend later. Knowing how Sadie might have been affected by previous abortion was important. Why did she flush and look away when Dolores asked her if she had any children? Her guess was right.

'Yes.' Sadie looked away again, dropping her eyes towards her clenched fist lying in her lap, her bowed head answering. 'Three years ago, when I was 18.' She never wanted to talk about it. It was her private secret, stuffed down deep inside herself. She did not think about it. But Sadie thought she should not lie in this interview about another abortion. They might examine her, know somehow. 'In Edmonton. I moved down here to Calgary last year. I don't know where to go anymore.'

Dolores was careful not to betray any judgmental attitude about Sadie's abortion. She continued her neutral questioning, for the sake of completing the pretense of the intake form. 'How many weeks were you when you had the abortion?'

'Eight weeks. I was very young and confused. I didn't know what to do. They gave me the abortion pill, RU-486, actually it was two different pills, and it took a couple of days. It was painful, and there was a lot of bleeding. It wasn't simple to do a home abortion by pills at all. I ended up in the emergency ward, because of the bleeding and an infection. I don't want to go through the pills again.'

'Before you can get an abortion this time, you'll be 12 weeks. You can't use the abortion pills anymore, it has to be a surgical abortion.'

'I want it done quick. I don't want any delays.'

This is a damaged young woman, Dolores thought. She has already had one abortion, and now she wants another one. What could she say to her to make a difference? She was seeing this too often, women wanting repeat abortions. Sometimes three or four repeat abortions. The first abortion led to emotional deadening, the numbness that made the next abortion easier. Or were they just using abortion for birth control, again and again? 'You said you were using birth control?'

'The Pill, and Rick used a condom, but it broke. We tried double protection, so it isn't our fault.'

No surprise. How often had she heard from the clients the contraception they were using failed? 'I meant the first time, your first abortion, were you using birth control then?'

'Yeah, the same thing. I didn't take the Pill every day, and the other time the condom slipped off. It was another guy. Rick and I have only been going out for a year. I broke up with my old boyfriend, left him behind in Edmonton. Then I came down to Calgary, and I met Rick.'

Dolores checked off the appropriate Condom and Pill sections on the intake form. 'How long have you been using the birth control pill?'

'Five years, since I was 16, but it failed when I was 18, the first time I got pregnant. The Pill makes me feel sick, and it made my periods hard to understand. Sometimes too much bleeding, then no bleeding at all other times. So I don't like it. I don't take it all the time. Now it looks like I'm pregnant again.'

Sadie sounded apologetic to Dolores, explaining why she did not use the Pill regularly. Sadie was well conditioned to look on the use of the Pill as responsible sexuality. 'So you first went on the Pill when you were 16? So young?'

'I became sexually active then. My mother took me to her doctor to put me on the Pill. She didn't want me to get pregnant.'

Dolores continued her professional interviewing, not betraying her personal opinion how wrong Sadie's Catholic mother was putting her young daughter on the Pill. She assumed the mother was Catholic if Sadie was. What good was she doing her daughter to help her fornicate? All the beauty of sexual love as God intended it for married men and women demeaned, reduced to teenage risk management. And how healthy was it to put a growing adolescent girl on a powerful hormone pill interfering with her still developing reproductive organs? She would discuss it all with Sadie later. For now she finished the questions. 'Did you ever have an IUD?'

'I tried it once, but it also caused me pain and bleeding. I got another infection from the tail end of the coil hanging down from my cervix into my vagina. I went into toxic shock, chills and fever, my body shaking. I had a red spot on my leg, and couldn't walk without pins and needles. I ended up in emergency, and they said I had sepsis, blood poisoning from the infection. They took the IUD out right away and pumped me full of IV antibiotics. Later they told me I shouldn't have had an IUD so young, they only use it for older women. The doctor I had was an incompetent quack. He did whatever my mother wanted.' Sadie raised her clenched fist lying in her lap and looked at her watch. These detailed questions took a long time. Rick would be impatient if she wasn't done when he got back. She didn't want him angry at him again.

Dolores was satisfied with the way the counselling interview was going. Sadie did not sound apologetic this time in her answer. She sounded angry at what he mother and the doctor did to her. She had gathered much information from Sadie through a few simple questions, getting a good overview of her whole sexual history. There was much here she could use in the counselling session after the pregnancy test and the video. She would take the opportunity to educate Sadie on what was wrong with all the birth control methods. In her experience the women knew nothing. They had never been told the facts by their doctors who just prescribed the Pill for them as routine.

Sadie was probably suffering from the effects of Post Abortion Syndrome too. Dolores understood what Sadie revealed in her answers, even if Sadie did not realize the significance herself. The IUD was not only contraception but an abortifacient device, designed to irritate the uterus and prevent implantation of already conceive embryos. Did anyone ever tell her the Pill was also an abortifacient? Inform her of the three ways the Pill worked: suppressing ovulation, so there was no egg, or changing the cervical mucus so sperm could not live to fertilize the egg, or also changing the endometrium, the lining of the uterus, preventing the implantation of a fertilized egg, the embryo, the child already conceived? Did anyone make it clear the first two ways were contraceptive, but the third way the Pill worked was an early chemical abortion? Probably not, most of the clients admitted they were never told the full truth about the Pill.

How many other unknown chemical abortions did Sadie have, besides her RU-486 abortion? Because of her use of the Pill and the IUD? The birth controllers got around the problem by redefining when life began, claiming not conception in the fallopian tubes but implantation in the uterus was the beginning moment of life. According to the redefinition, the prevention of implantation was not abortion. Life had not begun yet. Dolores wanted to give Sadie the real information in their talk later. She deserved to know the facts, the truth everyone was covering up. Sadie would have been spared so much grief in her young life, if only she had remained chaste and pure, if she had saved herself for marriage, if she had listened to the Lord and His Church as a good Catholic girl.

'Have you used any other birth control methods?'

'Yeah, I took the birth control shots for a while, but I didn't like those side effects either. Why is it the women who have to take all these things? All Rick has to do is put on a condom, or have a vasectomy. He says he doesn't want a knife used on him, so it all falls on me.'

'You're not the only one Sadie. It happens to many women. The men don't want to be bothered, but they want safe sex without children. The way nature designed us most of the details of human procreation fall on the woman. There are no pills for the men.'

'It's unfair.'

It was too soon in the intake interview to speak of God and his plan of human sexuality. So she spoke of nature. Sterilized men and women, sterilized temporarily by the surgeries, the vasectomies and tubal ligations, were neither God nor nature's plan. Human beings were living like animals now, neutered and spayed, mutilating their God given bodies, and living lower than the animals, people wallowing in their unnatural lusts. Dolores hoped she could reach Sadie on many levels in their counselling session to come, all the facts and all the morals.

Sadie was thinking about her resentments towards Rick again, wanting him to be more of a man for her. 'He's nothing but a sperm donor.'

'You mean your boyfriend?'

'And I don't like the way he keeps saying I'm getting too fat. I'm not overweight. He says he doesn't want a fat girlfriend. I accept him however he is, but he wants physical perfection in me. He's skinny, but he's got a pot belly from beer drinking, and he stinks of cigarettes. I can hardly stand the smell of him sometimes, but I don't say anything.'

'You're not fat. Look at me.'

'You look okay.'

Dolores smiled at Sadie, happy to see the developing

conversation she was building with her continued, woman to woman. Soon the intake interview questions would be completed. 'Have you ever used emergency birth control, the morning after pill?'

'Yeah once, but it made me deathly sick. I don't want to use it again.'

Did Sadie know the morning after pill also worked to abort already conceived embryos if it failed to prevent conception? Know it was an overdose of birth control pill hormones in one concentrated effort to try and stop implantation in the uterus? The birth control injections, the implants in the arms, they were all hormonal overdoses causing early chemical abortions. They were all essentially the same drugs, only the method of delivery was different. 'Have you ever had any sexually transmitted diseases?'

Sadie looked away again, rubbed her fingers up and down her clenched thumb in her fist, before looking at Dolores to answer this last question. 'My old boyfriend infected me with gonorrhea so I dumped him. He was unfaithful. He got it from someone else and gave it to me. I couldn't bear to have him touch me anymore. I was so worried. The gonorrhea was sore, burning when I had to pee. I had a bad smell down there, but it cleared up with the medicine.'

Dolores had to know this history how the sexual transmitted diseases might have affected Sadie's ability for conception and childbirth. The STDs harmed the women in many ways. All the birth control junk and all the sexual diseases poisoned the women's wombs. So many sterile women now. The women at first did not want children, and later when they started to realize what was important in life it was too late.

'And I had PID once, pelvic inflammatory disease, a very bad infection. But it didn't damage my fertility. I had an ultra sound to check me out. No scarring of my tubes. I have cysts on my ovaries, but it seems I keep getting pregnant.' Sadie's mouth twisted in a sardonic smile at her unstoppable fertility.

Dolores was worried about Sadie. She was far too young at twenty-one to go through so many reproductive problems already. She liked her, liked her honesty, her strong feelings. She needed her boyfriend's help and support. 'Is there any chance at all Rick might come in when he gets back? Can you persuade him?'

'Rick is a brute, a cold hearted brute. He *should* be here with me.'

'Do you feel alone with your pregnancy?'

'Absolutely alone.'

'We can help you with all of these things Sadie. Maybe show you some better ways.'

'I sure hope so. I'm thinking all I can do for sure is get my tubes tied. Or get a full hysterectomy, have them take everything out.'

'You don't really mean it, do you? You're too young for something so drastic and permanent. Your life and feelings can always change.'

Sadie did not answer her, instead studying her hands in her lap. Dolores decided it was time to move the session forward.

'If you will sign here please, giving your consent to the pregnancy test, we can do it for you now.'

12

Julie walked to the back of the house to see Mickey in his office.

'Someone is here to see you.'

'What's it about?'

'She has some papers in her hand.'

'Oh boy.'

Mickey walked along the hallway with Julie to the front of the house. The woman when she saw him spoke right away: 'Are you Mickey Finnegan?'

'I am.'

She handed him the papers. 'You have been served.'

The process server turned and walked out the door, and Mickey went back to his office to look at the new legal documents. He sat down at his desk and put on his reading glasses.

'What is it?' Julie asked, coming to find out.

'It's a Notice of Motion from the Craigenback Abortion Clinic. We have to be back in court again in three days, at ten o'clock in the morning on December 24th, in front of Judge Dockendorff.'

'What do they want this time?'

'They are asking for a court order signs be placed on our outside front door and our inside office walls we don't provide abortions or abortion referrals. They also want restrictions on our pro-life signs when we picket Craigenback's, so we can't use words like Kill and Murder.'

'Why?'

'They say abortion is legal, so we have no right to accuse them of wrongdoing like killing and murdering. They say it's slander and libel.'

'So now the court can tell us what to say, and what not to say?'

'It's what Craigenback and Sterne want.'

'How can they get away with that? Stopping our freedom of speech?'

'Sterne is a smart lawyer. It's why Craigenback pays her the big bucks. The good doctor is always lawyered up. They saw they got everything they wanted this morning cutting off our phone, so now they're pressing their advantage.'

'I feel completely controlled, even my words.'

'Interesting isn't it, the amount of control exercised by the advocates of freedom of choice?'

'Hypocrites. What can we do.'

'Not much time to prepare. They've probably these attacks for some time, ever since the new phone book came out, and not they're hitting us with punch after punch.'

'It never ends.'

Mickey saw the humor in it. He smiled. 'The crisis center is in crisis.'

'I don't like what they're doing. I hate it I have to see the abortion mill through our front window across the street. Now they are even inside here, with their signs on our walls. I don't like this at all.'

'I don't like it either. I'll try to fight it.'

'By the way, while you were out, the Catholic Women's League dropped off a donation of some baby clothes, a crib, and two infant car seats. I put them in the storeroom.'

'Great. I hope with all these legal threats we're facing from Craigenback, we'll still be here to give them to mothers who need them'

Julie turned and walked out of Mickey's office, returning to her station at the front of the house. Mickey watched her go, his headache bothering him, and growing worse. He reached in his desk drawer for the pill bottle and took another dose.

13

Dolores handed the intake card over to Sadie sitting at the other side of the desk for her to sign. Now she knew enough about Sadie to help her. No legal requirement existed for a signed consent to do a pregnancy test, but everybody always signed the form anyway, trained to be obedient patients, expecting it was a step in getting an abortion. Sadie signed the form.

'Come with me and we'll take a urine sample.' Dolores led Sadie partway down the central hallway to the tiny bathroom in the middle of the house. She showed her the plastic specimen container already set out on the counter of the sink. 'Come back to the room where we talked when you're done. During the test we will show you the video so you are well informed. It's 30 minutes. I will come back with your test results when the video is done.' Dolores gave Sadie the usual speech, and Sadie accepted it. Dolores recognized the familiar passivity, the clients so conditioned by medical routine. They gave the urine for the pregnancy test as requested, and then waited, only this time left with a video to watch. The clients accepted they were required to be informed before receiving the abortion referral, although no legal requirement for pre information existed. No one ever refused to watch. Some did turn it off halfway through. Some clients stormed out of the counselling room in the middle of the video, when they realized it was pro-life, but most people just watched it to the end.

After the complaints about the Crisis Pregnancy Center's phone listings became public, one of the local television stations sent an undercover reporter with a hidden camera, the reporter pretending to be a woman seeking an abortion. The reporter even brought someone else's urine with her to be tested positive for pregnancy. The television station wanted to expose the Center, to film the pro-life video and counselling session with a hidden camera and put it on the six o'clock news. Dolores did not mind the pro-life video was broadcast to all of Calgary. The news media usually covered up the reality of the dismembered bodies of the aborted babies. For once, the television news showed the truth about the killing of the unborn child. The news reporters wanted to convict the Center of showing pregnant women horrendous pictures, of using scare tactics. Truth did not matter, the worst thing you could do was hurt someone's feelings. The television station meant to show the pro-life counsellors were insensitive. Righteous indignation was the tone of the news clip. Imagine showing a pregnant woman in crisis gruesome pictures of aborted babies. The number of clients dropped off after the television news report, but picked up again as people forgot. The video and the talk with the counselor afterwards, those were the main things.

And the prayers. Dolores believed only the grace of God could touch the hearts of the clients. She knew her human limitations, knew only God could work inside the soul of another human being. She could not say anything to change another person. She was powerless. Whenever her day came to volunteer at the Center she went to the early morning mass at Sacred Heart church, and offered a holy hour of prayer. The volunteers always prepared spiritually for the pro-life counselling work of the day to come. They could not do such work on their own power. Where else could the strength to do it come but from God? They could not do a thing without the grace of God.

Dolores recognized Sadie's passive obedience as another irony of abortion. Angry feminists in rebellion for women's lib asserted their freedoms and rights to their own bodies, and ordinary women were still led around as much as ever. Led into abortions they were told to have and did not really want. Told by everyone, by their boyfriends, and husbands, and told by their fathers and mothers some of them, told by the news media, and by their schools, told by all the other powerful social forces supporting abortion. Told by the population controllers with their agendas to control the number of people, told by the eugenicists with their agendas to control the quality of people, wanting people without defects. Told by the climate change activists, to control pollution of the environment. Told even by their churches. The pro-abortion propaganda focused on unwanted children; you never heard about all of the unwanted abortions.

Left alone in the bathroom, Sadie passed some of her urine into the cup she held beneath her over the toilet bowl. She noticed the shower curtain hiding the tub right beside her, the plastic still damp with beads of water. The lady Dolores wasn't wearing any rings on her fingers. Maybe the middle-aged woman was unmarried, or divorced.

When Sadie came back to the counselling room Dolores was waiting for her with the television set already turned on, and the video player ready to start. The television screen showed white snow with the sound turned down.

'Does anyone live here?' Sadie asked, sitting down on the small couch beside the wall to watch the video, noticing how much of a home the house looked. 'It looks like someone took a shower in the bathroom.'

'Sometimes we freshen up. Sometimes Julie has to clean her baby. Now you just watch this dear, and I'll be right back with your test results.' Dolores pushed the play button, turned up the sound dial, and stepped out of the door of the counselling room, closing it behind her, leaving Sadie alone.

14

In the bathroom Dolores pulled on the protective disposable gloves, used an eyedropper to squeeze three drops of urine into the square foam pad of the little plastic pregnancy test, and waited five minutes for the test reaction. The first blue line appeared in the other foam pad, indicating the test was working properly. Then the second line revealed itself, faint at first, gradually darkening to a definite blue color. Sadie's test was positive, the second announcement of the presence of a new baby. The first sign was Sadie's missed period. Dolores poured the remaining urine into the toilet bowl and flushed it, put the specimen container and eyedropper in the trash can, and washed and sanitized her hands.

She brought the little pregnancy test with her, careful not to touch the urine pad with her bare fingers. She would show Sadie the actual test to confirm it for her. In happy times when a woman wanted to be pregnant, or changed her mind about abortion, the pregnancy test with its two blue lines became the first baby memento, cherished by the mother who would keep it forever and one day show her child. Dolores came out of the bathroom into the reception area, and sat down in one of the chairs placed there for waiting clients. Julie behind her receptionist's desk asked her in a low voice so Sadie would not hear them talking: 'How did it go?'

'She's pregnant.'

'You seem tense.'

Dolores nodded. When the pregnancy test was negative she felt relieved. The pressure was off. She would not have to fight to save the life of the child. The client could be educated for the future. But when the woman was pregnant she felt the responsibility weighing on her.

Julie noticed how Dolores was feeling. She felt it herself when it was her turn to counsel. 'It's funny, even we pro-lifers who love children seem happier if the woman is not pregnant.'

'It's just the terrible prospect of abortion bothering me.'

'She sure wanted an abortion the way she came in her.'

'She thinks she does. She doesn't know the facts. And doesn't know herself.'

'So what else is new?'

'I never want to start thinking of people as typical. Every soul is unique and important.'

'I didn't mean anything.'

'Nobody knows the truth anymore.'

Dolores rose from her chair and went over the pamphlet rack. She selected the ones she would give Sadie, based on what Sadie told her in the intake interview. She would give the pamphlets on Post Abortion Syndrome, on The Bitter Pill, on Natural Family Planning, and Resources for Single Mothers. She hoped she could Sadie off all the birth control junk. Dolores fingered her rosary beads as she waited for the video to finish, hearing the faint voices on the other side of the door of the counselling room.

Dolores thought of the magnificent development of the

preborn child, the same information Sadie was watching on the video. After two weeks the child was only one quarter of an inch long, but already the growth was awe inspiring. For the first two weeks the embryonic stem cells were all the same, then some unknown mechanism turned on the genes in the cells and differentiation started. She marveled at the amazing processes so early, before the woman even knew she had missed a period. Originally identical stem cells now began speeding to different areas of the body of the child, becoming the organs of the new human being. Between two and three weeks the basic structures of the heart and nervous system were already in place. At week three a tiny heart began to beat. At week five key organs like the liver developed, and the eyes appeared. The baby still only one quarter of an inch long contained as much varied information as an encyclopedia. The brain and nervous system grew at the rate of 4,000 to 5,000 neurons a second, and each of the neurons was as complex as a large city.

The facts were astonishing. If only people could appreciate once again their own dignity, and the wonder of the unborn child. Appreciate the beauty of God the divine artist at work, creating each unique amazingly complex new human being to live forever. But she knew from working with many clients the people had no formation anymore, had never received any spiritual education, and precious little scientific information either. God loved every human being into life. Would people ever again stand in awe of the mystery of conception and birth?

Dolores kept praying the Hail Marys on her rosary beads,

and remembered the first questions and answers of her child's catechism:

Who made me?

God made me.

Why did God make me?

God made me to know, love and serve Him in this world, and be happy with Him forever in the next.

The simple catechism told her the meaning and purpose of human life even as a child, if only she had the faith to believe it. She was a prodigal daughter who wandered far from home.

The video Sadie was also warning Sadie about the physical damage to her body from abortion procedures. The uterus could be punctured or scarred from the sharp curettes. Women could bleed to death from perforation of the uterus. The damaged uterus and cervix could be incapable of future pregnancy. The scar tissue of the scraped uterus might have trouble receiving embryos for implantation later, or the placenta might have trouble attaching to the endometrium. The cervix, once forced open for an abortion, would be weakened as a muscle for holding future babies. The video showed all the risky consequences the abortion system denied: infections, premature babies in the future, low birth weight babies, and breast cancer for the mother.

Sadie was watching the same realistic, graphic pictures of aborted babies on the video the undercover television reporter denounced. The dismembered bodies of babies torn apart, their severed arms and legs and heads in the grasp of the abortionist's forceps, showing her the bruised bodies of babies born dead but still intact after abortions induced by saline solutions or prostaglandin drugs. Aborted women were talking on the video about the emotional and spiritual suffering they went through for the rest of their lives, the guilt and the grief, the aching pain of loss.

Dolores heard the video end, and the click when Sadie turned of the television. She waited, listening for some moments to the silence in the counselling room. Julie listened to the silence too.

'Good luck. I'll pray for you.'

Dolores stood, knocked lightly on the door, took a deep breath, and whispered low: 'God help us,' turned the door handle, and walked into the counselling room.

15

Julie's phone rang in the waiting room. 'Family Planning, may I help you?'

She was repeating the general telephone greeting the Crisis Pregnancy Center devised applying to all the names in the phone book going to the same telephone number and same address. Family Planning covered all of them.

'Hail Purity.'

'I told you to never call me here.'

'I am your Commander in the Warriors. I decide. It's time we spoke again.'

'What do you want?'

'We've heard the Center is fighting an all front's war.'

'It's been hectic today. Mickey lost in court. The phone will soon be cut off. Dora was fired, more legal papers were served a few minutes ago, and a tough drop-in client wants an abortion.'

'What are the papers about?'

'Mickey has to be in court again Christmas Eve to try and stop Craigenback from controlling the signs on our front door.'

'So much for a free country.'

'I can understand why we need to do something more.'

'Drastic situations call for drastic remedies.'

Julie looked around down the hall to where Mickey was. 'I

really can't talk now.'

'Can you get the legal documents?'

'Mickey might leave them on his desk. He's reading then now.'

'If you can, scan them and save them in our joint email account, under a message in Drafts. Don't send the message, just save it. I will log on later and open the Drafts folder and see the documents.'

'I'll try.'

'Merry Christmas Purity.'

Julie hung up. The phone rang again. 'Family Planning. May I help you?'

The caller at the other end of the line did not say anything. Julie repeated her question. 'Are you there? Can I help you?'

Still the person at the other end of the line listened in silence. Julie hung up again. The phone rang again. 'Family Planning. May I help you?'

Silence and breathing.

'Are you there?'

Julie replaced the phone receiver back in its cradle. The phone rang again, almost immediately.

'Family Planning, may I help you?'

'This is Mayor Kathy Winters calling. My office is receiving many complaints about the anti-abortion deceptive counselling clinic. They're confusing everyone.'

'Yes Ma'am.'

'Can you send me any information you have so I fully understand the situation?'

'Our information is that the pro-lifers are providing their

clients with the facts and a choice. What's wrong with that?'

'Who is this?'

'My name is Julie. I volunteer here.'

'Here? Where's here?'

'The Crisis Pregnancy Center.'

'Son of a bitch,' the Mayor said, and hung up.

Julie smiled to herself for a moment. Then the phone rang again.

'Family Planning, may I help you?'

Silence and breathing.

'Are you there?'

No answer, and Julie ended the call.

Who could this be? Was it Dora or Sara? Or one of their friends? The government spying on them? Her commander in the Warriors keeping tabs on her? Craigenback's people harassing them? Julie wondered how long she could continue living with so much pressure at the Center when her baby Jeffrey needed her. He was her first and final responsibility. James Roberts had disappeared, and never acknowledged he was the father. She was all Jeffrey had.

16

'All done?'

Dolores sat in the chair beside the television, facing Sadie who sat on the small couch on the other side of the counselling room. The pro-life counsellors preferred to sit closer to the clients now when the time for the pretense of an abortion clinic was over. Dolores did not need to have an official desk between herself and Sadie anymore. She just wanted to be friendly to her, and help her. She saw Sadie was sitting on the couch with her arms folded across her chest, her hands clutching her opposite arms. Her upper body was half turned away from looking directly at the television or the counselor. Dolores gave her the news head on, the life changing results of the pregnancy test.

'Your test was positive.'

Sadie turned her averted head to look at Dolores. 'Could the test be wrong?'

'Sometimes, but not usually.'

Maybe there was hope. 'I can't be pregnant. Not now.'

'The pregnancy test detects a hormone called Human Chorionic Gonadotropin, HCG, a hormone never in your body unless you are pregnant. The new embryo sends out the hormonal signals so the unborn child can implant and grow in the uterus. It's an amazing fact of nature, that the child is in charge of his own growth and development.'

'I don't want any child in charge of me.'

'Don't you find it interesting the baby is not part of the mother's body, but is the one introducing new hormones in her body?'

'You can't say it's a baby already.'

'Here is your pregnancy test. The one blue line means it is working properly. The second blue line means it is a positive test.'

Sadie unfolded her closed arms and took the tiny test in her hands to look at it carefully. She tried to comprehend the awful news she was pregnant again. A baby was growing inside her. She blocked it out, placing the pregnancy test beside her on the arm of the couch. She did not look at it again.

'We can refer you to a good doctor if you like.'

'Will he do it?'

The Crisis Pregnancy Center only had one doctor for referrals. All the rest were involved in birth control and abortion, even the Catholic doctors. Thank God they had at least the one doctor.

'What did you think of the video?'

'It was biased.'

'What do you think of the baby's quick development?'

Dolores wanted Sadie to focus on her own baby, at possibly eleven weeks. How could she help her see the wonder of it in her tense depression, sitting on the edge of the couch, her whole body closed in on herself with her arms wrapped around her and eyes looking away? Dolores did not like the expressions *unborn child* or *pre-born child*. They made the child seem unreal, not human yet. How could she help Sadie see her baby was a child already, even before birth? She did not like the words *unwanted child*. The parents did not want the child; the child was not intrinsically unwanted as one of its own characteristics. The word *unwanted* put the stigma on the child.

Fetus did not sound human either. *Fetus* was now a medical, dehumanized scientific term. The pro-aborts tried to hide the humanity of the child with even worse euphemisms: the *product of conception*, or an *intra-uterine gestation*, for twins a double *intra-uterine gestation*. A gestation was not even a thing, it was only a process. Just like the phrases *termination of pregnancy* and *extraction* did away what was done to the child killing it. A pregnancy was another indefinite process, not the concrete, real body of a growing child. The abortion system not only did away with the babies, it removed the words to describe the killing, a neat two-step dance of evasion from reality. The impersonal termination of pregnancy avoided any human moral questions. *Termination of pregnancy* was only a *Procedure*, and what could be wrong with a medical procedure? They were only *Therapeutic Abortions, TAs*.

Why be so scientific and medical about everything with all the impersonal technical jargon? *Zygotes? Embryos?* Women had sex, they conceived, they would have a baby if they did not interfere with the natural order of things, and let nature take its course. When everything was framed in the medical model and made technically scientific it was easy to dehumanize the victim. Dehumanizing the victim through the careful selection of words was always the first step in mass genocide. Stamp out the cockroaches. If it was hard for the pro-lifers to find words to describe the full humanity of the child before birth, it was also hard for the pro-aborts to avoid the recognition of babies and killing without all the elaborate semantics talking around it. Dolores preferred the old fashioned charm of the words she said to Sadie now: 'You are with child.'

'I can't have this. Rick doesn't want it. He will leave me if I don't have an abortion, he already said so, and I still want him. I'm not strong enough to raise a child on my own.'

Dolores was amazed at the contradictions in Sadie. She made no sense. Before she hated Rick, did not want his baby after seeing him flirt with her sister. Now she was saying Rick was the one pressuring her to abort. For some reason she needed him. Dolores would have to take Sadie's declarations with a grain of salt. And unconsciously, Sadie had said the word *child*. She hoped it was something she could build on, help her break through her denial. 'So you do believe you have a child growing within you?'

'Not yet.'

'But you just said *child*.'

'It's my body.'

'The new human being inside you is not you Sadie, is not the father or the mother. The child is a separate human being with his own body, his own independent development.'

'It's not a human being yet so early.'

'The child only needs time and nutrition to grow and actualize from within.'

'It takes time to become a fully human being.'

'If the child is not human to begin with, nothing is added later to make the child human.'

'What?'

'The unborn children are not potential human beings, they are human beings with the potential to keep growing and developing, just like all of us do through our whole lives. I didn't know when I was your age I would develop to how I look now. I was once slim like you. I didn't know I was programmed in my genes to get heavier as time went on and I grew older.'

Sadie thought Dolores seemed sensitive about her weight. She had mentioned it twice now. 'It's hard to stay thin, I know. I have to exercise, and watch what I eat.'

Dolores was glad to see Sadie relating to her, staying in the conversation with her despite her resistance. Maybe there was a chance to reach her. She wanted to get back to Sadie's assertion she lacked strength.

'You're a capable person. You should never feel about yourself you can't raise a child.'

'But I don't want to do it alone. What can I do when my man is irresponsible?'

'If you want to get really scientific about it, the facts are all there now from modern research. The new child is a full human being from the moments of conception. The single cell zygote, which forms when the sperm and the ovum unite and the new human being is created, contains the entire human genome. Scientists discovered it from DNA sequencing. The single cell is a self-metabolizing, entirely unique and unrepeatable human being. All the objective evidence is there if you are willing to look. High school students learn it biology class. Humanity is not decided by size.'

Dolores could see Sadie blank out on her scientific lecture, staring downwards at her hands clenched in her lap. Technical words were used to dehumanize the child, but technical words were avoided when they proved the humanity of the child. If the facts of life did not matter, what more could she say to Sadie who did not want to hear it, but just wanted to do what she wanted to do?

'I'm not ready for children yet,' Sadie said into the silence as Dolores thought. 'Maybe later.'

'You only have a limited window of opportunity to have children. Did you know a woman is born with all of her eggs, and a man produces new sperm every day? As a woman ages her eggs also get older. After age 35 a woman's fertility drops like falling off a cliff.'

'I still have a big window. I'm only 21. I have years to go.'

'As long as you know. Many women thought they could put off having children, and then when it's too late they feel cheated. They were told they could have it all.'

'Cheated by who?'

'Just the general philosophy going around. Did you know that in in vitro fertilization, assisted reproduction in a laboratory, when they put an egg and a sperm together in a petri dish, and it's an older couple, they will use the man's sperm but not even allow an older egg? They insist on a donor egg in that situation.'

'Sounds unfair to the woman.'

'It is what it is. A woman's on a biological clock. A man can still have his own child, but the older woman can't. For many women it becomes an unexpected tragedy in their lives.'

'Like I said, I have plenty of time.'

God doesn't matter to her, Dolores thought, *and even the science doesn't make much of an impression. Reason and logic are not her concern. She is just a young woman trying to cope with life, overwhelmed by her feelings. Dolores knew all about it herself, the inner struggle for emotional self-control. She saw it in Mickey too.*

17

Dolores changed direction. 'How do you feel about the abortion you had before?'

Sadie's clenched hands became closed fists. Dolores never saw two clenched fists in a client before. She looked like she was angry enough to jump off the couch and attack her, the two fists a sign she was ready to fight. Suppressed pain glistened wetly in her eyes. 'I'm okay with it. It had to be done. I was way too young to have a child.'

There it was, the child again. 'Do you feel any guilt? Or grief? A sense of loss?'

'No.'

'Does the abortion ever come back into your mind?'

'No.'

'When you see a three year old child, do you think 'My child would be three now?'

'No, nothing.'

'Do noises like vacuum cleaners bother you, brining on any flashback to the abortion procedure?'

'No. What are you getting at?'

'We call those things abortion connectors, reminding women of what they may have put out of their minds.'

'No, I'm okay.'

'Was any other help offered to you besides abortion?'

Sadie was silence for a moment by the unexpected question.

She was thinking back. She beat a fist against her knee. 'No, I just knew and so did everyone else abortion was the best thing for me at that time in my life. I was a young teenager, only eighteen, a child myself.'

'Have you ever done self-punishing, self-destructive acts connected to your abortion?'

'No, I don't even smoke or drink or take drugs.'

'Did you have any depression?'

'No. I felt relieved.'

'Any suicidal thoughts?'

Sadie shuddered such an extreme suggestion could ever be associated with her.

'Of course not.'

'Do you ever dream about the child you aborted?'

'No.'

Dolores saw the continuing pain in Sadie, heard her repeated denials. She knew her disturbance was too great to force her to face it. Her body betrayed her, the clenched fists and glaring eyes holding back her tears. The pain was too much for her to talk about now. Maybe someday she would be able to talk about it, if anyone around her cared enough to listen that something important happened to her, and validate her experience. Abortion was not usually talked about that way, if at all. She tried another approach.

'Do you want children Sadie?'

'Yes. I have nothing against children when the time is right. I'm a normal woman. I have normal needs.'

'Abortion can have many side effects on a woman's body, like the video showed you, the damaged uterus and cervix.

A second abortion might permanently damage your ability to ever have children. I would not be giving you good counselling if I did not raise those possibilities with you. The desire to have children someday could be a risk factor, another reason for not having an abortion.'

'I don't seem to have any trouble getting pregnant.'

'Yes, but you might miscarry.'

'No fault then.'

In the face of her stubborn denials, Dolores decided she should not press Sadie anymore about her post abortion trauma. Denial was the most effective of defense mechanisms. Denial would never yield to direct frontal assault. Alcoholics in denial could never be told directly they had a drinking problem. They had to hit a personal bottom before reality broke through. Sadie's denial would not be broken today. She was satisfied she had at least alerted Sadie to the existence of physical and emotional abortion trauma was something common to many women. It was the best she could do for now. And something else was suddenly overwhelming her. 'I hate to do this, leaving you for a third time, but I have to go to the bathroom. I'll be right back.'

18

Julie saw Dolores come out of the counselling room, close the door behind leaving the client alone, and go into the bathroom. Dolores had tears in her eyes. Julie wondered what was going on in this unusual development.

Dolores sat on the closed seat of the toilet in the cramped washroom. She rubbed her eyes, wiping at the tears. Talking with Sadie had stirred her feelings about her own abortion. She tried to stifle the searing grief spilling out from the deepest recesses of her wounded mother's heart, the pain still tearing her apart. She had written a letter to her dead daughter Rachel after she named her, expressing her sorrow for aborting her. The tear-stained letter had helped. She did not burn it but kept it folded, stuffed in the pockets of her clothes, the letter to her daughter her constant companion. At times she would read it again. She felt for the letter, took it out of her pocket, and read it now.

My Darling Rachel,

Rachel, I am your mother Dolores. I aborted you 20 years ago when I was 21. I am so very very sorry. I never got to meet you, never got to see my sweet faced baby. I was under many pressures at the time. I didn't know what I was doing. I didn't have all the facts. Everyone around me told me it was the right thing to do. I didn't have any help in my life.

I was very young, and left alone, and I was scared. But all that's no excuse. I should not have aborted you. I should not have refused you life. It was wrong. I should have known better. I shouldn't have rejected you. I wish I was kinder to you. I didn't respect your human dignity. I should have let you live. I was very unfair to you. I was your mother, and I should have protected you. I should have died for you, not you dying for me.

The abortion must have been very painful for you. I can't even imagine what you went through. I thought I was doing the right thing, but I was wrong and blind. I know it now. I made the worst mistake of my life. I wasn't mature enough to treat you right. Handle the situation right. Do the right thing to help you, and help me. I was sick at the time, sick in my mind, sick in my soul. I was selfish. I was a selfish mother. How I wish I really loved you the way I should have.

I have regretted aborting you ever since. How I wish I never had the choice. Part of me died then too. I wish I had never done it. I always remember you. My loss has been heavy to bear. I wish I could have known, watched you grow up, become a lovely young woman. I have missed out on all the love I could have given you, all the love you would have given to me. Missed out on all the years, all the joys watching you grow up day by day. I missed watching you take your first step, missed hearing you say your first word, and going off to your first day at school. I miss all the happy times we could have had together, turning into happy memories. I never got to hold your hand walking in the park, or see you race as a star athlete in school. Above all, I have missed you, my darling daughter. You whispered goodbye, before I ever said hello.

I need your love and forgiveness now Rachel. I know now, too late, you would have been a real blessing in my life, not a burden at all. And you have missed out on knowing life. And you, my dear other children, you could not live because I destroyed my body in the abortion, and you all died before your births. I killed the only child I would ever have. What I did was unforgivable. I don't know how to ask you all to forgive me. Even if you did forgive me, I don't know if I could ever feel it.

The memory of what I did that day has haunted me. I have often dreamed of you. You are always with me in my heart. You are loved very much. I am sorry. I will be sorry for what I did to you every day of my life for the rest of my life. I have cried often for you. Please forgive me. It seems ridiculous to apologize. How can I apologize for killing you? But I am sorry. I am so ashamed. I wish I had never done it. I wish I had never done it.

Love,
Mom.

Reading her wrinkled and torn letter to her daughter Rachel, the letter she could never send, the letter to her two miscarried children, Dolores wept. She sat in the privacy of the washroom of the Crisis Pregnancy Center, trying to control the emotion raging within her, her large body heaving, not wanting to make any sounds. The loss of her child was always with her, an unbearable sense of the eternal loss of the greatest good. She was in hell. She stood from her seat and washed her flushed and tear stained face and reddened eyes clean in the bathroom sink. She put her much folded, precious letter back in her pocket.

She knew she was forgiven, after she went to confession with kindly Fr. MacIntryre at Sacred Heart parish, and accused herself of having an abortion, and the Lord forgave her. It was hard to enter the dark confessional, she was afraid to do it. She remembered her confession

'Forgive me Father, for I have sinned. It has been five years since my last confession.'

'What has kept you away so long?'

'I-I-had an abortion.'

'Have you suffered?'

'Yes Father. I regret it. I can never be at peace about it.'

'The Lord wants you to share in His peace beyond understanding. There are healing programs to help you work through your feelings. I am here in the Jesus' name to absolve your guilt, for His forgiveness to flow through me for you.'

'Nothing seems to help. I always feel guilty about it.'

'God loves you and forgives you. Your child is not lost, but living in the heart of the Lord.'

'I wish I could feel it.'

'You will in time. Remember forgiveness is not in the feelings. No more than faith is a matter of feelings. It's a matter of the spirit.'

'What I did was unforgiveable.'

'Abortion is a very serious mortal sin, but no sin is unforgiveable. Do not sink into despair, an even more serious sin. You must believe and hope in God's mercy.'

Dolores was weeping. 'I showed no mercy to my own child Father. I killed my daughter.'

'Don't beat yourself up. It's good to face the reality, but no sin is greater than God. He can forgive even the worst of sins.'

'I can't seem to forgive myself.'

'Turn it over, and let go of it. Don't keep holding on to it.'

'I do want to be forgiven. I want to feel at peace about it.'

'Pray.'

'I freely chose to do it. I ignored everything I knew better. I just wanted to do it.'

'I know.'

'I think about killing myself sometimes. I don't deserve to live if my daughter couldn't.'

'We don't know until something is lost forever how much it meant to us.'

'I felt relief at first, I was in a bad situation, but later the regret and guilt came. I can't stuff it down anymore. I can't bear it anymore.'

'Try to remember the worst of sins is a drop of water consumed in the infinite purifying fire of the love of God. In your weak moments think of the immensity of God's love. Plunge yourself and your sin into the boundless ocean of God's mercy and love. His understanding. He knows everything. Perhaps I sound contradictory, saying God's love is both a fire and an ocean. But both are true.'

'I will try to remember God loves me.'

'Even when you can't love yourself. We tend to focus too much on ourselves. Think instead of God. We are such small specks, and He is the infinite.'

'I will Father. But I find it hard to pray. I don't feel anything. My heart is cold.'

'Forgiveness and peace are yours for the asking.'

Dolores choked back her tears. 'I am asking Father.'

'Are you sorry for your sins?'

'Yes Father.'

'Say the act of contrition.'

'O my God, I am sorry for offending you, not only because I fear the loss of heaven and the pains of hell, but because you are all good, and worthy of all my love-I'm sorry Father, I forget the rest.'

'That's enough for now. That was very good. For your penance I want you to sit quietly alone in the Church before the Blessed Sacrament in the tabernacle, and ask God what He wants to say to you. Pay close attention to the thoughts coming into your mind, and the feelings in the depths of your heart.'

'Yes Father.'

'When you are in wordless prayer before the Lord, when you look at Him, and He looks at you, heart speaks to heart.'

'Yes Father.'

'And look above the tabernacle and see the crucifix, look at the mystery of God's love on the cross for you.'

'I will.'

'Don't try to understand it, just look at Him. He wants to

be part of your suffering. He can give it meaning.'

'All right Father.'

'When you look at Him, remember love came down. He gave everything for you. And we, even we, miserable sinners and poor wretches, may be lifted up by Him and reach perfection in love. May the Lord bless you my daughter. I absolve you from all your sins in the name of the Father, and the Son, and the Holy Spirit. Amen.'

'Thank you Father.'

'Go in peace. If I may make a suggestion, it might help you to name your lost child, now that you are facing the reality.'

'Thank you Father.'

Dolores remembered how she felt the healing touch of the Lord forgive her as Fr. MacIntyre said the precious words of absolution over her in the dark secrecy of the confessional. And that was all it took, just everything in her. What an unspeakable mercy of God to forgive her so simply for such an enormous sin. She followed the kind priest's instructions after her confession, sitting in silence in the dim church. The hushed stillness of the sacred space, the flickering light of the candles, the scent of the carnations and chrysanthemums in the flower vases places beside the tabernacle filled her senses with the beauty of life both physical and spiritual.

Her heart and mind were lifted to the thought of God. She listened for something new not of herself. As she prayed in silence the world dropped away from her. The muffled sounds of the noisy traffic outside the church went unheard, her constant shifting on the hard wooden pew gradually calmed and stopped. Distractions fell away, and she knelt on the on the kneeler before the golden tabernacle, the dwelling place of God awaiting her for so long. She looked and listened in the stillness of her concentration for His word He might say to her. A great quiet came upon her, and she felt waves of love and power sweep over her contrite soul. She was washed clean, and borne up in a peace she had never known. She felt risen from the dead, and she surrendered to His love as the Lord kissed her soul in a new spiritual marriage. In the quiet empty church, she felt His wordless presence beside her, stronger than flesh and blood could be, and the Lord spoke His word within her mind.

She heard the name Rachel whispered in her mind, and knew the name of her daughter, Rachel weeping for her children because they were no more. And she knew what her penance for her sin would be now, she knew she was going to be a pro-life activist serving the other mothers, and the other unborn children. She wept in gratitude for her release. She could not help Rachel, she could not undo what she had done to her, but she could make amends by substitution. She would give her personal witness about abortion as someone who had been there. Good would come from Rachel's death, her death was not meaningless. Dolores still kneeling opened her closed eyes and looked at the tabernacle. She looked ahead, above, and from side to side, and still felt the invisible love surrounding her. She felt as if her crucified Lord hanging on the cross of wood on the wall behind the tabernacle was smiling at her in his last agony, happy for her. His love would stay with her, and go with her now, away from the tabernacle and out of the quiet church when she entered once again into the busy streets of the city, a woman who looked the same but a woman forever changed.

After those blessed moments of prayer the days passed, and she clung to her new peace, but still at times she found it hard to forgive herself. Sometimes she was fine. Then the pain returned, and she struggled anew for self-acceptance of what she did to Rachel. The remembered the peace of soul in church after her confession when she first felt the presence of the Lord, but it seemed she would not be released from her prison of pain until she had paid the last penny.

Maybe it was the devil, Lucifer the light bearer, the fallen angel far more intelligent than any human being, maybe it was Satan who would not let her feel forgiven. The devil knew her weak spot where he could torment her still, her non-acceptance, her wish she had never done it. In the silence of the Crisis Pregnancy Center washroom, in the darkness of her regret, she knew she must hold on in faith to the promise of the Lord. She had gone to confession, and she was forgiven. She believed in the assurance of the Church and God, despite the frequent feelings of remorse plaguing her, in the face of the devil who clutched at her still. A new attack came upon her now, and hell reached out for her again.

Please God, take this away. It hurts. It hurts.

Her thoughts went back to Sadie. She was the same age now at 21 she herself had been when she aborted Rachel. It was Christmas time. What kind of Christmas would Sadie have, planning her second abortion? She believed in the power of prayer. Prayer changed things. The Crisis Pregnancy Center witnessed many miracles, many changed hearts and minds, changed decisions about abortion, the greatest miracles of all. Dolores had faith there could be a miracle for Sadie too. She was worried about her. Sadie knew what she was doing, but she also didn't know. She didn't know in her search for love and happiness in all the wrong places she was dimly searching for the God who was the source of all true love and happiness in Himself. No one else would ever love her as He did.

Sadie too was one of the holy innocents in her ignorance. Dolores prayed for Sadie, and for Rick, and for their baby, raising her prayer of petition to God through His mother Mary, asking for her intercession. Mary would understand. She was a mother too, the mother of God. They tried to kill her son as soon as he was born, and she had to flee with him into Egypt. They did kill her son in the end. May knew what it was like to lose a child. Dolores took her miraculous medal of the Blessed Virgin Mary from inside the neckline of her dress, and held the holy medal in her folded hands clasped together in prayer in the washroom of the Crisis Pregnancy Center:

> *Mary my mother, please help Sadie. Please help this poor mother Sadie in her brokenness and her need. Show her the way Mama Mary, ask Jesus your divine son to send His help, and His light, and His power to help her in her darkness and distress. Send her support through many people in her pregnancy. Help her do the right things, and let her baby live. Help her to choose life. Help her to choose life for her baby, choose life for herself. Show*

her the way. Your son cannot refuse His mother anything. Please holy mother, you ask Him, ask your son Jesus to do something for Sadie. Amen.

When Dolores finished her prayer she was surprised to hear a voice whisper 'Mom.' She looked around. Was she going crazy? No one else could be in the bathroom. She heard the faint whisper again: 'Mom.' Then it hit her. It was Rachel talking to her. She heard the whispered voice yet again: 'I forgive you Mom. I am here with Jesus waiting for you. I love you Mom. It's all okay. I am happy now.'

Dolores placed both her hands on the sink to steady herself. She did not want to cry again. Sadie was waiting for her. Sadie needed her. But she felt such joy she had to stay a moment longer, stay with Rachel's voice. How hard it was to watch Sadie wanting to destroy what she herself could never have, and now wanted so much, her own baby. How hard it was to watch her throw her child away, like nothing.

Dolores was gone for a long time. Sadie opened the door of the counselling room and saw Julie sitting at her receptionist's desk. 'What's going on?'

Julie smile at her, making light of it. 'Our counsellor's having a breakdown in the bathroom.'

'What?'

'Just joking.'

Dolores opened the door and came out.

'I'm ready for you now Sadie.'

19

Dolores and Sadie went back into the counselling room together, Dolores closing the door behind them, leaving Julie alone at her receptionist's desk with her baby Jeffrey playing on the floor, Mickey still reading the legal papers from the Craigenback Abortion Clinic in his office at the back of the house. The mailman came, and Julie walked back to Mickey's office with the letters. 'Here's the mail Mickey. And Dora called. She said your line was busy.'

Mickey did not want to alarm Julie by telling her about the phone call from the Warriors of God.

'Yeah, I got a call I had to deal with.'

'Dora left you a message. The Pro-life Intergroup Association wants to have a meeting on the last Thursday of January in the basement of Sacred Heart Church.'

'The committee hasn't met in a long time. Why now?'

'Dora said people are concerned at everything going on, and want to have a more united pro-life movement.'

'I sense a trap. Dora was angry when I fired her this morning. Now all of a sudden a meeting has been arranged with everybody. Why is she trying to keep in touch, and why is she involving others? Doesn't she know she shouldn't be calling here? She's been fired.'

'I guess it's all still new and she can't let go.'

'It's hard to fire someone who thinks she's the boss. Let me know anything else Dora does.'

'I will. I got some frightening calls today, silent calls with someone breathing at the other end of the line, someone not speaking at all.'

'How often?'

'Three times already.'

'Keep a record. If we start getting harassing phone calls, the telephone company can trace them.'

'Do you think there is any connection between Dora and the silent phone calls?'

'I don't know. It is something new.'

'It's really creepy, silent breathing phone calls.'

'Don't let them get to you.' Mickey was sorting through the mail. 'What do we have here? It's a letter from Bishop Blair.'

'Read it out loud Mickey.'

He held the letter for a moment, savoring the design of the official logo of the Calgary Catholic Diocese on the envelope. He opened the envelope and scanned the letter in silence. Bishop Blair kept his distance from the controversial pro-lifers. He would never meet in person with them, despite Mickey's repeated requests for an appointment. Sometimes he replied to them with a letter, but mostly he remained silent. A letter from him was a rare event. Mickey had petitioned His Excellency Bishop Horace Blair to excommunicate Nathan Craigenback and Lester Dockendorff, complaining of the scandal of a Catholic doctor doing abortions, and a Catholic judge legally protecting him, but the Bishop did not want to intervene. In his letter of reply Mickey read the Bishop believed in education, and an appeal to the heart for repentance rather than any heavy handed exercise of ecclesiastical power. He also rebuked Mickey for the deceptive practices of the Crisis Pregnancy Center, and advised him to bring his pro-life work within the teachings of the Catholic Church for honesty and truth. As Mickey sat at his desk reading the letter Julie watching him saw a pained expression cross his face.

'What's wrong Mickey? What does he say?'

'Listen to this:

> Thank you for taking my examination of conscience for me. Bishops are not disciplinarians or executioners. We are teachers and pastors. I do not approve of your harsh hardline stance on abortion. You are not the only pro-life apostles in this Diocese. I am comfortable with my position, and I hope I can stay there. Take the log out of your own eyes first, before the take the splinter out of anyone else's eyes. Judge not. The pro-life movement attracts its share of kooks and crazies and disgruntled misfits beyond the Canadian social norm of tolerance and respect for differing beliefs. We do not impose our own beliefs on others. The Church must ever exercise charity in prudence. We do not tear out the weeds lest we damage the wheat. We do not politicize communion. I will not use the body of Our Lord as a weapon. Communion is for everyone. We are all sinners. Whenever I think of you I will think of the Lord's prayer. I advise you to do the same. My work as a Bishop in the Lord's vineyard is extremely busy, and I have neither the time nor the inclination to enter into a pen pal relationship with you. Please take me off your mailing list.

Julie had to sit down herself. 'It's unbelievable. Did he really write it?'

'I feel like the excommunicated one,' Mickey said. He was reading the letter again. Julie was still trying to understand the Bishop's letter.

'He doesn't like us. He doesn't respect us. He sounds so superior to us.'

'He's a snooty one, always looking down his nose at us. Blair is a virtuoso of aristocratic reserve and smooth diplomacy. Bishop Horace Blair is one of the elite masters of the universe.'

'Is this a bad place? Are we bad people?'

'The Bishop and the priests keep their distance from pro-life because they can't control it the way they control everything else. It's only we ordinary laymen who keep pro-life going. I'm afraid we have no leadership. We are on our own.'

20

Dolores and Sadie were seated back in the counselling room. Sadie saw Dolores' eyes were red, and her skin on her face was puffy. 'Are you okay?'

'I'm fine. Let's continue. We don't have much time. Sadie, do you believe in God?'

Dolores believed helping the clients explore their spiritual beliefs was a necessary aspect of abortion counselling, something the nurses at Craigenback's avoided. Dolores knew deep down in every human being was the fundamental idea of God.

'I don't go to church anymore. I was raised by my family to go to Sunday school when I was a kid. I know the story. There must be something, but I don't think about it much. I don't like talking about religion, what I believe is nobody's-'

'Do you ever pray to God for help? For guidance on what to do in your life? Have you prayed about this abortion decision?'

'I did say 'God help me' when I first thought I might be pregnant. This is a disaster.'

'Do you think God wants you to abort this child?'

'Why would God want me to be pregnant when it is the wrong time and nothing is right, and I can't possibly look after a child by myself, and I know Rick will leave me and I'll be a single mother? I don't want to be alone. I have to finish school. This will ruin my life. I just started a new course in hairstyling, and it will give me a way I can make some good money. I have to finish the course. I can be independent, not have to rely on him. He's unreliable anyway. This is just not the right time to have a baby.'

'Are you intimidated by a baby?'

'Of course not.'

'God came to us as a baby, at the first Christmas.'

Sadie laughed. 'I'm hardly the Virgin Mary.'

'But you are a mother carrying a child created by God. There's great dignity in that.'

'This Christmas is different. You're talking about a long time ago.'

Dolores heard many clients blame God before, blame the wrong time. She was familiar with all the rationalizations, even claims the abortion was for the child's sake. Heard it was a lousy world to bring a child into it, as if they were doing the child a favor it kill it, especially if the child would be disabled. Sometimes a wife and husband came, came even with their other children, seeking an abortion for the latest unwanted child. They too argued they wanted an abortion for the sake of the family's needs. What a sad delusion. How would a child feel when his parents killed his brother or sister? What would it do to the love and security in family life? How would killing a sibling damage the sense of safety of the already born children in the family?

Then there were the hardened sinners, the married woman pregnant from an affair with a man of another race, the woman wanting to hide her adultery. How could a white woman explain to her white husband giving birth to a black child? There was no explanation to deceive him the child was his. And should she deceive her husband if she could? Those were hard babies to save. What kind of marriages could they be, hiding such secrets? People were only as sick as their secrets, but they did not want to face exposure.

There were those who trotted out all the usual arguments how unfair it was forcing a raped girl of thirteen to have the baby, or force an incest victim to give birth. Hardly any of the millions of abortions were for reasons of rape and incest. The extreme cases used to justify abortion were only pro-abortion propaganda. Even in rape and incest, the innocent child never raped or molested anyone. The guilty rapists were not executed, why kill the innocent unborn child, the second victim of the sexual assault? Why punish the innocent girl with a second act of violence committed on her body with an abortion after the rape or incest? Why were so many pro-lifers, especially the politicians, willing to negotiate away the lives of those babies? So they could appear to be in the *reasonable* mainstream, keep the news media off their backs, and get votes? They were all false, all the arguments in favor of abortion. They should have the courage to say it. And what about the sex selection abortions? Why should the announcement: 'It's a girl,' be a death sentence when the parents wanted a boy?' What hypocrisy, aborting the girls in the name of women's rights.

Her first client Linda two years ago came back into her mind, talking to maybe her last client Sadie. Linda was a teenager who said she wanted an abortion because she was a model, and the baby would ruin her figure. Dolores did not like her at first, appalled at the shallowness of her reasons for an abortion. But after seeing the video Linda suddenly dropped her sophisticated façade and said: 'I know if I destroy my baby I will destroy me.' Then she told the truth. Her Catholic parents were pressuring her to have the abortion. The father of the baby was one of the teachers at her Catholic school, and she was underage. Her parents wanted to cover up the disgrace and scandal of her pregnancy. Linda herself did not want an abortion. Dolores was able to help her have her baby, and her parents eventually accepted the situation. The clients can be such actors, Dolores thought. I must not pre-judge what they say, and wait and see. Could there be another miracle with Sadie today?

'Sadie, do you really want an abortion, or are you being pressured by others or circumstances?'

Sadie started adjusting her sweater, shrugging her shoulders and straightening the collar of her blouse, although it was not bent. 'I'm not saying abortion is good. This is all just a mistake, something went wrong again with the birth control.'

'The birth control is all junk. The IUD and the Pill contracept *and* abort. You never know how the Pill works at any given time, if it works at all. You may have had several chemical abortions besides on surgical abortion.'

'I don't understand what you're talking about.'

Dolores reached for the large laminated poster rolled up beside the television, the one with the large diagram of the female reproductive system. She went to sit beside Sadie on the couch. 'Let me show you what I mean with this chart.'

'I'm not interested. It's too technical. Birth control must be okay if the doctor prescribes it.'

Easy does it. Don't get upset. She would have to be patient with Sadie's stubborn resistance. 'Do you have all the facts? All the birth control methods have a failure rate. They give people a false sense of security. Didn't the doctors tell you? And then people turn to abortion to back up the birth control failure. So birth control doesn't prevent abortion. Birth control leads to abortion.'

'I don't use abortion for birth control. I'm not irresponsible.'

Dolores put the poster down. She could not force Sadie to look at it. She would have to explain it to her with only words instead of pictures. 'You mentioned the confusing effects of the Pill, sometimes no bleeding, sometimes too much bleeding.'

'Yeah, I don't like it.'

'Did anyone ever explain to you the Pill does not really regulate your cycle as they claim? The Pill shuts down your cycle, and substitutes Pill controlled monthly bleeding to give a woman the feeling she is still having her monthly cycle. But the Pill can be erratic. Sometimes it makes the woman bleed too much, and other times not bleed at all. And when the woman's natural cycle has been suppressed for too long, it can shut down completely. She can't go off the Pill and have her natural period again. She no longer has cycles. Medically it's called amenorrhea, the loss of monthly menstruation.'

Sadie's head tilted towards Dolores. She looked interested in this information. 'I never heard of this before. You mean a woman, even a young one, is like a woman after menopause?

No more periods?'

'I'm afraid so.'

'Now I get my strange bleeding on the Pill.'

'The doctors should have explained the risks to you. Do you see how you can't always trust the doctors anymore? The Pill can also cause blood clots, leading to heart attacks and strokes even in young women. Did they ever warn you about those risks?'

Sadie leaned away from Dolores, sinking deeper into her chair. 'That's all a side issue. I came here for abortion.'

'Do you think you might feel bad having a second abortion?'

'It's not a human being yet. It's just a bunch of cells.'

'I hope you're not saying the child is like a tumor. Some people are that hard core. They deny everything about the baby.'

'I'm sorry, I just don't believe something so tiny is a human being like you and me.'

There are no small murders, Dolores thought. But if she started talking about murder she would lose Sadie. 'We have some amazing photographs now of the inner world of the unborn child in these books, just like you saw in the video. Please come back to the desk.' Dolores returned to the seat behind her desk and removed a book from the shelves. Sadie returned to her chair in front of the desk, but objected to the picture book. 'Please, I've seen enough. My mind's made up.'

Dolores saw arguing when life began was not the way to reach Sadie. She replaced the book, and sat down behind the desk, getting ready to shift her approach. She started to speak again, but then saw Sadie rubbing her forehead with her hand as if she had a headache. After a moment Sadie looked at Dolores. 'I took my pet hamster to the vet once when I was a little girl. It had damaged its leg. The vet said they couldn't do much for it, but they could do an x-ray, a dental type x-ray since it was so small, to see if the leg was broken. My mother didn't want to pay the money, nearly $200, but I cried and cried, and she finally paid for it.'

'What happened?'

'The x-ray showed the leg was broken, but they couldn't put a tiny splint on it because the hamster would just gnaw it off. They said the leg might heal on its own, and it did, but the little guy limped afterwards, walking funny for a hamster. They only live a couple of years, and then my pet died.'

'Why do you think you cared so much?'

'It was a living creature in pain. She felt things. I loved Sunshine.'

'Your pet's name was Sunshine?'

'Yeah.'

Sadie was humane, and she was planning an abortion. Dolores would not push it any further. She had seen surprising and contradictory admissions in clients before, like the time with Linda. Strange though that Sadie brought her pet's pain up herself. Was her subconscious mind making connections she was consciously denying about abortion. But Sadie quickly auto corrected.

'The unborn fetus does not feel any pain.'

'Newer studies show they do. Some people are even trying to pass laws limiting abortions, calling them the Pain Capable Act.'

Sadie remained silent and Dolores felt it was not the moment to try and ram the point through. She decided not to interfere with what Sadie was saying now. Maybe she would work it out for herself, since she brought it up herself. Dolores changed her approach again. 'Can your parents help you?'

'My parents are divorced. They have their own problems.'

'Do you have any family members, relatives who can help you?'

'I have a twin brother, Sean. We aren't close anymore. He went with Dad after the divorce, and I went with Mom. We havn't talked in years. We've all gone our own ways.'

'Are you really so alone? You said before you were alone, but I thought there might be someone.'

Sadie dropped her eyes.

'I've been left in a ditch.'

21

'How fast can I get it done?' Sadie asked again.

Dolores did not answer her. She was thinking of Frank and Teresa. They came wanting an abortion, and Dolores tried to convince the unborn child was a human being. Frank challenged her: 'Name one.' He sat back in his chair, tipping it back, his hands clasped behind his head, elbows sticking out at the sides, relaxed and satisfied he won the argument, disposing of millions of abortions as of no single human significance.

'Rachel,' Dolores said. 'Rachel.'

'Who?' Frank asked.

'My daughter.'

'Your daughter?'

'My child I aborted, and named later. Frank, if you named your child right now, the act of naming will help you and Teresa. Can you say, 'I am going to kill you tomorrow, little Teresa, or little Frank?'

Frank had stood up immediately and commanded Teresa they were leaving, terminating the counselling session. Maybe Sadie could take some straight talk. Nothing else was working. 'I know this is a tough situation for you Sadie. But two abortions might make you feel very bad. They might deaden you inside. We can't always block things out, stuff our feelings. They have a way of coming out, bothering us in other ways.'

'I can't think about the future now.'

'Do you think you might be doing something selfish in an abortion?'

'No. I don't appreciate you telling me I'm selfish. I do lots of things for other people. I don't want to talk to you anymore.'

'I didn't mean to judge you. I was just exploring possibilities in counselling.'

'Rick is probably back and waiting. He could come in here and ask what is taking so long. He's done it before.'

'Of course he does.'

'So what do I do now? Where do I get the abortion?'

The most difficult time Dolores had to face in all of her client sessions had arrived. The moment of truth must be faced. She took a deep breath: 'I'm sorry, we don't do abortions here.'

'So where do I go?'

'We are a pro-life center. We will do anything to help we can, but we cannot be part of getting an abortion. Abortion is wrong, so wrong we cannot do it, or refer to someone who will do it, or refer you to someone to refer you. We cannot be any part of killing an unborn child.'

Sadie jumped to her feet, the chair she sat on falling backwards on the floor with the sudden force of her movement, and she slammed her fist down on the desk. 'You told me you would help me here.'

'I'm sorry about the confusion. We don't believe abortion is helping you. It will hurt you, and kill your baby. We are always here to help you. Even if you go through with an abortion, you are always welcome to come back if you need help.'

'You lying bitch.'

'I'm fighting for the life of your baby. Can't you feel it?'

'Leave me alone.'

'Please take this pamphlet with you, explaining Post Abortion Syndrome. And these other pamphlets about support services for single mothers.'

Sadie remained standing in her anger, and paced back and forth a few steps in front of the desk, her hands clenched in fists, breathing hard and struggling to regain her self-control. She turned and stopped in front of the desk, Sadie looming over Dolores. 'Can you just tell me where abortions are done in Calgary? You don't have to refer me, just tell me where they are done.'

Dolores shook her head sideways.

'I'm sorry, that would make me part of getting an abortion. I must say no to you. You are a mother now, and nothing, not even an abortion, can change that. Please sit down.'

The quiet sincerity of Dolores hit Sadie hard. She reached for the fallen chair and straightened it up again, and sat down. Dolores kept trying to reach her. 'I am pleading with you for the life of your child. Even if it seems too hard for you to be a mother, if you have love in your heart you can move mountains. Many women have done it. Here, let me show you.' Dolores reached for the photograph album she kept on the side of her desk, the pictures of the happy clients of the Crisis Pregnancy Center, the smiling mothers with their babies. Dolores opened the photo album and turned it towards Sadie so she could see the pictures. Sadie began to look at the photos in the album. Dolores wanted to tell the stories of the women: 'This first one is a picture of Linda and her son Scotty-'

Sadie drew back. 'I don't want to see anymore.'

Dolores left the photo album open on the desk in front of Sadie. She tried again. 'May I show you something else?' She swiveled in her chair and picked up one of the life size fetal models, the one of a 12 week unborn child, and extended her hand for her to take it from her. 'This is exactly how your baby looks now at 12 weeks, and the exact size, just so you know.'

Sadie refused to take the plastic model in her hands. She folded her arms across her chest again. 'Take it away. I don't want it.'

Dolores placed the fetal model on the desk. She opened a drawer, and brought out the applications of childless couples who hoped the Crisis Pregnancy Center could help them find a child to adopt. Many of the couples were on waiting lists for years with so few children to adopt anymore. 'These are some smiling photos and descriptions of people waiting for years to adopt a child. They could give your child a good home, and help you out of your problems. Phillip and Melanie here-'

'I don't want to see any more of these kinds of things. I would never give my baby up for adoption.'

'I don't understand. Are you saying you love your baby too much to give your baby away for adoption, but you are willing to kill your baby in an abortion?'

'Adoption is out of the question.'

'Wouldn't the temporary pain of giving a child up for

adoption be better than the life-long problem of guilt from having an abortion.?

'I will lose my own life, my own plans, to be pregnant for nine months, and then give the child to another woman. I can't do it.'

'Surrendering for adoption is an act of unselfish love.'

'Forget it.'

'It's not like you're giving up a child. You're helping your child. Your own child. You will always be the birth mother.'

'I'm not interested.'

'You're pregnant now. Babies call for self-sacrifice. They take us out of our own natural self-centeredness.'

'I have a right to my own life. That's not selfishness.'

'Killing our children will not help us as women achieve our dreams.'

'You have some nerve to keep saying *killing, killing*. It's one huge guilt trip here.'

'Do you know yourself?'

'Yes, I know my own mind.'

'You're still young at 21. You have much to learn.'

Dolores hated falling into the lecturing, parental tone she just used with Sadie. She wanted to be a detached, professional counselor; instead, her humanity burst through. The picture books, the photo album, the charts, the plastic fetal model, the adoption applications lay all around them, ignored by Sadie who would not look at them. 'I know myself well enough. I know I want an abortion. I said that the minute I came in here. I know I can't look at some things. After my first abortion, I couldn't even look at the films in health class in school. One time I tried to watch one about how a woman's body works, and I fainted.

'The video must have been hard on you to watch today. I give your credit for watching the whole thing.'

'It was hard, but I watched it because you said I had to if I wanted an abortion. You lied to me.'

'I'm glad you saw it. You might be glad too someday. It's the truth.'

'I wish you would stop hammering away at me about *the truth*.' Sadie leaned over and buried her face in her hands, and closed her eyes.

22

Dolores continued trying to reach Sadie, in the precious few moments of time she had left with her.

'The adventure of a new life has begun in you Sadie. It's true, it's beautiful, and it's good. A new baby in the world.'

Sadie raised her head and opened her eyes to look at Dolores. 'You make babies sound like little angels.'

'They are. Adorable little angels.'

'Babies cry and scream all night long. I had a girlfriend, the only thing she could do was get up from bed and take her colicky baby for a drive in the car in the middle of the night. Nothing else would stop the crying. Babies have disgusting dirty diapers you have to clean up after them. They puke on you. After crying all night they sleep all day and the mother is trapped at home like she's in a jail, bored and lonely with nothing to do. She can't even have a decent conversation with another human being. How long can a grown woman talk baby talk all the time without going crazy?'

'Sure, babies are a lot responsibility and work. They're born helpless. But where did you get such a negative attitude towards motherhood? There are many rewards for a woman mothering a baby.'

'It's all work with a baby, especially without a man to help you.'

'Babies aren't drudgery, making you miss out on the exciting things in life. Mothering a child is a blessed activity. Most of us are not important people in the world, but for one person, your own baby, you are the world.'

'Do you have children?'

'No.'

Sadie made a dismissive wave. 'Then how can you set yourself up as an authority on motherhood?'

'I can still love children, even other women's children.'

'Easy for you to talk. Babies are expensive. It costs a fortune to raise children, to feed and clothe them, give them medicine, send them to school.'

'You don't need a fortune to have a child. Day by day, little by little, there are enough resources to meet the needs of the moment. God provides. People don't starve to death in North America.'

'It's a hard struggle to survive here, everything costs so much. You idealize everything. The world is overpopulated. There are too many people already. No need for me to bring one more.'

'The problem is not too many people. The problem is an unfair distribution of the world's resources. A small number of people control most of the world's wealth.'

'Well, they are not going to give it up. It's unfair to bring a child into the world to live in poverty and hunger.'

'Are you really going to have an abortion for the child's sake? Is that what you are telling me?'

Dolores knew what she said was true, puncturing Sadie's rationalizations she heard many times before, but she hated the fact she was arguing with her. Arguments were not the purpose of the Crisis Pregnancy Center. She was making mistakes as a counselor in this difficult session, losing control. But she could not help challenging all of the false reasoning. Sadie had taken in every bit of the propaganda for abortion. 'You seem to be very negative about everything. We can always live with faith, hope and love whatever our circumstances, no matter how tough.'

Sadie just looked at Dolores. The lady seemed to feel genuine motherly concern for her and her baby. This was a different kind of counselling from the social workers she had seen before. Why was this woman, a stranger, begging for the life of her baby? What was it to her? The heartfelt feeling of Dolores came through to Sadie more than her words. 'Who are you? Are you for real? I have never heard anyone talk like this in my life.'

'I am someone who knows abortion won't change any of the problems in your life. Abortion changes nothing, and will only be the beginning of a far worse problem, post abortion trauma.'

Sadie did not get what Dolores had just revealed to her. 'I told you. I have seen the single mothers at school dragging themselves around after being up all night with their babies. They are exhausted. I just can't do it. I won't.'

'Have you asked the mothers how they feel about it all? Do you ever hear a mother say she regrets she had her baby? I don't. I hear the regrets from the women who had abortions.'

'I object to you painting such a rosy picture of motherhood. It's not real.'

'You make your fertility sound like a curse.'

'It is when you're not ready for it, not expecting to be pregnant, not wanting it.'

'Your life may take a detour with the baby, but it doesn't have to be a dead end.'

Sadie grew excited, nodding quickly in agreement, although it was not what Dolores meant. 'That's it, it would be a dead end for me.'

'Beyond the dead end, sometimes you can see a little path.'

'What path?'

'It's the women who kill their children who have no future. The mothers who love their children, who give them life, they have a future. The child is the future. The child is the path.'

'I don't feel anything for this child. Especially when it's *his*.'

'Women often abort early in pregnancy when they don't want the child, all due to hormonal fluctuations, and later those feelings pass and they want the child, but then it is too late.'

'You're reducing my own mind and my freedom to choose to hormones?'

'Sadie, a new human being has been totally entrusted to your protection and care. You have been given a great responsibility, a great dignity as a mother.'

'I told you, it's a responsibility I don't want. Not right now. You can't tell me what to do. It's not up to you. I will make my own choice.'

'Choose life. I beg you, choose life.'

'I'm not having this baby. How many times do I have to say it?'

'This is tragic. A mother's interests should never be in conflict with her child. But abortion does, it pits a mother against her child.'

Sadie struck back. 'You're older than me, but I find you naïve. Women have always wanted to abort their children. They throw themselves down stairs, pound their bellies with their fists, take herbs and drugs, sit in hot tubs, stick coat hangers inside themselves, all kinds of things.'

'Woman is the guardian, the custodian of life. Women deserve better than abortion.'

Sadie would not listen to Dolores anymore. She was still stunned someone would say no to her getting an abortion. She just assumed was her woman's free right. She thought it was unreasonable for Dolores not to even tell her where they did abortions. She was being treated like a child not able to make her own decisions. She was annoyed information was being kept from her.

'You told me pregnancy is a matter of conscience. You don't really believe that. You lied to me in so many ways, just to get me in here, and keep me here to listen to your propaganda.'

'I have told you the truth.'

'You told me abortion is a medical procedure, told me I had to watch the video to give my informed consent. That was a lie too.'

'They call it a medical procedure, but abortion doesn't cure any illnesses. Pregnancy is not a disease. Make the right choice Sadie.'

Sadie exploded.

'I have no choice. Rick doesn't want the baby.'

'You always have a choice. We can help you if Rick won't.'

Sadie dropped all of her pretense and said something so honest Dolores was speechless.

'It might sound harsh, but if it is between me and the baby, the baby has to go.'

Dolores looked at her in silence, wondering what else she could say if anything to reach her. Sadie looked back at her in silence too. She did not want to talk anymore. She never expected such challenging questions when all she planned on was getting a free pregnancy test and an abortion at a family planning clinic. Dolores felt the responsibility to keep trying to save the baby.

'Are you finally admitting the baby inside you is a human being?'

'I don't want this kid inside of me.'

'So you do know it.'

'Sometimes abortion is necessary. Done in sorrow maybe, but it has to be done. If the baby is a human life, it is a life worth sacrificing. The mother's life comes first.'

'Don't you feel the sense of right and wrong we all have? I don't really need to tell you anything, do I?'

'No, please don't tell me anything more about the baby.'

'So the real question is not when life begins, is it Sadie?'

Sadie did not say anything.

'The real question is when love begins.'

Sadie still did not say anything, looking down at her hands in her lap, avoiding Dolores' penetrating eyes. Dolores wondered what more she could say to her, and then she knew.

'Have you gone to confession about your abortion dear?

There is nothing to fear in confession. You look so unhappy. It might help you.'

Sadie raised her eyes to look at Dolores again. Her mind took in these unexpected words in a family planning counselling session. Was it possible another miraculous revelation was coming, as happened before with Linda? Would Sadie reveal the truth of how she really felt about her abortion?

'I am free to do whatever I want.'

Dolores's hope was disappointed.

'Sadie, you bought the lie promiscuity is okay. You bought the lie birth control would protect you. Now you are buying the lie abortion is the way out.'

'They might be lies for you, but not for me.'

'It might be true for me I like ice cream and not true for you. But there are truths the same for both of us. The same for everyone. There is objective reality.'

'Everybody's doing it, that's the reality.'

'But those people are not living in the truth.'

Truth again.

'Truth? It's only someone's opinion. You don't know truth for me. We all have our own truths. We have that right.'

'This will be your second abortion. Think about what is happening to you. Abortion changes you. You won't be the same woman anymore.'

'This is the last one. I won't let this happen again.'

'What can you do?'

'I'll get my tubes tied.'

'At 21? Giving up your ability to ever have children?'

Sadie was silent, playing with her fingers. Dolores kept

pressing her. 'I thought you said you wanted children some day.' But Dolores saw Sadie would not answer her anymore. Was she only saying things now to say something, not lose the argument? Was it only pride driving her? Saving face? Resentment? Or was Sadie trying to provoke her, knowing she wouldn't like the comment about sterilization?

'Do you think tying your tubes will make you happy?'

'Yeah, I'll be happy, no more worries like this.'

'Define happy.'

'Living the life you want. No one telling you what you have to do.'

'Including God?'

'People are free to live the way they want as long as they're happy and not hurting anyone. I don't judge anyone, or interfere with them. I want to be left alone to live my own life too.'

'Frankly, I don't think you should be having sex because you're not married.'

'I knew it. You're a judgmental Christian.'

'I'm just going to lay the truth out there. You can do what you want with it. I'm just going to tell you the truth. Everything you're doing, the sex, the Pill, all that stuff is just not good for you.'

'Now you sound like a lecturing mother.'

The conversation with this difficult client was like a running battle. How would it end? Was there any chance she might change her mind about abortion? Or were they only debating from their fixed positions, talking past each other, with no chance of change at all? Was it all a waste of time? Dolores wanted to know the truth about Sadie.

'What do you really believe Sadie?'

'I believe I'm free to do whatever I want. That's the truth. That's reality.'

Dolores challenged her.

'Or whatever Rick wants?'

23

'I don't allow no one to abuse me,' Sadie said. 'Not Rick, not no one. I'm not taking any crap.'

Dolores was intrigued by this new avenue Sadie opened up. She sounded so determined to defend herself.

'Have you been abused before?'

'My mother was. My father dominated her so much she became a controlled woman who lost all her confidence. She used to argue back, but after a while she submitted to everything, even if she disagreed. She couldn't make any decisions anymore, she was so beaten down. She could never assert herself. I swore it would never happen to me.'

'What did your father do? Did he hit her?'

Sadie looked away at the painful memories still affecting her. 'Yes. He would hit her so hard it would knock her down to the floor. One night he was so drunk he even tried to set the dog on her. I had to save her. Then he passed out.'

'That's horrible.'

'If I had a gun I think I could have killed him.'

'It's lucky you didn't.'

Sadie did not answer Dolores. She looked towards the door of the counselling room, as if she wanted to get out. The memory of another terrible night at home came back to her. She was only seven at the time. 'I want a divorce,' Sadie's mother had shouted at her father. Sadie cringed under the covers in her bedroom, not wanting to hear her parents' fight, not able to bear it, but the house was small and the walls were thin.

'Kiss my royal Irish ass,' Sadie's enraged father shouted back.

The drinking of her parents always ended in the angry quarrels, both of them losing emotional self-control, and she would provoke him and he would hit her. The pattern was always the same. The next morning the threats to leave were forgotten, but the sullen resentments, the dull angers between her parents filled the bleak morning air of the hangovers. No smiles and laughter filled her home, Sadie finding her escape with the teachers at school, and her friends on the playground.

When his father hit her mother the night she was remembering now, her mother shrieked: 'Don't hit me again, please, no.' and her father said: 'Stop it. Stop all this nonsense.' The tension was so unbearable and her twin brother Sean crawled out her bedroom window and went running to the next-door neighbor's house to hide in her friend's home. Only later when she hoped her parents had passed out for the night did Sadie and her brother dare to return to the quiet, darkened house and their own bedrooms to pass the rest of the night. But this night her parents were still at it. Her brother fell asleep, but Sadie heard them speaking in the darkness in their bedroom through the thin walls of the house, the voices low and tense.

'Don't touch me. I don't want to do that.'

'Be quiet. You're my wife.'

Sadie heard her mother submit.

In the darkness, she vowed by the crucifix hanging on her bedroom wall she would never let herself be abused by a man like that, but she could not do anything to help her mother, she was too small; she could only stay silent, helpless, alone in her room, hoping her father would not come in. Her hand felt the baseball bat she kept under the covers beside her. She never needed to use it yet, and she hoped she never would. She wondered as she lay there: *How can my parents get divorced? We're Catholics, and the Sunday school teacher said marriage was for life.*

Sadie returned to herself, and looked at Dolores sitting behind her desk, waiting to talk some more with her. 'Where did you just go in your mind?' Dolores asked. 'You were quiet for a few moments there, staring at the door, but like you were far away, looking at something else.'

Sadie did not want to get into it all. They had talked long enough. 'I was just thinking of some private stuff.'

'I had a hard time too when I was a child.'

'Your family was bad?'

'Not my real family. Distant relatives. Family in name only. My mother died when she was giving birth to me. When I was eight, I watched my father die in front of me during my birthday party at a picnic in the park. My dad was known to everyone as a great kidder, especially when he had a few in him, and when his swim in the pond at the park turned deadly, he started waving his arms and crying out: 'Help. Help."

'What happened?'

Dolores let it all out, the memories she usually kept to herself.

'Everyone started laughing at him. They thought he was joking again. I saw he was really in trouble, and I started screaming: 'Help him. Help him.' I saw him go under the water. I rushed into the pond after him even though I couldn't swim, and then they came running, but by the time the people at the picnic reacted it was too late. I watched him disappear under the water and never come up again. They found him later, the weeds at the bottom of the pond wrapped around his legs trapping him, his arms waving in the current, his head upturned looking at the surface of the water above him drowning him, still reaching for the world of air just beyond his reach. My uncle told me how they found him later.'

'How horrible to watch your father die. And at your own birthday party.'

Dolores began scratching her right arm with her left hand.

'I was an orphan after that. I had no parents anymore. I was sent to live with my aunt and uncle and cousins, who didn't love me. They used me like a slave for the chores on the farm. If my dad was still alive he would never have allowed it.'

'Why are you scratching your arm?'

Dolores looked down at the arm and scratching hand. 'I caught poison ivy in the park the day my father drowned, and for the rest of my life on every birthday I break out again. I wasn't aware I was scratching myself again just now, talking about it.'

'But you grew up okay?'

'I never went near water again. I can't go swimming. I avoid it. And for years I used to pray: 'Please Lord, send someone to love me' It's all I wanted after those mean relatives.'
'Did you find love?'
'Still hoping.'

24

In a shared moment of silence after speech, the two women looked into each other's eyes, reading each other, getting to know one another. Dolores decided to deepen her self-disclosure, to tell Sadie about her abortion, when she heard the front door of the house open, the tread of heavy steps in the waiting room, and Rick asking where Sadie was, and heard Julie say: 'She's there, in the counselling room.'

Rick banged hard on the counselling room door, opened it, and stood in the threshold. 'What's taking so long?'

Dolores did not like the smell of beer surrounding him.

'I have to go,' Rick said. 'What's going on?'

Sadie rose from her chair to pacify Rick, putting her hand on his arm. 'She's pro-life Rick. We can't get an abortion here.'

'Rick, won't you join us for a talk? It's important, the way Sadie is feeling.'

'No, we have to go. It's been long enough. Come on Sadie.'

'I really would like to talk to you about your options, your alternatives to abortion.'

'We talked about it already. We can't afford a baby right now. It would lead to big problems.'

'So will an abortion. Why can't you just welcome this new baby into your world?'

Rick scowled at Dolores through his bloodshot eyes. 'I've

heard about these fake abortion clinics on TV.'

'You've got us all wrong.'

'We both want an abortion. It's what we want. What's it to you?'

'No woman really wants an abortion. Not like she wants something good in life, like a white wedding dress. Or a man's love. Or wants to be happy. A woman only wants an abortion like an animal caught in a trap wants to gnaw off its own leg.'

'It's a fetus, not alive yet, lower than an animal.'

Dolores never tired of trying to teach the truth to all the false denial and resistance she heard over and over. 'The child's heart beat starts at three weeks, brain waves start at six weeks. We use the pulse of the heart and brain waves to determine death. Why not apply those simple tests to determine the life of your child now eleven weeks old? It's your own son or daughter we are talking about.'

'I don't want to be preached at.'

Dolores was provoked and tired of it all: 'You know Rick, you're right. I am a Christian. I go to church every Sunday, and I get preached at.'

'I told you I don't want you preaching any sermons at me.'

'What's wrong with a sermon? I like a good sermon. My priest preaches a sermon at me every Sunday, and I love it. He is preaching the word of God, the words of life. A good sermon is saving me. Who are you, you don't want to be preached at? Who do you think you are?'

'I'm not religious.' Rick was unsteady on his feet and leaned against the doorjamb for support. 'We have freedom of religion in this country. Freedom of abortion. The Church does not control me.'

'You are free to accept God, and free to reject Him, but you will be responsible for your choice, and liable to His judgment.'

'Some freedom, if you get punished for it.'

'You are making a fatal misunderstanding of freedom. If it isn't God, something else will control you. You won't be free. You will be in captivity to your alcohol, your sexual desires. Punishment enough for you, right there. Enslavement enough of your freedom.'

'You people are religious fanatics here. Not counselors at all.'

'You have a duty to worship God as His creature. It's the first commandment. Worship God. You have a duty to a woman if you sleep with her. You have a duty to the child you fathered, if you're a man.'

'Rick's shoulder was slipping down the doorway. 'I don't believe in your punishing God, in heaven and hell.'

Sadie was watching Rick talk to Dolores, learning some more about her boyfriend. Dolores was so provoked by Rick's arrogance she could not help herself saying what she really thought. 'So you don't care about anything except yourself?'

'What do you worship lady? Human rights for fertilized eggs?'

'So you're a young person who knows everything. Nobody can tell you anything.'

'I know your type. Church on Sunday and the missionary position in bed and lots of kids. You're all hypocrites you

Bible thumpers. Pompous assholes telling everyone else what they should do with their lives. Smiling and shaking hands in Church, peace be with you, and hating each other, cheating each other, gossiping and backstabbing the rest of the week.'

'You must be Catholic if you know about the sign of peace. What makes you so angry about Christians? Sure, we're all sinners. There's always room for one more sinner in Church. One more hypocrite in Church. Why don't you come too?'

Sadie was surprised to discover Rick was Catholic too. He never mentioned these things, they never talked about them. She watched him taunt Dolores in a way she would never do herself.

'Sin is fun. I love it when Sadie and I do what we do. I bet all you Christians like it too, but you won't admit it. You sanctimonious Christians make me sick.'

'Rick-' Sadie tried to stop him.

'I'll tell you something. Sadie loves sex too. Sometimes she says she doesn't, but she doesn't mean it. I can tell from her moaning she loves it, and when she says no then I just take her.'

'Was he trying to shock her? Dolores knew what life was about. 'That's rape, even if she's your girlfriend. Even if she was your wife.'

Rick laughed. 'Well, dear old Sadie likes a little bit of marital rape now and then. She says No and means Yes. You should hear her screaming, the pain and the pleasure all mixed together. It's a real turn-on.'

'Rick, don't you have any of the real human purposes of sex? Of love and respect for a woman? Concern for her emotional wellbeing? Of respect for the procreation of children? In a permanent marriage? However fallen the world is, there is still purity in people.'

'Purity?'

'Yes, purity and chastity, self-giving love, self-denial and self-control. Not self-indulgence in recreational sex using women for your own pleasure. Sex as entertainment. Sadie isn't some actress in a porn movie to satisfy your sick desires you see other people doing. You say you know my type. I know your type too. You watch pornography, don't you?'

'What of it? It's legal. I like sex. There's nothing wrong with it.'

'Don't you know all the harm of putting that dirty filth in your mind? It's disgusting.'

'I like what's dirty. The porn I get in my email is called Your Daily Dirt. Nobody hides it. Rape em and scrape em, that's my motto.'

'You're deliberately trying to offend me. Have you no decency left?'

'A pretty little sermon. What I'd expect from a self-righteous Christian like you.'

Dolores felt a little scared of Rick, but she didn't think he was going to get violent. He was still on a verbal level, and he was not making any threatening gestures towards her. She could feel his anger, but she could not back down on what she believed. 'There's nothing pretty about the way you see the world, the way you are living.'

Rick crossed the line in his drunkenness. He leered at her, licking his bottom lip with his tongue.

'The repressed sex starved Christian. I bet you haven't had it for a long time.'

'Rick, stop it,' Sadie said.

'Get out of here,' Dolores said, standing from her seat. 'You're not going to assault me, even verbally. Get out, or I'll call the police.'

'We should be calling the police about your phony clinic here.'

'You can boast of all your sex, but abortion is the ultimate sexual perversion. Killing the child who comes from sexual intercourse meant to create new life. There's nothing phony in what we do here.'

'But you know something lady? It's not against the law. You can't call the cops about our abortion.'

'I wish I could.'

Rick took a lurching step towards her. Dolores cried out: 'Mickey. Mickey.'

Mickey came running from the back of the house. 'What's going on?'

'You're the man we saw on TV,' Rick said when he saw Mickey. 'The idiot getting arrested.'

'Yeah, it's him,' Sadie said. She turned to Dolores. 'You told me you weren't connected to him. You're all a bunch of liars.'

'Sadie, let's get out of here,' Rick said.

'We're always here for you Sadie,' Dolores said in a last attempt to let her know. 'A lot of support is available. Many people are willing to help you. You're not alone. Don't forget your pamphlets.'

Sadie was silent in the presence of Rick, yet surprisingly nodded goodbye to Dolores, and she took the pamphlets Dolores extended towards her in her outstretched hand. Some connection had been made between them.

'Don't you want to go to heaven?' she cried out in her last desperation, her concern for them.

Rick took Sadie by the arm moving her out of the room.

'Please think some more what you are about to do,' Dolores said to her departing back.

Sadie did not answer her. Rick and Sadie left, Rick swaying on his feet, Sadie clutching the pamphlets in her tense right hand. Rick looked back over his shoulder, and took his parting shot. 'Drop dead.' He slammed the front door of the Crisis Pregnancy Center behind them. They were gone. Sadie's positive pregnancy test with the two blue lines was left behind on the arm of the couch in front of the video player, forgotten.

25

Dolores was disappointed her talk with Sadie was cut short by Rick's intrusion. The conversation might have gone somewhere if she more time. They were getting close as women, sharing their pasts. She wished Rick joined them. She wanted him to know how abortion would harm Sadie. He needed to know. She could not believe he didn't care anything at all what happened to her. She regretted she did not have the time to teach Sadie about Natural Family Planning, how it could be a safe and effective natural birth regulation with no harmful side effects and still respected the purposes of human sexuality. Sadie probably believed all the lies about NFP, that it was risky and ineffective, and difficult to practice. All the woman had to do was learn how her body naturally worked and make some daily observations. She wished she had more time to discuss the sexually transmitted diseases, and the need for chastity and self-restraint. Some of the STDs caused cervical cancer. Promiscuous young women did not know all of the risks they were taking. They did not even see themselves as promiscuous if they only had one boyfriend at a time. Good old-fashioned lust now led to millions of murders of unwanted children, millions of damaged men and women, and millions of sexual diseases, and they still didn't get it.

When Sadie and Rick walked out the door, Dolores made

the sign of the cross over herself and prayed: 'Forgive them Lord, they know not what they do.' She was concerned about Sadie. A coerced abortion was bound to hurt her. Mickey, Dolores and Julie stood at the front windows of the Crisis Pregnancy Center, watching Sadie and Rick outside on the sidewalk, talking beside the car. They could not hear them, but they could see they were arguing, Rick leaning his hand against the car door to steady himself, his other arm pointing back at the Center.

'It seems this session went badly,' Mickey said to Dolores.

'Not good at all. I lost it. I got mad and argued with them. I was lecturing and preaching. I didn't have enough time with her. The boyfriend was in control, pressuring her.'

'It's impossible sometimes. And yet other times we see the beautiful miracle of a woman changing her mind, deciding to have her baby.'

'That's God's action. I don't seem to be a persuasive counsellor.'

'You have a great heart for the unborn and the women, which is the most important thing.'

'I wasn't good today. I hate it when fights happen. We were just talking at each other, the usual arguments on both sides. We connected for a couple of moments, but I don't know if she heard me.'

'When the clients throw out smokescreens of denial, they can suck us into arguing back. There isn't much we can do to avoid it.'

'But I can't help feeling something got through to her she didn't want to admit. She didn't admit any bad feelings from her first abortion either. Her boyfriend was still drunk from his hangover. He was useless.'

'Have you ever noticed denial operates in both alcoholism and abortion? Nobody has a drinking problem, and no one has an abortion problem.'

'I don't think the pro-aborts would appreciate the linkage,' Julie said. 'They think they stand for a human right, not a human problem.'

'Don't be discouraged Dolores,' Mickey said. 'Or too hard on yourself, down on yourself. It isn't up to us to save the world. We can only do what we can. The rest is in God's hands.'

'It's so hard to watch them choose abortion. I wish I was a better counselor. I feel like such an amateur. I wish I was a better Christian.'

'We're all amateurs. I'm an amateur lawyer. I know it. But no one else is doing anything. And there is such power in the law. If only the Catholic lawyers cared about real justice for the unborn, instead of going along with the abortion system to advance their careers.'

'You're pretty good in court Mickey,' Julie said, 'from what I've seen. You can hold your own and speak up. You might lose a lot, but they can't steam roller over you.'

'I'm afraid they can, and did this morning. But you're right, there is a certain equality in court, in all the traditions and procedures. When I'm sitting at the lawyers' table, I am equal in rights to whoever is sitting at the table on the other side. It could be two or three lawyers on the other side, a whole team. It could be lawyers from some huge entity, like the government or some large corporation. But it is still just two tables, the two parties in the case, equality.'

'Except it isn't equal,' Dolores said. 'Judge Dockendorff favors the big establishment pro-abortion side, favors those tables and teams of lawyers.'

'You can't get around the real world politics of it. But in theory, in principle, and in practice, it's just the two sides at the two tables, with equal rights to speak, no matter how much more powerful one side may be. I find that an inspiring tradition.'

Dolores did not want to say anything to discourage Mickey in his passion for the law, the way the law should be. His idealism for the law meant so much to him, and she knew it. Mickey wanted to encourage Dolores and Julie too in their counselling work. 'Even if we aren't the best people to be doing it, we are doing it. Someone has to do it. I would gladly step aside if some of the big shots really started working on stopping abortion.'

'Me too, I feel the same way,' Dolores said 'I would step aside if the doctors and social workers really worked against abortion.'

'You are the best people to be doing it,' Julie said.

Mickey shared some more of what happened in court earlier in the morning.

'Abortion is a normal way of life now. Or should I say a normal way of death? Look at Craigenback's abortion mill across the street, freely operating, just like any other business, another customer service. Judge Dockendorff said an abortion clinic is no different than a barber shop or auto mechanic.'

'This is normal?' Julie asked.

Mickey rubbed the back of his neck, his constant headache pulsing at the base of his skull. 'It is a strain sometimes.' He tried to bring some sunshine into the grim day. 'I saw something hilarious in the courthouse today. A lawyer got on the elevator bent half over, carrying a stack of law books piled in his hands and arms, and I asked him how he did, and he said: 'We pleaded guilty."

Mickey and Dolores laughed. Dolores always laughed at his jokes. But Julie said: 'I don't get it.'

'He studied the law very hard and concluded his client was guilty.' He laughed again. 'But seriously, even if the law is corrupted by the killing of the innocent in abortion, I have to keep believing in the law. The principles of fairness are a beautiful system if properly used. The right to confront your accuser, and cross-examine him in a public trial is a powerful instrument. The requirement for evidence to back up an accusation is a protection not to be taken for granted.'

'Oh Mickey,' Dolores said, 'here we go again. I already told you how I feel about the law.'

Mickey had to tell her. 'While you were busy with the client, we were served some new legal papers from Craigenback and Jessica Sterne.'

'Again? So soon?'

'I have to be back in court in two days, on the morning of Christmas Eve. They want to put signs on our front door and on our office walls that we do not provide abortion services.'

'Their signs on our walls? I can't believe it. I can't stand this. Judge Dockendorff might as well be sitting in a corner of the counselling room, monitoring what I can or can't say to someone like Sadie. Why don't they just send the sheriff to seize all of our furniture. They already took our phones.'

'We also got a nasty letter from Bishop Blair today,' Julie said.

'Can I see it?'

Mickey handed the letter to Dolores who read it in silence. She handed it back to him without a word.

'Well?'

'No comment.'

Mickey decided to needle her a little. 'I'm thinking of suing Bishop Blair for defamation of pro-life. I have a libel and slander case from the things he has said and written about us.'

'You can't sue the Church. If you do I'm quitting.'

'Everybody sues the Church, sexually abused children, native children forced to assimilate into Church run residential schools. Why not libeled pro-lifers?'

'You can't sue the Church. The Church is the body of Christ, the Church is our mother, Holy Mother Church.'

'The people who have taken over and are running the Catholic Church in Canada aren't Catholic anymore. Don't let your respect and reverence for the Church make you deferential to them. They exploit the submissiveness of Catholics.'

'I can't be part of suing the Church. I mean it. If you sue the Church I'm leaving. For all the bad priests, there are just as many good men who give up their lives to serve God and humanity.'

'I'm surprised you are so middle class, so conventional. It would make a great lawsuit, pro-lifer sues Catholic Church for non-support and defamation.'

'You have no chance of winning that lawsuit before any judge or court in Canada.'

'I had a tough one yesterday,' Julie said. 'She was taking Accutane for acne, and then found out she was pregnant. She was terrified her baby will have birth defects. I tried to re-assure her, but she was determined to have an abortion.'

'Did you tell her the baby is a human being with problems, and we should do our best to treat the problems, and not eliminate the human being?' Dolores asked.

'She wouldn't accept it. She was so afraid. It's a tough situation. People need a lot of faith in God, and a lot of respect for human life, and a love of a deformed baby, not to abort for disability reasons.'

'You sound like you accept some reasons for abortion Julie.' Mickey said.

'No, I know abortion is always wrong. But I understand how it might seem kind to the child by some people. They're mistaken, but I understand how they could feel that way, think that way.'

'Be misled that way. It's really one of the most horrendous reasons for abortion, because the child will not be perfect and have problems. People should not consider it for a second. It isn't right. They even have new euphemistic jargon for it now, saying a baby with disabilities is *incompatible with life*.'

'You know how seductive and apparently reasonable pro-abortion arguments are,' Dolores said. 'They always appeal to a false compassion.'

'People are confused and deceived when it comes to abortion, even the nicest and smartest people,' Mickey agreed. 'Did you educate Sadie on all the birth control lies?'

'I tried but there was little time. She was anxious about the boyfriend and wanted to get going. I mentioned some things.'

'Was she here for an abortion because of failed birth control?'

'As usual. But she didn't see the connection. She said the doctors must know what they are doing.'

'They have such touching trust in the world and authorities around them.'

'Did you use the charts to show NFP instruction? It's important we do it in every counselling session.'

'I'm sorry. There was just no time for everything. She refused to look at the posters how her body works. I did give her the NFP pamphlet to take with her.'

'Good.'

They peered through the venetian blinds of the front window as they talked, watching Rick and Sadie still standing on the sidewalk talking beside their parked car. Rick looked angry, and Sadie looked like she was calming him down, explaining her brush with the pro-lifers. Rick pointed at the house. He turned around and came back to the front door. Dolores caught her breath at the coming confrontation. She was glad Mickey was there. It might be good if she could appeal to Rick again for the life of his baby, to urge him to protect Sadie and his child. She did not see him as he paused at the closed front door of the house. Some moments passed. He did not come in, but walked quickly back to the car and got in the driver's side. Sadie pulled on the dented door to wrench it open and got in the passenger's side. Rick started the car and drove away, belching some blue smoke from the rear tailpipe, Sadie crying beside him.

26

Between the time the Crisis Pregnancy Center was served the legal documents on December 21st, and the court hearing on December 24th, Mickey only had two full days to prepare his defense. Dolores came to sit in the public benches of the courtroom to support him, as much as she hated the law, lawyers, judges and courts. No one else was there just before the Christmas holiday, except Craigenback's lawyer Jessica Sterne, her silent co-counsel sitting beside her, the court clerk, the two extra security guards, and Judge Dockendorff. The court did not usually hold hearings this close to Christmas, and no reporters were present.

Jessica Sterne stood to address the court.

'Your Honor, the Craigenback Abortion Clinic is asking for an emergency order requiring the Crisis Pregnancy Center to place prominent signs on its front door and office walls stating the Center does not provide any birth control or abortion services. You have protected the rights of the Craigenback clinic, and the rights of the public, with your order preventing the Defendant from false advertising in the Yellow Pages of the telephone directory, The order we seek today extends the protections needed against these anti-abortionists. Their telephone line has been disconnected, but the advertising in the phone book will last for the entire coming year. Some people might see the listings and go to the address without calling first to make an appointment. The public needs this extra protection from the fraudulent tactics of the Crisis Pregnancy Center. Thank you.'

This emergency hearing should not take too long, and soon he would have his Christmas break. He only made himself available on this late date just before the holidays to oblige Jessica Sterne.

'Mr. Finnegan, what is your response to these very serious allegations?'

'Your Honor, my response is this attempt by the abortion clinic to interfere with a crisis pregnancy center hardly show respect for freedom of choice. It's all about social control under the guise of freedom and the law. Will signs be placed on the front door and office walls of the Craigenback Abortion Clinic they do not give all the facts about abortion or provide alternatives to abortion?'

Jessica Sterne objected. 'Your Honor, I refer you to the transcript of the radio talk show interview of a counsellor from the Crisis Pregnancy Center, Dolores Cruz. On page 29, starting at line five-'

Mickey objected. 'I was given no notice this evidence would be used today.'

Jessica Sterne leaned over the space between the two tables separating the lawyers, and handed Mickey a copy of the affidavit of radio talk show host Martin Schiefle, with the attached transcript as Exhibit A. 'These documents are already on file from the first hearing Your Honor.'

'This is not correct legal procedure,' Mickey objected again.

'Not at all-' Jessica Sterne began to reply.

'Be quiet Mr. Finnegan,' Judge Dockendorff interrupted. 'Objection overruled. I want to hear the evidence.'

Jessica Sterne began reading from the affidavit exhibit, the transcript of the radio interview between Martin Schiefle and Dolores Cruz:

> Dolores Cruz: Let me repeat, we are not deceptive and dishonest. All the confusion over the use of names from the lying use of the words Family Planning and Birth Control as code words for abortion by the other side. They are the dishonest ones. We simply try to educate our clients when they arrive at the Center on the truth about abortion.
>
> Unknown Caller, Self-Identified as Dolly: I know for a fact you let people think they are at an abortion clinic when they first come in.
>
> Martin Schiefle: Is it true? Do you let people think they are at an abortion clinic?
>
> Dolores Cruz: Our counselling sessions last on an average of one to two hours, sometimes longer. By the time the client leaves the Crisis Pregnancy Center she completely knows what we are about.
>
> Marting Schiefle: But what about right at the start?
>
> Dolores Cruz: People can be confused at the beginning. It takes some discussion to clear up all the confusion about

abortion.

Martin Schiefle: But do you tell the clients right away at the start of the session you are pro-life?

Dolores Cruz: The term pro-life has become so loaded with false meanings and associations, so many stereotypes, we want to discuss some things first to aid communication. Does the Craigenback Abortion Clinic tell its patients abortion kills a human being? Do they tell the women how dangerous abortion is for them? No, they don't.

Sterne stopped reading from the transcript evidence. 'There you have it Your Honor. A complete public admission the Crisis Pregnancy Center does not inform people the Center is pro-life.' Sterne sat down, confident in her position with Judge Dockendorff's court.

Mickey stood to speak, but before he could say anything Dolores spoke from her place in the public benches behind the guard rail. When she was interviewed on Schiefle's radio talk show, she recognized the voice of Dolly on the telephone was old Sara, disguising herself as someone else. Dora and Sara often assumed false identities to protect themselves in their public pro-life statements, even though they criticized Mickey and the Crisis Pregnancy Center for being dishonest. Dolores let is pass during the show. She was disappointed Dora and Sara were attacking the Crisis Pregnancy Center on the radio show, but she wanted to speak now? 'Your Honor, I am Dolores Cruz. I can tell you the transcript just read is taken out of context. It does not tell the whole truth about my interview on the radio show.'

'You are not a sworn witness today in this hearing Ms. Cruz,' Judge Dockendorff said. 'Please sit down. You have no legal standing to speak to the Court.'

'But you just read what I said,' Dolores objected.

'Your Honor,' Mickey said, quick on his feet the way lawyers have to be, 'the Defense calls Dolores Cruz.'

Dockendorff's head quivered without actually shaking from side to side. He managed to control his reaction before showing too much of what he felt. 'Mr. Finnegan, this is an informal Chambers hearing. It is not a full trial in open court. That will come later. We do not hear live witnesses in Chambers hearings. You should have filed a sworn affidavit in reply to Ms. Sterne's affidavit evidence. We proceed by way of affidavit evidence in Chambers. Perhaps you should obtain legal advice.'

'You Honor, we didn't know Ms. Sterne was going to make these arguments. It's only fair we have a chance to respond. We were only given two days to prepare for this important hearing.'

'Mr. Finnegan, everything has been properly done according to the rules of court. It is you who are out of order.'

'I request an adjournment so I may cross-examine the affidavit evidence of Martin Schiefle. I have that legal right, to cross the evidence used against us.'

'Request denied. You are not going to delay this hearing by an adjournment strategy.'

'But the right to cross examine your accuser is fundamental

to our system of justice-'

'Motion denied.'

Dolores still wanted to speak. 'Your Honor-'

'Please sit down Ms. Cruz, or the Bailiff will have to remove you from this courtroom. You have no legal right to speak to this court today. You can testify later as a witness at the full trial, if you follow proper procedure.'

Dolores resumed her seat. Jessica Sterne was relaxed and smiling. Mickey was outraged. 'How can you deny my right to cross examine on an affidavit?'

'I have my ruling Mr. Finnegan. It is not your place to argue with a judge. These proceedings will not be delayed. The public interest is at stake. There are limits to everything. You have no right to unbridled cross-examination.'

'With all due respect Your Honor, what is the legal basis of your ruling I cannot cross examine the evidence being used against me?'

'Because I am doing it.'

Mickey shifted his argument. 'Freedom of speech is a two way street in constitutional law. We not only have the freedom to speak our pro-life opinion to the public, but the public has a freedom of speech right to hear it. The public do not need legal protection from our pro-life speech, they actually need protection of their right to hear pro-life. These signs Ms. Sterne wants on our pro-life center warning people away from us are actually an infringement of the public's rights, not just ours.'

'Mr. Finnegan, I am afraid you are forgetting again of what I must constantly remind you. The constitution, and your opinions about abortion and the alleged killing of human beings are not before me. Only truth in advertising, business rights, private property rights, and the right of the public to be protected from fraud are before me in your many cases with the Plaintiff Clinic.'

'They are the ones bringing the many cases Your Honor. Our rights and freedoms are enshrined in the constitution. Freedom of Religion. Freedom of speech. Freedom of thought, belief and opinion.'

'Mr. Finnegan, the abortion clinic is a private business establishment. The government is not limiting your rights and freedoms. The constitution is meant to limit the intrusion of the government and their agencies into the lives of private citizens.'

'But once the court grants a civil court order to the private abortion clinic, all of the enforcement machinery of the government is activated, with police and arrests, courts and trials, fines and imprisonments. The civil court order to a private party becomes state interference with our lives as private citizens.'

'The state is not moving against you. You have no state enforcement to fear if you obey any order the court makes, as you should.'

'But that becomes a legal fiction, that the state is not moving against us. Like the legal fiction the unborn children are not human persons deserving of any legal rights and protection, whatever the reality is.'

'Be that as it may, I am ruling you cannot rely on constitutional rights in this case.'

Mickey shifted his approach again. 'Your Honor, in light of your comments the Craigenback Abortion Clinic is a profit making business, I now wish to make a formal, verbal motion in this hearing the Clinic display signs on their office walls their counselling is biased by a financial conflict of interest. It they make their money doing abortions, how can their counselling be objective and disinterested? It is a clear conflict of interest.'

'Motion denied.'

'So you think it is fair justice our telephone is disconnected, and signs put up on our front door and office walls, but the abortion clinic has a free hand?'

'Mr. Finnegan, I am not here to debate the law with you. I am hereby ordering signs be prominently displayed on the front door and office walls of the Crisis Pregnancy Center that the Center does not provide birth control and abortion services or referrals.'

'Will you also order the Craigenback Abortion Clinic to put us signs on their walls they do not provide the options of childbirth and adoption?'

Jessica Sterne spoke. 'Your Honor, this is absurd. What business advertises what it does not do?'

'It's no more absurd than–'

'Mr. Finnegan, I have made my ruling. You have no motions before me today.'

Dolores watched and listened to poor Mickey try to fight on as Sterne and Dockendorff steam-rolled over him. She dug her fingernails into her palm to restrain herself from saying something angry, and getting herself thrown out of the courtroom. Angry outbursts were not her style, but she felt a fury rising within her, and knew again why she hated the law, and hated to come to court.

27

Jessica Sterne decided to press her advantage, now that she had everything she wanted, and saw Judge Dockendorff and Mickey were openly fighting.

'Your Honor, we are also asking the anti-abortion picket signs protesters bring to the Craigenback Abortion Clinic be limited to exclude inflammatory words, and exclude naming private individuals. The signs say things like Abortion Is Murder, and Abortion Kills Children, and House Of Horrors.' The name of Dr. Craigenback is displayed as Doctor Death, and his nurse Sincerity Burstall as Nurse Death. We want these derogatory signs prohibited.'

'But those simple words go to the heart of pro-life. Abortion is wrong because it takes a human life. To suppress those words that abortion is killing is to suppress pro-life.'

'I find for the Plaintiff words as Kill and Murder are defamatory. The laws of Canada permit abortion. The laws of this land do not restrict abortion, or consider abortion the killing of a human being. The Criminal Code in Canada for a century has defined a human being as someone who has proceeded completely outside the mother's body at birth. The Fetus has no legal standing, no legal personhood, no legal rights to prevent abortion. The Supreme Court has made that clear. I must follow the law. To make accusations of killing on public signs is a libel of the Plaintiff, which is legally a legitimate business in the eyes of the law. You may use words such as Respect Life or Right To Life on your picket signs in a general way, but any words on your signs implying abortion kills or murders a human being are hereby prohibited.'

'So we must put up signs saying we are pro-life at our office, but our pro-life protest signs on the sidewalk in front of the abortion mill are not to be displayed at all? I don't think you are being very fair to us as.'

Judge Dockendorff leaned over his elevated bench, looking down directly at Mickey beneath him. 'I warn you Mr. Finnegan. This court has always tried to bend over backwards and give you some leeway as an untrained layman in the law, someone who is not a professional lawyer. But if your tone turns into contempt of court you will be sanctioned.'

'Your rulings today are simply denial, court institutionalized official denial abortion kills children.'

'I'm sorry you do not grasp the intricacies of the law. Abortion is not before me. Only the laws on defamation and fraud are before me today.'

Jessica Sterne spoke again. 'Your Honor, the Plaintiff is also concerned at the picketing of Dr. Craigenback's home, and the home of Sincerity Burstall. I don't know how they found those private addresses, but they have been coming there too with the same offensive signs, harming the reputation of the Plaintiffs with their neighbors. We ask the court today for a restraining order to prevent the home picketing, and also an order prohibiting pro-life picketing of our law offices.'

Mickey had remained standing throughout the court arguments back and forth, too involved in the urgency of the hearing to sit down. 'We have every right to express our opinion abortion is socially unacceptable by picketing the homes of those involved in it, and then think they can go home and fit into the community, be normal people just like everyone else. Abortion is such a terrible evil, we have to bring those responsible for it to public attention. Abortion is socially unacceptable.'

He wanted to end this special emergency hearing Jessica Sterne had rushed through the day before Christmas.

'Mr. Finnegan, a man's home is his castle, and his entitled to privacy. What you are doing picketing private homes is what the law terms watching and besetting. It is illegal. I am forthwith granting an emergency order to prevent you land your associates from harassing Dr. Craigenback and his staff, including the legal counsel he retains, from any other locations than the Craigenback Abortion Clinic. I mean, you are not to harass them there either, but you may express your opinions in the socially acceptable way I set out earlier today in general signs, and set out in previous orders of staying 50 meters away from the clinic. You are now ordered to stay away two miles from the private homes of the clinic staff. I find it is your anti-abortion activities harassing doctors and nurses in their homes which is socially unacceptable. And I daresay community standards in Calgary agree with me.'

'But you have no trouble invading my home where I live, cutting off my phone, putting up signs on my front door and walls-'

Dolores stood again in the public benches at the back of the courtroom, watching Mickey walk into dangerous territory, losing his Irish temper.

Judge Dockendorff banged his gavel hard on his elevated desk, the sharp crack of sound ending it. 'Mr. Finnegan, I have made my rulings. My wife is waiting to go shopping. Today's matters are concluded. Court is adjourned. Merry Christmas everyone.'

The court clerk called out: 'All Stand.'

As they stood in respect for his office while Judge Dockendorff exited the courtroom, Mickey and Dolores looked at one another across the railing separating the lawyers' tables from the public benches. There was nothing they could do. The Crisis Pregnancy Center, and the pro-life protests, had all been smashed, with a few pieces of paper, and a few words, on Christmas Eve, in an informal court hearing with nobody there. The painkiller pills Mickey took before the hearing were wearing off, and a pounding headache was pulsating all over his head, and growing worse. His hand rubbed the stiffness of the sore, tight muscles at the base of his neck. It hurt.

28

Sadie and Rick sat in the living room of their rented apartment. Sadie was troubled. 'I don't know Rick.' She curled her legs up under her on the sofa, Rick in the easy chair sitting across from her. It was Boxing Day, just after Christmas.

'After talking to the counsellor yesterday, I have doubts. I don't feel good about it.'

Rick leaned forward, his hands gripping the arms of the big chair, careful not to spill the bottle of beer balanced on the chair. 'They weren't counselors at that place. An abortion would be the best thing. It's not human yet so early. Best for the kid too. We're not ready to be parents. Either one of us.'

'I know I said I wanted it too, but I don't like the idea.'

'Why the hell not?'

She looked away, rubbing her hands over her eyes. 'It's all so ugly. It scares me to do it again. I'm farther along this time. Here I am doing it again. What has happened to me?'

Rick was standing above her now. 'It's just another medical procedure. Day surgery. You're out in a couple of hours. Nothing to it. Like pulling a tooth.'

Still Sadie did not look at him. Rick turned his back on her, walked over to the window facing the city street, and stood looking out at the passing cars, the people on the sidewalk walking by. The late afternoon winter sun was shining behind the branches of the old maple tree on the front lawn outside of their squat apartment building, the branches casting dark shadows like bars on the window glass. Green trash bags full of torn Christmas gift-wrappings leaned against the curb, and a Christmas tree lay on its side waiting for the garbage truck tomorrow. It was only Boxing Day but Christmas was over for Rick already.

He turned to Sadie, 'You will get some unbiased counselling at the abortion clinic from professionals, not like those anti-abortion fanatics. Just check it out. One of our options.'

Sadie closed her eyes and shook her head. 'I don't know Rick. I don't know.'

'Let's just go and find out.'

'I feel like I am crossing a line, a big line.'

'You should go to the appointment tomorrow for the counselling, then go for the procedure the next day. It's the mature thing to do. The responsible thing.'

Sadie opened her eyes and looked at him. 'Why are you so relentless?'

"I'm only talking sense.'

'Don't manipulate me Rick. Don't pressure me. I'm pregnant. We are talking about our baby. Or what could be our baby.'

Rick tried a sincere approach. 'Let me get you a can of the beer you like. You must be thirsty.'

"Thanks.'

Rick went into the kitchen and opened a can of beer for Sadie. He added one of his Cytotec pills he used for his ulcers to full can of beer, stirring to dissolve it. He did not want to shake the beer. He had heard Cytotec could induce contractions when used by a pregnant woman and cause an early abortion. He returned to the living room and handed the can. "Here you go'

Sadie reached up her hand from where she was sitting. 'Thanks, that was thoughtful of you.'

Rick, still standing, made his sincere speech. 'Sadie, I would love to have you as the mother of my children someday. But now is just not the right time to start a family. We both need to be further along in our work and life goals, when we can afford to give our baby the best. If you have the abortion now, we can plan our future lives together so everything is perfect.'

'You really mean that?'

Rick's jaw tightened, irritated at her resistance. She was always oppositional and argumentative about everything, always had her own opinions contradicting him. Why couldn't she be more easy going, go along with him, be submissive? Why did she always have these changing moods about everything? Who was manipulating who?

'Are you using this to get me to marry you?'

'Is that what do you think of me?'

'Is it mine?'

'How can you say that to me? I haven't been with anyone besides you. You know that.'

Rick craned his neck to the side, looking out the window again. Sadie wanted to talk about all of it. 'When you had sex with me, weren't you agreeing to be a father? Agreeing to the possibility anyway?'

He looked at her then. 'Why do you think I used condoms?'

'But can't we accept the baby anyway, even if it was unplanned? A mistake?'

'You're a Catholic woman, you knew what you were getting into.' He looked out the window again. Sadie sensed his absence, even though he was standing right there in front of her, but turned away from her, looking out the window. 'Why do you have to say such hurtful things?'

Rick turned and looked at her then. 'So now I have to put up with the hurt feelings routine?'

Sadie stared at him, and replied: 'Yes I feel. I can feel how ice cold you've turned.'

Rick remained silent, and turned away from her again to resume looking out the window. Should he use the genetic disease in the family excuse he did not want to pass on to a child? That might be going too far. Sadie was not believing him even at his most sincere. She might demand tests to prove it. Maybe the Cytotec would solve the problem, with no need for further discussion.

Sadie was surprised at the conversation. She resented his continual pressure on her. She received no encouragement from him, no input from her, no choice really, never any question about his decision for abortion. She was only an obstacle he had to clear out of the way. She was pregnant, and he was not happy about it. She watched him standing by the window, his back all she could see, his head looking outside, and she felt his stubborn absolute refusal. She saw he wanted out. Was he looking out the window at other women walking by? What did he really want? Someone who was not pregnant? Someone else? She knew in this moment nothing she could say would ever get through to him. The chasm of the unresolved pain between them widened, driving them ever further apart.

'What kind of love is this?' she asked. She still sat alone separate from him on the couch with her legs curled beneath her, and as she raised her can of beer sipping it, she burst into tears.

29

Rick made a right turn from Center Street, driving Sadie in his dented Mustang with the broken door and taillights to her appointment at the Craigenback Abortion Clinic. He stuck his left arm out of the open car window in the winter air to make the turn signal. The pro-lifers were already lined up on the sidewalk for their annual Feast of the Holy Innocents demonstration. They held the protest every year on December 28th during the Christmas Season, in remembrance of the unborn children killed by abortion. In the Catholic Church the Feast of the Holy Innocents was the memorial of the children killed by King Herod seeking the life of the newborn Jesus, and the pro-lifers saw the present day killing of innocent children by abortion the same kind of injustice.

The pro-lifers stood behind the 50 meter buffer zone, an invisible line ordered by Judge Dockendorff to keep them away from the clinic patients and staff, after Mickey acted as a lone ranger two months before, locking the front doors of Craigenback's with a padlock. He was frustrated the authorities would not close the abortion clinic down after he proved it was located in the wrong city zone for a business or medical clinic. Craigenback should never have been allowed to operate his abortion clinic in a residential neighborhood. After the civil disobedience, Craigenback got the injunction for the buffer zone, a double twisting of the law, the court ordering police protection of an illegal clinic. The other prolifers, especially Dora and Sara, blamed Mickey for getting them all removed from the sidewalk right in front of the clinic.

Dolores held one of the toned down protest signs Judge Dockendorff allowed on Christmas Eve, a sign saying **I REGRET MY ABORTION**. Julie stood beside Dolores, holding her own sign with a drawing of a baby crying and the words **WHY MOM WHEN I HAVE SO MUCH LOVE TO GIVE YOU?**, and Mickey was there too with the words written on it **ABORTION IS EVERYONE'S SIN**. Dora and Sara stood together on the sidewalk, keeping themselves apart from the others, avoiding Mickey, Dolores and Julie. Dora held a protest sign proclaiming **HOUSE OF HORRORS**, and Sara's sign said **ADOPTION IS THE OPTION**. Their own choice of signs which said **ABORTION KILLS CHILDREN**, now censored by Judge Dockendorff, were no longer displayed. Some of the deeply religious protesters held signs with Christian messages proclaiming **LORD FORGIVE US AND OUR NATION** and **JESUS FORGIVES AND HEALS**. No one wanted to be arrested for displaying an illegal sign, although Charlie Kelly pushed it close to the limit with his hand lettered poster which said **ABORTION STOPS A BEATING HEART**.

The whole issue of words on signs, the question of what was a legal or illegal sign, had become an absurdity in the conflict, but the jeopardy was real enough, with possible consequences of arrest. Charlie was one of the more aggressive pro-lifers, and he resented Judge Dockendorff's limitations on his freedom of speech. He was prepared to be arrested over the injunction on pro-life protest signs, and argue about the interpretation of words. Was his sign implying abortion was killing or murder, or only reporting medical facts unborn children had beating hearts? Charlie knew the law often involved subjective wrangling over words and hair splitting over commas. But today during the quiet Christmas holidays no police drove by to monitor the demonstration. Charlie was arrested once before, for sitting in front of the doors of Craigenbacks' and refusing admittance to anyone. But the great majority of pro-life protesters would never attempt to directly interfere with a woman's physical freedom. As they picketed the abortion clinic, walking back and forth on the sidewalk, the pro-lifers holding their signs beyond the buffer zone, many of them prayed, holding special rosary beads colored in baby pink and blue.

Dolores walked over to join Dora and Sara. She wanted to show some Christmas spirit despite their differences. Sincerity Burstall the abortion clinic nursing director walked by to go to work, and took a verbal dig as she passed: 'Too bad you weren't aborted.'

'Too bad you weren't aborted,' Sara said right back. 'Baby killers.'

Sincerity taunted Dolores too. 'Do you have your camera today? Are you taking pictures of the women going into the clinic, violating their privacy?'

'I only bring my camera to protect us from false accusations.'

Sincerity tossed her head at her. Dolores saw the woman

walking beside Sincerity Burstall filming the confrontation instigated by Sincerity on her cell phone. The whole incident was a set up. Dolores worried Sara fell into a legal trap with her comment back to Sincerity, giving the abortion clinic evidence to remove the pro-life protesters even further away. She walked over to tell Mickey what just happened. Mickey was standing now among some pro-lifers who held the court approved signs saying **RIGHT TO LIFE** and **RESPECT LIFE**. Mickey could not understand how Judge Dockendorff allowed the signs while objecting to the other signs. Didn't the simple signs say it all, that abortion takes a human life, especially when the words were printed on a protest sign held on the sidewalk in front of an abortuary? He voiced his concerns to Dolores, when she came over to join him. 'What do you make of it, what Dockendorff ordered about the signs, about his logic?'

'What logic?'

'Remember what Dockendorff said when I asked him what the legal basis was for his order?'

'I remember something about the law of defamation. He said it was libel to accuse Craigenback of murder when abortion is legal.'

'Remember what else he said?'

'What are you getting at?'

'He said it was legal because he was doing it.'

'I didn't understand that.'

'I think he meant he has the legal power and authority as a judge to make any decision.'

'He does, but it sounds kind of arrogant, one man alone

does what he wants, imposes his personal opinion on the whole city because he went to law school and was appointed a judge?'

'Apparently he can decide for all of us.'

Dolores shuddered. 'That's enormous power.'

'Maybe we should appeal. One thing about the law, everyone is presumed to know the law except the judges. They can always be reversed on appeal.'

'But all the courts support abortion, from top to bottom. Mickey, we have another problem. I just heard Sara fight back with Sincerity Burstall. They both said to each other 'Too bad you weren't aborted."

'Oh boy. We have to talk to Sara again. It won't be easy.'

'Sincerity Burstall's friend filmed it all.'

Mickey shook his head. A man came walking down the street and without a word tore the sign young Julie was holding right out of her hands.

'Hey.' Julie said.

'Get a life,' the man said. He tried to tear up the sign, but it was not made of cardboard, the sign was thin but strong corrugated white plastic. The man grew frustrated he could not tear up the sign. He tried folding it, but the reinforced plastic resisted his efforts to crush it. Finally the man threw the sign on the ground and stomped on it with his feet, but he was not able to destroy the sign, and walked away down the street in defeated silence, fuming. Dolores and Julie laughed, amused at the man's actions. Julie picked up her battered sign, dusted it off, and continued her protest. Her sign was crumpled and creased, but she still used it. She felt there was something significant in a battered pro-life sign just like the torn and bruised babies.

Dolores recognized Rick's car as he drove by the buffer zone, and pulled up at the front door of Craigenback's 50 meters away. She saw Sadie emerge out of the passenger side, and it seemed Rick was saying something to her through the open door of the car as she leaned inwards, but was not getting out himself. Sadie looked around, and recognized Dolores standing there at the buffer zone limit, wearing a long green dress this time, but with the same bright red shoes, and holding a pro-life protest sign. The woman looked like a bright Christmas ornament. Sadie looked across the street and saw the Crisis Pregnancy Center she went to by mistake last week. Sadie heard since then how the pro-lifers deliberately set up their office close to the abortion clinic, which was also in a house with sign outside. She was confused before, but she knew where she was now, and exactly what she wanted to do. No point in having Rick's baby. She was through with him, and would soon be leaving him. She would make a new start after the abortion, breaking all ties to her past with him. She knew where he was going now, to have a beer, leaving her to face the abortion appointment alone. All he was good for was the money he gave her to pay for it.

When she saw Sadie get out of Rick's car Dolores wanted to talk to her again. She took a risk, and trudged forward through the winter slush on the sidewalk into the buffer zone, following after her. Dolores was not a pro-lifer who broke the law in civil disobedience, and she did not want a confrontation, but she could not let Sadie whom she knew, on this day of all days, go into the abortion clinic alone without anyone trying to help her. She was careful not to touch Sadie when she reached her. She wanted to give her some encouragement with a comforting touch, but the pro-lifers were warned touching anyone could be charged as an assault. Sincerity Burstall was vigilant, constantly monitoring the sidewalks outside the clinic through the video surveillance security cameras. Dolores called out: 'Sadie, let's talk. You don't have to go in there.'

Sadie stopped and turned around towards Dolores, facing her. 'We already talked. I've made my choice.'

'You can still change your mind. There's still time. You still have a chance.'

'Please, I have to go. They're waiting for me.'

'You don't have to do this. We can help you.'

Sadie turned her head away. 'I have to go.'

'I hope nothing I said hurt you. I was only trying to help you.'

'I know.'

Dolores remembered how she lost it, became angry, and started arguing with Sadie and Rick. 'Sometimes it's hard to help someone, and it's so easy to hurt someone. I hope I didn't say anything wrong or hurtful to you.'

'I understand you're pro-life.'

Dolores felt pressured at how little time was left. 'I had an abortion myself, when I was your age. I didn't tell you before. It's the biggest regret of my life. I'd like to talk to you more personally, as a friend.'

Sadie looked at her again. 'So that's why you're standing in the street holding that sign **I REGRET MY ABORTION**?'

Dolores hoped she could get Sadie away from the pull of the abortion clinic doors. 'Yes, that's why. Would you like to go for a coffee and talk it over? They can wait for you. We didn't get to finish last time.'

'No, I can't have anything to eat or drink. They told me that yesterday. Are you trying to trick me again?'

'I didn't mean it that way. Just to talk.'

'We talked plenty. Except you wouldn't tell me where abortions are done, and the abortion clinic was just across the street from you and me the whole time.'

Dolores tried one last time. 'Sadie, here we both are, outside the abortion clinic. The day of decision has arrived. The day of choice. Are you really going to murder your baby today?'

'Leave me alone. I have to go.' Sadie turned away from Dolores to walk into Craigenback's.

'If your baby could talk to you,' Dolores said to her retreating back as Sadie walked away from her, 'what would she say?' Dolores tried to speak for Sadie's voiceless child as Sadie kept walking away: 'Mommy, please let me live.'

Sadie half-turned: 'It's too late. The abortion already started yesterday with what they put in me. And I was having bad cramps a few days before that. It's just way too late.'

Sadie kept walking. The siren song of abortion had whispered in her ears, and she was deaf to anything Dolores could ever say. A van pulled up to the curb, and a young man jumped out. The man approached Sadie. 'Merry Christmas. Would you like a portable ultrasound? We can show you just what your baby looks like, and how far along you are. It's free.'

'What are you talking about? An ultrasound? Here? In the street?'

'Inside the van. We are all set up to give free ultrasounds. Many women change their minds about abortion when they actually see their baby.'

'Not here in the street. You people are too much.'

'We just want to help you.'

'I don't want any more of your help. I want to be left alone.'

One of Craigenback's volunteers walked towards Sadie, the clinic worker in street clothes wearing a bright orange vest emblazoned with ESCORT on front and back. 'Do you need some help getting into the clinic? Are they harassing you?'

'Yeah, I want to go inside.'

'Leave her alone,' the escort said to Dolores and the ultrasound technician. 'This woman has a legal right to access this legal procedure without being forced to run a gauntlet of people trying to change her mind. How can you be so insensitive at such a difficult and private moment in her life?'

'We're trying to help her. You're not,' the man said.

'You're both inside the court ordered buffer zone, and you can be arrested. You better get out of here, and don't try this again. We have your license plate number on our cameras now.'

The man went to move his van out of the buffer zone, and Sadie turned and walked toward Craigenback's front door, the escort holding her by the upper arm. But when they reached the front steps, Sadie hesitated. Rick, who was watching it all before driving away, saw Sadie stop at the foot of the stairs. He got out of his car, and walked over to Sadie, took her by the arm, and walked her up the steps to Craigenback's front door. He buzzed the doorbell with his free hand, spoke into the intercom, and when the door swung open he pushed Sadie through the doorway. 'Get in there.' Sadie's head snapped around to take a last look at Rick. Dolores could only watch. Tears were on Sadie's cheeks, and her eyes flashed at Rick. Dolores could do nothing more than what she did, even trying to speak for Sadie's child to his mother, 'Mommy, please let me live.' She had to let her go, and Dolores walked back with her picket sign out of the no man's land of the buffer zone to her legal spot on the sidewalk 50 meters away.

That baby doesn't have a friend in the world, Dolores thought. Last week she found the pamphlets she gave Sadie and Rick stuck in the mailbox outside the front door of the Crisis Pregnancy Center when she left work that night. Rick only came back and paused at the door without coming in to return the pro-life information. Powerless, she watched this other door at Craigenback's swing shut on Sadie, taking her away from her sight. Sadie had walked away from her, walking her baby to death.

'I can't believe someone would abort their child,' Sara said, having come up to Dolores to watch Sadie walk into the abortion mill.

Dolores was annoyed at her righteousness. 'I can't imagine the pain and confusion Sadie is going through to believe abortion is her best choice, even though I talked to her a long time, and got to know her. Even if I did it myself a long time ago. We think we understand a lot about it, but to me a mother aborting her child is a strange mystery. I can't penetrate how she feels. I can't judge it.'

'Abortion is wrong,' Sara said. 'I can judge it.'

'But can you judge that woman's soul, Sara?' Dolores asked her.

'Yes I can. She is a sinner.'

The man who was unable to tear up Julie's plastic protest sign returned, coming down the street and holding a hunting knife in his hand. Julie was frightened at the sight of him, and dropped her sign, and ran away. The man picked up the sign with the words **WHY MOM WHEN I HAVE SO MUCH LOVE TO GIVE YOU**, and sliced it in two, using his sharp knife with the long serrated blade. He cut up the two sections again into smaller pieces. No one went near the man wielding the hunting knife, the pro-lifers just watching him from a safe distance. He looked around smiling, satisfied this time at his success destroying the pro-life sign. He walked away down the street, still holding the knife in his hand swinging at his side. Mickey took out his cell phone, and called the police to report the dangerous assault on the pro-lifers.

30

Sadie stood in front of the Plexiglas window in the reception area of the Craigenback Abortion Clinic, waiting for Sincerity Burstall to admit her for her appointment. The abortion clinic was built like a fortress. Steel security bars covered the thick, plate glass outside windows, opaque to any view of the inside. An outer steel door led to the reception room, the door controlled by a buzzer lock. A second steel plated door stood electronically locked at the other side of the reception room, the entrance to the inner offices where they performed the procedures. A uniformed security guard wearing a holstered gun stood just inside the front door, buzzing in the women who identified themselves over the intercom. Sincerity was seated behind the bulletproof glass shielding the clinic staff.

To complete the security, Dr. Craigenback wore a bulletproof vest, and carried a small handgun under his medical scrubs. The gunsmith recommended a snub-nosed Smith & Wesson .38 Special as a popular gun for self-defense, lightweight and easy to conceal. He could wear it in an unobtrusive shoulder holster going about his daily routines as an abortion doctor. Craigenback felt empowered possessing the fable handgun, carrying it with a light swagger in his walk, imagining himself a romantic figure. He received death threats, and wanted to protect himself.

Sincerity bent her head down to speak to Sadie through the

opening in the Plexiglas. 'Do you have your health card?'

Sadie slid the card through the opening.

'How will you be paying the extra fee today? Visa, Mastercard, debit or cash?'

'Cash.'

'Do you have the $50 off Christmas coupon valid for the month of December?'

'No.'

'$500 please.'

Sadie extended the folded bills through the opening. Rick gave her the money, and warned her it was the last she would ever see from him if she didn't go through with it.

'Take a seat.'

Sadie sat in one of the chairs in the waiting room. Six other women also sat in chairs placed around the walls. They all sat in silence, their faces blank, staring straight ahead or leafing through a magazine, avoiding eye contact with the other abortion patients. One of the women stared downward at the floor. Sadie thought the waiting women looked tense, despite the relaxing music playing on the ceiling speaker, with the sounds of ocean waves and zithers. A bronze statue of an Egyptian goddess stood on a display table in one corner of the waiting room.

During her counselling appointment yesterday, Sincerity told Sadie she would have a suction curettage at her first trimester stage of pregnancy, the dilators prying open her cervix, and a suction machine removing the contents of her uterus. Then curettes, sharp spoon shaped knives, would be used to scrape the sides of her uterus to ensure the abortion was complete, with no body parts left behind.

'Today a nurse will insert laminaria sticks in your cervix, a simple procedure to soften and dilate your cervix for tomorrow's termination of pregnancy. The laminaria won't hurt. It only takes a couple of minutes.'

Sincerity gave her the consent form to sign after the information. Sadie could not be bothered reading the form, but had asked as she signed her name, looking at the nurse.

'Is is dangerous?'

'No, abortion is safer than childbirth, ten times safer. It's one of the most common medical procedures, in the country, like cataracts.'

'I've heard it can be dangerous. I saw the video at the Crisis Pregnancy Center last week.'

'They tell lies there. They're not professionals, but we have all been to medical school here. We are the abortion experts and caregivers. They are the compulsory pregnancy party, based on religious fanaticism.'

'Some of the pictures of abortion looked scary.'

'That's what they do, scare people with horrible pictures. It's disgraceful.'

'But are the pictures true?'

'Medical waste never looks pretty. It's not for laymen.'

'What about side effects afterwards?'

'You will lie down in our recovery room for a few hours. You should be able to go home later today. We can give you analgesic pills with codeine in it if you have any pain. It's similar to menstrual cramps. Don't have a bath but take showers for the next two weeks. If you have any heavy bleeding or clotting, which is rare, you should go to emergency at the hospital. If you experience any infection regular antibiotics will take care of it. Your family doctor can give you a prescription. We just do the TAs here.'

'TAs?'

'Therapeutic abortions.'

'Any long term side effects?'

'No. just think of your cervix as a muscle. Like your hand is a muscle. Try and experiment now if you like, opening and closing your hand.'

Sadie opened and closed her clenched hands.

'You see? Your cervix is the same kind of muscle. It can open and close without any pain or damage.'

'I see what you mean. I don't feel any pain closing and opening my hands.'

'Of course not. It's what they're made for. Abortion won't hurt you.'

'They told me the heartbeat is already there at 21 days.'

'No, there's no heartbeat yet. You're only 12 weeks. Don't worry, it's not a baby yet. Only at birth can you speak of a baby. It's always best not to wait too long, the sooner you have an abortion the better, the easier it is, the safer it is. Those anti-choice places, they do a terrible thing in delaying women from abortions, making it more dangerous for them. They just apply psychological and moral pressure on a woman to hinder an abortion because of their religious beliefs. I often have to correct what women have been told by them. They are just dumb. Closeminded.'

'So what is in me right now?'

'Some tissue growing inside your uterus, an intra-uterine gestation.'

'Then why do I feel like I'm being selfish, doing this?'

'Cultural conditioning. Religion. Everyone else's expectations for you. Abortion is a positive decision. A pro-life decision. Pro your life. It's okay to be selfish. There's nothing bad about putting yourself first. As women we're told everything else comes first before us. Selfishness just means thinking clearly about what is best for you and what you can deal with.'

'I can't deal with a baby now, I know that.'

'Right. What is the point of being selfless in having a child?'

'It would be a mess now.'

'Right. My job here is wonderful helping women like you. We do more good here than someone working in a heart transplant unit.'

Sadie was taken into a procedure room where the nurse inserted the laminaria sticks in her cervix. Then the first appointment was finished. Sincerity walked Sadie to the front door yesterday. 'See you tomorrow morning at 11.'

Dr. Craigenback complained lately about the loss of business, telling Sincerity her job was to process the women faster. He gave her a clear directive: 'Business is so slow since those new pro-life ads in the phone book, you've got to get more women in here.' He kept costs down with an assembly line system, doing three procedures an hour. Individual screening and counselling were trimmed as a cost saving measure. Otherwise, the abortions would be too expensive. If the women wanted abortions the clinic would provide the service, if they had the money. Sometimes the women would be hesitant, tearful and doubtful. Craigengack told his nurses they were not paid for words. They should tell the women to make up their minds because other women were waiting who wanted their abortions.

Sincerity Burstall's job may have been to sell abortions, but she also firmly believed in abortion rights. Her work was more than a job, it was a cause and a ministry. Safe medical abortions meant freedom for women, empowerment for women instead of the dangers of childbirth or dangerous back alley abortions. A women's destiny need not be controlled by her biology. She saw the abuse of women in her own family, with her drunken father and her battered mother taking all of his abuse, her wifely duty to keep the family together for the sake of the children. The priest told her mother to obey her husband, and offer up her sufferings as her sacrifice. Sincerity was not going to end up like her oppressed mother.

Sitting in the reception area now on the day of her procedure, Sadie noticed the eerie silence prevailing over the soothing music. She could feel it, the clinic as silent as a morgue. Her head began to ache, the pain so excruciating she stood up and walked over to Sincerity's nursing station and asked her for an aspirin.

'You really shouldn't, the aspirin will thin your blood just before the procedure.'

'My head is killing me. What harm can some aspirin do?"

'I'll give you two regular Tylenol instead.'

Sadie returned to her seat and waited for the pills to take her headache away. One of the young women sitting in the waiting room changed her seat to sit down beside her, speaking to her in a low whisper. 'My name is Sandra. What's yours?'

'I'd rather not say.'

'I've got something you need to see.'

'What are you talking about?'

'Do you mind if I show you some pictures about babies and abortion?'

'Who are you?'

'I'm someone who cares. I don't want to upset you. I'm here to support you and your baby.'

'I've already seen the pictures they show across the street. I just talked to the woman again outside. Some man wanted me to have an ultrasound. When will you people stop invading my privacy? I want to be left alone.'

Sandra slid out of her chair and knelt on the floor in front of Sadie. She took a small package from her coat pocket. 'May I give you this little Christmas gift? It's a pair of hand knit baby booties. Only a little token from me, but think of the wonderful gift you could open. Your very own baby. And here is a beautiful red rose for you, a flower from heaven, a gift from St. Therese, The Little Flower. You and your baby are not alone. You are loved, more than you know.'

The security by the front door saw Sandra showing the pictures and handing the gifts to Sadie. He walked over to the two sitting women, grabbed Sandra's arm, and pulled her to her feet. 'What do you think you're doing?'

'We were just talking.'

The guard looked at the pictures in her hand and took

them from her. 'You're not supposed to be in here. Get out, or I will call the police, and take your propaganda with you. You can join your friends beyond the buffer zone. I should search you for your hidden video camera and tape recorder. We know about undercover stings at reproductive clinics.'

'Take your hands off me.'

'Get out. Now.'

Sandra looked around at the women sitting in the waiting room. 'You don't have to do this. People are willing to help you.'

Sincerity Burstall and another nurse walked through the inner door into the waiting room and stood around Sandra, talking over her so the women could not hear her clearly. 'Don't listen to her,' they said. The security guard still holding her by her upper arm and Sincerity escorted Sandra towards the front door, Sincerity telling her: 'You don't know about real life. You're living in a bubble. You're not here to make someone's decision. You don't know the reason women make real decisions.' When they reached the door the security guard shoved her outside. 'You're a psycho,' the guard said, 'get the hell out of here.'

'That's what I'm trying to do, pray and love the Hell out of here,' Sandra said.

'Just go now.'

Sincerity turned to calm the waiting women. 'I'm sorry about this. An anti-abortion infiltrator disturbing the peace.'

'She seemed like a peaceful person,' one of the women said.

'You can't trust her peaceful surface,' Sincerity said. 'These people don't work alone. They're all from the Dark Ages.'

No one said anything more, and the nurses left the waiting room, returning to their inner offices behind the steel door and bulletproof glass. After they left, and as Sadie continued to sit waiting with the other women, the inner door to the abortion procedure rooms swung open again. A woman clothed in a medical gown with no street clothes underneath ran into the waiting room. A nurse was pursuing her, grabbing her from behind. The woman turned on the nurse. 'Leave me alone. I'm sorry. I've changed my mind. I thought I could do this, but I can't.'

'Please come back. We can talk about it. You can get your clothes. You can't leave like this.'

'I want to get out of here. You have no right to keep me here.'

A male attendant came out of the back rooms, standing behind the nurse for reinforcement. The nurse tried to ignore the startled eyes of all the women staring at her now. 'Of course you can go. We just want to help you calm down.'

'Get the guard away from the door and let me go. Now.'

Sincerity Burstall came out from behind the bulletproof glass a second time, and nodded to the guard, who opened the front door. The distraught woman looked around the waiting room, the women sitting in stunned silence. 'I'm ashamed of myself I ever considered it,' the woman said. She fled the abortion clinic through the front door, running out wearing the medical gown flying behind her, and she ran down the street, never looking back.

'Excuse me nurse, what is happening?' one of the women asked.

'Everything's okay. Some women get upset. She was a little hysterical. She might even have been another anti-abortion infiltrator. We get everything here. I don't know how she will survive in the winter cold without her clothes."

'What's going on?' another woman asked. 'She seemed real enough to me.'

'Don't worry about it," Sincerity said. 'She just wasn't sure.'

The patients did not say anything more. The women continued their waiting. A few moments later a woman sitting near Sadie, the one staring at the floor, got up and walked out the clinic's door. She did not say anything, but as she passed Dolores and the other pro-lifers standing outside on the sidewalk with their protest signs, she smiled and flashed a thumbs-up sign. She had changed her mind.

Sadie's suppressed doubts, her ambivalence began to rise within her again, but she did not want to think about it anymore at this last minute. She emptied her mind of any more thoughts, waiting and wanting to get it over with, accepting her fate. The decision was made. It was too late to back out now. The laminaria inserted in her cervix had already started the abortion. This was a terrible but necessary step to be free of Rick, and start a brand new life—Sadie saw Sincerity through the Plexiglass answer the telephone, argue with someone, slam the phone receiver down, quickly dial another call, say a few brief words, and push a button on the wall. A ringing alarm filled the waiting room with its insistent clanging, and Sincerity ran from behind her glass cocoon through the steel door into the room of waiting women.

'Everybody out. We have a bomb threat. Wait outside in the

parking lot. The police and the fire department are on their way.'

Sadie and the four other women still waiting for their appointments followed Sincerity, the security guard, and the nursing assistants out the door, gathering in the parking lot beside Craigenback's. The pro-lifers picketing outside on the sidewalk heard the alarm, and saw the abortion clinic, all of its staff and patients, hurry out the door and stand in the parking lot in the cold winter air. Then they saw Dr. Craigenback come out of the house on the other side, and stand on the narrow sidewalk leading to his back yard, smoking a cigarette, waiting separate and alone, taking a break from his work

31

Sergeant David Ryan was driving his patrol car in the area when the call came over the police radio to investigate the bomb threat at the Craigenback Abortion Clinic. He quickly answered the call, arriving with his partner. The other policeman stood guard over the people, keeping the clinic staff and patients standing in the parking lot separate from the pro-life protesters on the sidewalk. Sgt. Ryan searched inside the building for a bomb. Mickey watched the show from the crowd below, and he was not happy with the Catholic policeman Ryan participating in the charade of the phony bomb threat. He suspected Craigenback orchestrated the bomb threats to deprive the pro-lifers of their legal rights to protest. The abortionist did not want them at his clinic at all, even 50 meters away behind a buffer zone.

'Look at this make-believe,' Mickey said to Dolores. 'Ryan is Catholic, his wife is a friend of Dora and Sara. He shouldn't be playing along with this.'

'He has to do it. The motto of the police is to serve and protect.'

'He knows it's all a public relations game. The only thing he's protecting is his job, covering himself. He should charge Craigenback with making false alarms. This goes on all the time. Why is he responding to the abortion clinic's complaints, and ignoring my call about the man with the knife attacking us?'

'I wonder how those women can stay and wait through this to have their abortions,' Julie said. 'It's like a fire drill in school, everyone ordered out, and ordered to wait, and ordered back in. They're all only following orders.'

'So is Sgt. Ryan,' Mickey said. 'My point exactly.'

Dora and Sara heard Mickey, and they came over and both lashed out at him.

'Leave David Ryan alone. He's a brave man, just doing his job.'

'Shame on you Mickey Finnegan, criticizing a good policeman.'

'Did it ever occur to you, if this was a real bomb threat, the people standing in the parking lot and on the sidewalk still wouldn't be safe? They are all still too close to the house. This is all political theater, for show.'

Dolores spoke up to the two women. 'I don't agree with Mickey about David Ryan, but I don't agree with you either Sara, telling Sincerity Burstall she should have been aborted. That's not pro-life. I'm appalled.'

Dora defended her friend Sara. 'Mind your own business, you're not the boss of us.'

'Mickey, what can we do about this?' Dolores asked him. 'This can't go on.'

'Nothing. We can't do anything. We're powerless over her. You know I've tried already.' He turned to Dora and Sara. 'We might have to apply for our own injunction to remove you from the demonstrations. Do you want that?'

Dora was infuriated. 'We're getting our own lawyer. You

won't speak for us in court anymore. The very idea. Pro-lifers asking for an injunction to silence pro-lifers. Are you going crazy?'

'Good luck if you can find a pro-life lawyer in Calgary.'

'I have a cousin who graduated from law school who will help us.'

'What experience does he have, and how much is he charging you.'

'None of your business. You won't be saying bad things about us in court anymore.'

'I'm afraid it's the truth. You damage our pro-life presence here.'

'You're no one to talk. You do more harm than good with all of your stunts, just attracting attention to yourself. You aren't the only pro-lifer in this city. It's only the newspapers who like to build you up to make us all look bad. We've started our own pro-life group, WUFF, Women United For Families.'

'WUFF? Sounds like a weak bark to me.'

'Wait till you feel our bite,' Dora said.

'Is publicity what it's all about? The newspapers and TV? You've been getting your own lately, and it's bad for all of us, your verbal fighting with the clinic staff. Are you trying to take over as the pro-life leaders?'

'No one is the pro-life leader. The pro-abortion news media elected you the leader with all the news stories about you. None of us ever elected you leader. You are not qualified to be a pro-life leader.'

'I agree. I'm not qualified to even be a pro-life member. But who is? The professional people qualified to do it don't want to. Is your cousin the law school graduate the new pro-life leader and spokesman?'

'At least he's not a criminal, deceiving people with a fraudulent counselling center.'

'You may be pro-life,' Mickey said, 'but you're mean.'

'Crook, crook, crook,' Sara said. 'You've made your deal with the devil.'

'I paid my debt to society,' Mickey said, 'but you're still mean.'

'Why don't you get a job and get married and live like a normal man?' Sara said. Dolores listened intently to what Mickey might say in answer to her question.

'My passion is pro-life and the unborn children. Don't you respect what I do as a full time pro-lifer is important work?'

'So you aren't looking for normal happiness Mickey?" Dolores asked him.

'Too bad you weren't aborted,' Sara said to Mickey.

'That's it. Sara, we have to talk.'

'Leave me alone,' Sara said, and walked away from him, putting her hands over her ears so she wouldn't hear him. 'Don't talk to me Mickey, the pro-aborts, they're the ones you should talk to,' Sara said, Mickey trailing behind on the sidewalk in front of the abortion mill, still trying to talk to her holding her hands over her ears. The same thing happened before. There was no way to get through to Sara if she did not want to listen. Mickey was surprised again at her primitive defense mechanisms.

Dora came over and said to Mickey, 'Leave her alone.

Are you going to assault her too?' Dora had not forgotten how Mickey took her by the arm to escort her out of the Crisis Pregnancy Center when he fired her last week. Mickey ignored what she said.

'Dora, both you and Sara refused to sign the pledge and code of conduct for our pro-life protests here, promising not to argue or be belligerent with people. We all signed it. Why can't you two? Instead we have these problems.'

Dora and Sara walked away from Mickey. 'You're not our leader, get that straight. We have our own group, independent and separate from you.' Dora said as she left him. As they walked away Sara said to Dora, 'He looks down on us. He thinks he's better than us.'

'Don't worry,' Dora said. 'If Mickey Finnegan think's he's somebody because he got some newspaper interviews and was on TV, he's riding for a big fall. We'll get him. We'll bring him down.'

'I don't know even know what he's talking about half the time,' Sara said.

'We need a normal person speaking for us. Not some criminal.'

Julie still resented the two Christian women who caused her so much trouble for being a single mother. 'You got it Mickey. They're pro-life, but they're mean.' Then she asked Mickey and Dolores both: 'Why does it have to be this way, all the divisions in pro-life, all the infighting, when we are all on the same side?'

'Because people care so much,' Mickey said.

'I don't understand.'

'It's not so unusual. The people who care so much about the same things can fight each other the most.'

'I still think it's weird.'

As the pro-lifers talked, they saw the weekly arrival of the biomedical waste truck, driving down the alley to the back door of the clinic. The back alley was visible from the front sidewalk where the protesters stood, only the clinic parking lot between them. They watched the truck driver carry out the containers of body parts from the back door of Craigenback's, the round drums looking like ice cream containers, sealed with red tape. The drums of biomedical waste would be taken out of town for incineration. Other times Craigenback used the garbage disposal grinder in the sink of his clinic, depending on the length of pregnancy, and the type of abortion and type of tissues. The abortion clinic stopped disposing the medical waste in the dumpster in the alley at the back door when the pro-lifers went through it, and found the discarded parts of babies. The smell of the decomposing bodies of the babies covered in crawling maggots was horrible, but Fr. MacIntyre from Sacred Heart agreed to hold a funeral service for the dead children, with burial in the Catholic cemetery, and it was in all the newspapers. The clinic also stopped using the garbage disposal in the sink when the drain lines got clogged with body parts, and had to be dug up for repairs.

The Craigenback Abortion Clinic also had a profitable sideline business selling fetal organs and tissues. The biomedical tissues were in great demand, and could be sold either fresh or frozen, for several uses from cosmetics to vaccines. Dolores shuddered at the sight of the disposal truck. 'I feel sick.'

'It's unimaginable to me,' Julie said. 'I can't understand it. The unwanted babies killed and thrown in the garbage, or flushed down the drain, or burnt in the dump, or used for spare parts, or used in other ways.'

'Business as usual,' Mickey said.

'Don't say unwanted,' Dolores said. 'Unwelcomed by some, but they are not unwanted. Other people want the children. Some people wait for years to adopt a child and never can. Some of us want them to live among us even if we never know them.'

'But the other people have no legal right to them,' Mickey said. The pro-lifer watched the driver finish his weekly pick-up of containers, and drive away down the alley.

'How do you figure the truck driver made his regular pickups during a police investigation of a bomb threat?' Mickey wondered aloud.

32

'Craigenback Abortion Clinic. May I help you?'
 'It's Maureen from Biohazards Recycling.'
 'Oh yes.'
 'We are running out of livers and hearts, and low on brains.'
 'I'm looking out at a full waiting room now. We should have something for you soon.'
 'Can you ship them without the arms and legs showing? Some of our staff get upset.'
 'Sure, we can remove them.'
 'They don't like the heads either.'
 'We can cut the heads off and split the faces and take the brains out.'
 'Good.'
 'No problem.'
 'We received the notice your rates are going up.'
 'We're still one of the least expensive around. I will send you our detailed rate chart per part.'
 'Why the extra cost?'.'
 'Our expenses have increased even more than that. It takes a lot of careful manipulation of the procedures to get the parts intact.'
 'Yes, you do a good job. We are very pleased with the quality of the material.'
 'Thank you. I'm pleased to hear it.'

'When will you know about your inventory?'

'I'll call you tonight, just before closing at five. That work for you?'

Can I please talk to Dr. Craigenback about something?'

'He's outside right now.'

'Outside?'

'Yes, we have a policeman investigating a bomb threat, so we had to clear the building.'

'What are you doing inside? Isn't it dangerous?'

'No. the bomb threat is only to get rid of the protesters for good. I am in locked basement office. No one will find me here.'

'I see. Can I call you at five?'

'I'm afraid I will be out of the office then. How about meeting me for a drink at Callahan's around six?'

'Fine, I can do that. Look forward to it.'

'My treat for a nice glass of wine.'

'Yum'

'Til then.'

'Maureen, I can hardly wait.'

'Can you bring the fresh body parts with you? We'll take whatever you have. We are doing some big important experiments.'

'Can you bring the cash?'

'See you then.'

'By the way, in the future we can harvest fresh parts every day, and Fedex the parts freshly overnight.'

'Good to know.'

'Bye.'

33

A mother with her little girl who lived in the neighborhood came down the street towards the pro-lifers standing with their protest signs at Craigenback's. The mother was holding her daughter by the hand. The girl was excited seeing the crowd of people, and said to her mother: 'Mommy, Mommy, let's go see the pro-lifers.' The girl's mother had explained to her before who the people were standing on the street with their signs, but the little girl did not really understand everything. Her mother did not want to get into a discussion about abortion when her girl was so young. The girl had asked her mother before: 'Mommy, why are those people standing on the sidewalk?'

'Some mothers don't want their children, they can't look after them, and these people want them to want them.'

The little girl thought a moment and asked: 'What do the mommies do with their children they don't want?'

'They go to the place the people are standing in front of, and they leave them there.'

'Who looks after the children then?'

'No one does dear, the children are just gone.'

'Gone where?'

'You're too young to understand now Nancy. We'll talk about it later when you're older.'

'Why don't those people on the street look after the children if they want them?'

'They say they will, but other people say they don't. It's too hard to explain dear.'

'Mommy, let's go. This place scares me.'

The Craigenback Abortion Clinic was an intrusion in the quiet residential neighborhood. People going to work and school had to stand at the bus stop right in front of the clinic with protesters all around. Craigenback should not have been there, his commercial clinic was in the wrong residential zone, but the city planners gave him an exemption. Mickey went to court to have Craigenback evicted, but Judge Dockendorff threw the case out. The law did not matter when it came to abortion. Whatever the law said, Craigenback was above the law, laws big and small and no one was going to shut him down. The girl's mother was not happy to walk through the gauntlet of protesters on the public sidewalks, but it was the way they had to go, and she tightened her grip on her daughter's hand. 'Hush Nancy. We'll just walk by minding our own business. Don't get involved. Mind me now. Let them be. Don't talk to those people.'

Dolores did not say anything to the little girl and her mother as they walked by. She could tell the mother wanted to avoid them, and Dolores did not want to be accused of harassment as the mother dragged her little girl through the pro-life protest in silence. Nancy was waving and smiling at the pro-lifers with her free hand, and saying hello, but her mother stared stonily ahead. The children in the neighborhood, with a school and playground just down the street from Craigenback's, were one of the reasons Judge Dockendorff restricted the pictures of aborted babies on the pro-life signs. No one wanted to upset the children. In court, Jessica Sterne complained of the insensitivity of the pro-life protesters, holding their ugly signs in the presence of the children in the neighborhood. Dolores looked at her own sign, **I REGRET MY ABORTION**, and remembered the exchange in court months ago. Judge Dockendorff had restricted the pictures on signs before his more recent prohibition of the words KILL and MURDER on the signs too.

'If the pictures of aborted babies are too horrible to look at,' Mickey had said to Judge Dockendorff, 'maybe it's something we shouldn't be doing.'

'Mr. Finnegan, your anti-abortion signs with the graphic pictures, are offensive to civilized standards of public discourse. So too are your signs in front of this courthouse referring to me as Judge Death, and Dr. Craigenback as Doctor Death. All such signs and gruesome photographs and drawings of abortion procedures are hereby prohibited.'

'What about our freedoms of speech and religion and opinion judge?'

'No freedom is so absolute it cannot be limited. Your callous disregard for the feelings of the children in the neighborhood with your graphic signs is terrible. The children must be protected from you.'

'The children have to be protected from the pro-lifers? Isn't that an inversion of reality? Ironic?'

'It's perfectly logical.'

'Only in a twisted world. What of the feelings of the children killed behind the walls of Craigenback? I suppose that's all right since it can't be seen and offend anyone. Who is protecting those children?'

'What children? Children exist in law at birth. We have been over this many times Mr. Finnegan. I repeat, no rights are absolute.'

'Except for abortion, the super right which shall not be limited with any restrictions whatsoever, or even publicly criticized.'

'Mr. Finnegan, I have made my ruling. Your protest signs are limited, your protest presence within 50 meters of the clinic is limited, and my patience with you is becoming very limited. Court is adjourned.'

Dolores felt bad for Nancy and her mother, and all the other residents of the neighborhood where the Craigenback Abortion Clinic was operating, but what could the pro-lifers do? Accept abortion clinics as a normal part of life, and not protest because Craigenback located his clinic in a house in a city neighborhood? Some people driving by honked their car horns as a sign of support for the pro-lifers, while other drivers gave them the finger, yelling obscenities out their car windows. Dolores waved back at the friendly car horns. Most simply drove by ignoring them, intent on their destinations, and pedestrians walking by were mostly indifferent, except for the two teenage girls who came by now, and grabbed Julie's sign out of her hands a second time, shouting at her: 'You fascists get out of here.'

Mickey came over to Julie's defense. 'You girls leave her alone. We have legal rights to be here, freedom of speech and freedom of peaceful assembly. You girls can be charged with assault and destruction private property.'

The girls threw Julie's sign down on the sidewalk and walked away, but not without a protest of their own. 'You shouldn't be allowed to be here. Fascist pigs. Our bodies, our lives, we have the right to decide.'

Dolores said: 'Julie, please try to hold on to your sign.' They both laughed. Another car drove up to the clinic's front door, and a man got out, ready to take his wife and teenage daughter inside. The women turned their heads, and came over to talk to Dolores and Julie, who were now standing alone, but the man came over to usher his family back towards the front door. He threatened the pro-life women: 'When we come back out, I'm going to put a bullet in your head if you try and talk to us.' The man opened his coat, and showed something bulging inside his jacket pocket, implying he was armed. The clinic escort came over wearing her orange jacket, and told the couple with their daughter they would have to wait in the parking lot instead of coming in the front door because of the ongoing bomb threat investigation

Dolores and Julie ran over to Mickey and told him about the man threatening to shoot them. Mickey walked over to the policeman in the parking lot guarding the clinic patients, and reported the incident of the man's threat. The policeman said he would look into it, but told Mickey he was trespassing inside the buffer zone and should leave the parking lot immediately. Sgt. Ryan was intent on searching the property looking for the alleged bomb. He did not want the pro-lifers complicating his job with charges and counter-charges, suspecting Mickey of playing politics. The reporter for the

Daily Record who had just arrived ignored the accusations from the pro-lifers about the threats to them, concentrating all of her attention on the bomb scare. The television news cameras filmed the incidents with the girls assaulting Julie and her pro-life sign, and the man threatening the pro-lifers he had a gun, but they too were more interested in the allegations of a bomb at the abortion clinic.

'Craigenback should never have been allowed to set up his abortion clinic here on this street,' Julie said. 'Now we have violence in a residential neighborhood, with men threatening us with guns. It makes no sense. Violence does not belong here. It's out of place.' Mickey could only nod at the young woman's insights.

Dolores made sure she took some pictures with the camera she always carried for protection of the pro-lifers, just in case evidence might be needed later in court. She knew Mickey found it annoying the way the women like Dora and Sara banded together in twosomes, but she understood the need for security in the women participating in such a dangerous activity as their pro-life work. She would never want to be standing alone on the street protesting in front of Craigenback's.

'Oh no,' Dolores said, when the local Ku Klux Klan member who liked to attend their pro-life rallies came walking around the corner, carrying his sign, dressed in his white sheet and hood. He usually came when the news media were present, and all the attention immediately went to him. He was a mysterious stranger who never spoke, parading in silence with his sign saying **RIGHT TO LIFE**. 'Mickey, do something.'

'What can I do? We have no authority to tell anyone what to do. We can't control who shows up at our pro-life demonstrations. We can't even handle an old woman like Sara.'

34

Sgt. Ryan finished his investigation of the bomb threat, finding nothing as usual. He also questioned the man who had arrived late with the two women. The man denied threatening the pro-lifers, and when the policeman patted him down he found no gun in his pocket. Sgt. Ryan was also suspicious when he saw the Klansman arrive, and wondered about a link between the Klan and the bomb threat. The mysterious man refused to answer any questions, and Ryan concluded he had no evidence to interfere with the white sheeted stranger. He reported to Sincerity Burstall the situation was all clear.

'Thank goodness. We don't want anyone dying here.'

Sgt. Ryan adjusted the visor of his police cap with his hand, shrugged his shoulders, and looking directly into Sincerity's eyes from beneath his hat said to her: 'Babies die here every day.'

Sincerity remained silent, not snapping back at the policeman, and Sgt. Ryan quickly left the abortion clinic. Never before was he so bold to say something pro-life in his official duties. He was worried he might be in trouble if Sincerity Burstall made a complaint to his chief. As Sgt. Ryan tried to get away from the abortion clinic Mickey approached him. 'No one from the police has responded to my call about the man with a knife attacking our signs. Here is the sign, cut to pieces. He could have injured one of us.'

'Where is the man?'

'He's gone now.'

'We saw him too,' Dora and Sara and the other pro-lifers chimed in, clustering around Sgt. Ryan, someone they knew, a Catholic like themselves.

'I took his picture,' Dolores said.

'I never got a call from dispatch about a knife assault. Do you know where he is, or who he is?'

'No, he was a stranger.'

'There's nothing I can do. Maybe he lives in the neighborhood. If you see him again call us then. Be careful.'

After the police and fire trucks left, Sincerity and the clinic escorts ushered the remaining women standing in the parking lot back into the clinic, Sincerity at the back of the line as if she was shepherding stray sheep back into the fold. During all this time, Dr. Craigenback was leaning against the outside wall on the other side of his clinic, dressed in his medical scrubs, smoking a cigarette, waiting to return to work. He tossed the butt on the ground, and stamped it out with his foot. He saw Fr. MacIntryre arrive, and begin setting up his portable altar on the sidewalk outside the buffer zone to say Mass on the Feast of the Holy Innocents during the Christmas Season. Grandstanding nut, Craigenback thought to himself. Mass belongs in a church. It should be dignified. Not out on the street in front of my place of business. Dolores and the other protesters approached the priest to take part in the open air mass. Nothing he could do to stop it. Complaints had been made to Bishop Blair, but for some unaccountable reason

Blair would not interfere with the elderly priest. He seemed afraid of him. Well, Blair was a bishop, and bishops were politicians, and played both sides. It was also too much when Blair allowed MacIntyre to hold the funeral service for the aborted babies found in his dumpster. It was only medical waste. Tissues. The crazy pro-lifers even went through his garbage, and now he had to put a lock on the bin, and use the garbage disposal in his sinks. Craigenback shook his head. What could you do about those people? He allowed the women to say some prayers and goodbyes himself if they wanted it, in the clinic's chapel, but few did. He walked back inside, the bomb scare over for now, eager to catch up on his backlog of interrupted procedures.

Sincerity gestured to Sadie sitting in the waiting room to come to the Plexiglas window. 'Dr. Craigenback will see you now.' Sadie's turn had finally come. The torture of the morning's long wait with all the upsets made her increasingly uncertain. Two more of the waiting women left when they were standing in the parking lot, refusing to wait anymore, and they did not come back. But Sadie followed Sincerity's directions, as she buzzed the inner steel door open, and waved to Sadie to come inside. They walked down a short hallway to the procedure room, even more silent than the eerie stillness of the waiting room. Recovery rooms for the post-operative patients were also down this inner corridor, and Dr. Craigenback's office. The disposal room was at the far end of the hall, by the steel plated back door. Sincerity showed Sadie where to undress, put on the medical gown, and lay down on the table. She gave her the sedative which would leave her awake during the procedure, but deeply relaxed. Sadie took the pills, undressed, put on the medical gown, and lay down on the table, waiting some more. The table was still damp and stained from the fluids of the previous patients. Sadie's nostrils were assaulted by the heavy antiseptic smell of the medical clinic masking the odors of the other women, and she smelled something else: depression and desperation, hopelessness and fear. She smelt it all soaked into the bloodflecked walls of the dreadful room where abortions were done.

Sincerity gave her some last instructions, following clinic policy to keep the women calm. 'One last thing. We have a chapel here. If you would like to pray afterwards, or have the remains baptized, or write a goodbye letter, we can provide the service for you. Sometimes it helps a woman to find closure.'

'No thanks. I don't want anything like that.'

'Edward, will you give her the anesthetic please?'

'I keep thinking about the baby's heartbeat I heard on the video across the street.'

'It's just sounds, dear. Vague internal sounds.'

Sincerity could not bring herself to say the word heartbeat. She leaned down and whispered to Sadie lying on the table, building an intimate private bond with her. 'I'll tell you a secret. I had two abortions, and I am proud of it. They saved my life, or I wouldn't be where I am today. We are entitled to children by choice, not by chance. You should be proud too. You're a brave woman. You're doing the right thing.'

'Am I?'

'A woman has a right to a safe and satisfying sex life, the right to sexual pleasure without unwanted children. Just like a man.' Sincerity squeezed Sadie's hand for support, and Sadie squeezed her hand back.

'What if the baby is born alive?'

'We just leave it alone in a basin until the end comes. It won't last long.' Sincerity was not going to tell Sadie how Dr. Craigenback handled the dreaded complication of live birth after abortion, when he would twist the necks of the aborted children to finish them, or snip the back of their spinal cords with scissors.

'Do they cry out? Or move?'

'It's just sounds and spasms and twitching. They aren't really alive. We don't harm them. We just do not resuscitate.'

'Can I get in trouble?'

'No. It's not killing baby when the intent was a legal abortion. It's not a baby. It's just an unfinished abortion.'

'Will I have to see it?'

'No, we take care of everything. Besides, it can only happen in late term abortions when labor is induced, and sometimes the product of abortion still seems alive.'

'The lady across the street had a different opinion.'

Sincerity breathed a heavy sigh of disapproval, and curled her lip, disappointed Sadie was not understanding her explanation. 'Everything those people say is medically inaccurate. And extreme. It's just a routine part of the job. With your first trimester abortion there is no chance of a baby born alive. The instruments vacuum out the contents of the uterus. There's nothing left to be called born alive. Don't distress yourself. It's impossible.'

'I was so worried. I would feel really bad.'

'Those anti's are good bullies. Don't listen at all to their life-threatening medical misinformation. Everything they say about morality is false too. Abortion is actually about motherhood. Women who choose abortion are making well thought out decisions, responsible choices for their own lives, and for the lives of the children they will have later, when circumstances are right. Abortion makes for better families. I'm surprised women are not beating up the anti-abortionists left and right, with all the harm they do.'

'That's it. That's right. This isn't the time for me to have a child. You make sense.'

'Ignore those fanatic people with their agendas to control women.'

'Thank you so much.'

'Always remember Sadie, abortion will make you happy and free. What the anti-choice people say is all just sexual shaming. Don't let them get to you.'

Sincerity left the operating room, and Edward the orderly stepped forward to inject Sadie with the local anesthetic in her cervix. He was not medically qualified for the work, but Craigenback trained him to do it to save costs. He directed Sadie to put her feet in the stirrups, and opened her vagina with the speculum. He injected her cervix, warning her: 'You're going to feel a pinch as the needle goes in.'

Then Edward left Sadie alone to wait for the doctor while the freezing took effect.

35

After a long wait, Dr. Craigenback finally came in. Sadie turned her head to look at him. He paused standing still, with a grin on his face, and slowly directed his eyes up and down her body, in a sexual kind of way. He wore a white surgical gown stained from his earlier procedures, a cap over his hair, and a medical mask over his mouth. Surgical gloves hid his hands, the gloves stained red. All she could see of him were his eyes behind his thick glasses. Sadie felt scared, but all she wanted by now was to have everything over with. A nurse came in behind him. Sadie was fully prepped and draped for the procedure. The doctor did not engage in any small talk to establish a relationship with his patient. He would never see her again. He removed the sheet to uncover her body from the waist down, and clamped a tenaculum on her cervix to keep it in place for the insertion of the dilators. He did a quick ultra sound of her abdomen, singing hymns:

'Jesus, Oh Jesus, take the sinners down by the river, Oh Jesus.'

After a quick glance at the ultrasound monitor Craigenback turned to the nurse assisting him. 'A double gestation.'

The screen was turned away from Sadie, so she would not see the pictures, and the sound was turned off so she would not hear the heartbeats. The nurse looked at the screen, frowned, looked at Sadie, and said without thinking: 'Twins.'

Sadie, a twin herself, struggled to get off the table. Craigenback directed the nurse to hold Sadie, and Edward hearing the commotion ran into the room, using his strength to pin Sadie down to the table. Sadie writhed beneath his arms.

'I've changed my mind. Please, let me go.'

'It's too late,' Dr. Craigenback said through his surgical mask, the words muffled. 'One of the twins would probably have gone anyway.'

Sadie stopped struggling under Edward's grip on her, but tears were streaming down her face. 'Let me go, please. I'm really nervous. I don't want to do this anymore.'

Craigenback slapped her in the face. 'Shut up.'

'What are you doing to her?' the nurse asked.

Craigenback turned on her. 'You be quiet too. She's hysterical, and I'm calming her down. I know what I'm doing.'

Dr. Craigenback asked the nurse for the dilators, and began to pry the cervix open. Sadie started struggling again against the force of the attendants holding her down, twisting her body from side to side on the table. "No. No. Stop.' Sadie thrashed beneath them, trying to break free and get off the table. Edward cursed in the struggle. 'Hold still,' he commanded her. 'If you don't stop it you'll get hurt.'

'I want my babies. I can't go through with it. I want them now.'

'Hold her tighter Edward,' Craigenback said. 'I can't work like this.'

He knew he had to finish the procedure, or face a complicated legal situation for him for an interrupted half-abortion. Sadie kept writhing trying to get up, and her kicking legs knocked over the tray of instruments beside the operating table. Craigenback bent over, picking up the largest dilator from the blood splotched floor. 'Hold her steady.' Edward bore down with all of his strength on Sadie's arms and chest. Her back was bent, her legs hanging off the end of the table during her fight to get off the table. Craigenback pushed himself between her legs, keeping them spread apart with his hips. He ignored Sadie's protests, his practiced rhythmic hand and elbow pushing the dilator in and out of her vagina to pry open her cervix. He inserted the tube of the suction machine into her opened uterus, and turned on the power. It sounded to Sadie like a roaring suction machine as loud as a compressor, the noise filling the room along with her own screams. The force of the suction dismembered the contents of the uterus, the suction tube aspirating the products of conception, both the fetus and the placenta sucked into a glass jar connected to the hose. The jar filled with a red, bloody mass of tissue. Sadie passed out, going limp, unconscious on the table. Craigenback put her feet back in the stirrups along each side of the table. Regaining consciousness but still held down Sadie shuddered, twisted on her side, and vomited.

Edward made Sadie lie flat on the table. She passed out again. Craigenback inserted the sharp curette into Sadie's uterus, scraping the sides to remove any remaining pieces. His hand was shaking after the struggle, his foot slipped on the bloody floor, he lost his balance, and the curette sliced into Sadie's uterus. She groaned, even though she was anesthetized, and unconscious, lying limp on the table. Craigenback was alarmed the patient was feeling pain. Blood started pouring out of her perforated uterus through her cervix and onto the white cloth of the operating table. The curette had punctured her uterus and cut an artery. They could not stop the bleeding, and the nurse ran back to Sincerity Burstall, and whispered to her to call the ambulance from emergency at the hospital. Sincerity dialed 911, spoke to someone, and then turned back to the nurse.

'What's going on? They want to know. 911 wants to know what's going on. I need an answer.'

'All I know is she is unconscious, moaning, and bleeding.'

Sincerity relayed the message to 911, then turned back to the nurse.

'They want to know if she's breathing.'

'She's non-responsive, bleeding more than they would like.'

Sincerity reported to the 911 dispatcher, listened, then turned to the nurse again.

'What's her color?'

'Grayish, like ashes. Her lips are turning blue.'

'A gray color,' Sincerity said into the phone, listened again, and relayed back to the nurse. 'They say do chest compressions. They'll send paramedics with a non-breathing bag, and IV blood transfusions along with the ambulance.'

The nurse ran back into the operating room to tell them, but no one was there, except for Sadie lying alone on the table, unconscious. The ambulance arrived silently, a Code Two, driving down the alley to the back door with lights and siren turned off. The paramedics found Sadie covered in blood, her legs spread apart in the stirrups, blood saturated towels pushed in a pile on the floor. Edward was gone, and Dr. Craigenback disappeared into his office. Sincerity whispered to the nurse, 'If they ask you any questions, just play dumb. We don't know what happened.'

Sadie was treated by the paramedics, placed on a stretcher, shrouded in several sheets, and taken out the back door and put in the ambulance. Sincerity and Edward held a large black plastic tarp between the back door of the clinic and the waiting ambulance, so the pro-lifers protesting on the front sidewalk could not see past the parking lot what was happening in the alley. But the protesters could see someone was carried on a stretcher, wearing an oxygen mask on her face and an IV bag attached to a pole beside her. The rest of her body was hidden by all the sheets. In the ambulance her pulse collapsed, and the paramedics worked hard and fast to stop her falling blood pressure. They had come to Craigenback's before.

'What's going on?' Julie asked.

'He's injured another one,' Mickey said.

'Oh God,' Dolores prayed, making the sign of the cross over her head and chest. 'When will it all end?'

'I hope it wasn't Sadie,' Julie said.

Dolores was shaking. 'I hope it wasn't anyone.'

'It had to be someone,' Mickey said. 'This can't go on forever. There goes another holy innocent, not knowing what she was doing.'

'There goes another fool,' Julie said.

Julie took her cell phone out of her pocket, to take pictures of Sadie carried out of Craigenback's to the ambulance, but the clinic escort came over and stood in front of her, the escort waving her arms and jumping and down blocking Julie's camera, the escort standing right in front of her face, dancing and weaving, shouting obscenities, and giving her the finger. 'I wish I was your sister, so I could sneak in and poison your cookies,' the escort said. 'You're a predator, a bottom feeder.' Julie could not take any clear pictures with the escort's interference. When Sadie was loaded into the ambulance, the doors closed, the driver drove away, and only then the escort left Julie alone.

'They always take the injured women out the back door for the ambulance,' Julie said. 'Like throwing her out in the trash.'

'I hope you don't mean women who have abortions are trash,' Dolores said.

Julie was taken aback.

'I didn't mean that. I meant the abortion clinic treats them like garbage.'

'Okay.'

'What are we really accomplishing, being here?' Julie asked

'I think it's worth it if one child can be saved from dying, unloved and alone in a trash can,' Dolores said. 'The children are treated like garbage too, just thrown away, utterly abandoned in death.'

Sadie survived, but the doctors at the hospital told her later they had to perform a hysterectomy to save her life from the massive bleeding, and the infection risk from her cut bowel also damaged when Craigenback's curette slipped. They removed everything, her uterus, her ovaries and fallopian tubes. The doctors told her she would need hormone replacement therapy for the rest of her life./ They also informed her in their opinion the scar tissue from the cuts on her uterus, and the lacerations of her vagina and cervix, would have made future pregnancies impossible anyway. One of the doctors at the hospital tried to explain what happened to her in detail as she lay recovering on one of the beds.

'You were unconscious when you arrived here, due to your blood loss, and you were septic, with a high fever, and elevated white count. We had no choice. We had to save your life. We called the doctor at the clinic to find out what happened, but we never heard back from him. He abandoned you to our care. We could not wait for your consent, we had to act to save you.'

The words were only a blur of sounds to Sadie, who turned her face to the wall. The kindly doctor tried to encourage his battered patient.

'You are still alive Sadie, and only 21, with your whole life ahead of you.'

36

The Daily Record did not report a woman was taken by ambulance to the emergency ward of the hospital from a botched abortion at the Craigenback Abortion Clinic, the newspaper disregarding the photographic proof the pro-lifers sent to the news editor. Mickey wrote a letter of complaint to the publisher of the newspaper, Jeremiah Patrick. He sent copies of his letter to the other news outlets in Calgary, accusing the Record and the other media of a pro-abortion bias always slanting the news against pro-life, and covering up the facts about abortion, not reporting the truth of the news to the public. Jeremiah Patrick wrote back to Mickey, and sent copies of his letter to several other people, including Bishop Blair:

> Thank you for your latest vituperative letter devoid of all common sense and professionalism accusing a fine newspaper with a long history of impartial journalism of bias. We pride ourselves on covering all the news, without fear or favor. I cannot allow my staff to be harassed by your fanaticism. I suspect you have the rack ready for me in your zealous inquisition of all those who fail to adhere to your opinions. I have instructed my editors to no longer accept any press releases from you and your organization. You will no longer be interviewed by our reporters. We will find someone else to

speak for the anti-abortionists. We will not give coverage to splinter fringe groups, and individuals such as you who are disreputable in the eyes of all. We shall not defile the columns of our newspaper with your strident raving and ranting. I advise you to unplug your overheated photocopier. I warn you the defamatory words you have publicly expressed about the Daily Record are actionable in law. Govern yourself accordingly.

Mickey showed the letter to Dolores, who was struck by the vehemence of the attack on Mickey. 'It's so over the top it's self-indicting. Maybe he has a bad conscience as a Catholic running a pro-abortion newspaper.'

'It's Patrick who has libeled me,' Mickey said. 'Defamed me and pro-life, and published the disparagement by sending it to third parties. I have a libel case against him. It would make a great trial. I can see the headlines now: News Media Defame Pro-life.'

'Mickey, forget what the law books say. When it comes to abortion, they all just ignore the law, even the judges. You can't interfere with abortion, or criticize the integrity of the authorities who support it. They just won't allow it.'

'But a libel trial against one pro-abortion newspaper might have an effect on all the others. It's not about me. It's an opportunity for a pro-life initiative, an example some pro-lifer wouldn't take it anymore, and sued the news media for libel.'

Dolores leaned both her elbows on her desk, and put her head in her hands. Then she looked up at him. 'Mickey, for all your intelligence, I'm surprised how naïve you can be. I know you. You can study law books on libel, and you can file a lawsuit against Jeremiah Patrick and the Daily Record, but you can't win. They will give the case to Judge Dockendorff and he will rule against you. None of the news media will even report on the trial. Publicly, it won't exist, just like that poor woman taken to the hospital didn't exist. The media will just spike it.'

Mickey was undeterred. 'I'm sorry Dolores, but I have to do this. I feel called to do it. I don't have the money to hire lawyers to take on the deep pockets of the newspaper, but I never had any money for lawyers to defend us against Craigenback either. It should be done. Someone should sue the pro-abortion news media for constantly defaming pro-life.'

'But Dockendorff already said it's pro-lifers who defamed Craigenback with our protest signs. He's not going to turn around and admit the pro-choicers defame pro-life.'

'It's the principle of the thing. The law must be upheld,' Mickey said, wanting justice. He studied the law on defamation, thick, heavy books, and filed a claim in the court to restrain Jeremiah Patrick from circulating his libel letter around Calgary. The lawyers for Patrick and the Daily Record sought an emergency court hearing in early January to dismiss Mickey's claim. They argued the purpose of the law of defamation was to protect one's good name and reputation in the community, but in the case of Mickey Finnegan, he was a disreputable anti-abortion activist with no reputation, good name or standing in the community to protect. Judge Dockendorff agreed with the lawyers for the newspaper, and dismissed Mickey's lawsuit for defamation, ruling the publisher Jeremiah Patrick and the Daily Record were entitled to their freedom of speech and freedom of the press. Mickey could not dictate to professional journalists; news judgments belonged to them.

Mickey could not restrain himself as Dockendorff read out his written judgment, although he usually played the judicial game of due decorum and formal protocols.

'Dockendorff, how can you take away our pro-life freedom of speech on our protest signs, disconnect our telephone line, order us what to say and not to say in our counselling sessions, and then turn around and say the news media should have their freedom of speech? You contradict yourself with your double standard. You just look for legal sounding reasons to favor abortion. It's completely unfair. You are an unjust judge. You should remove yourself from any more of my pro-life lawsuits with your record of pro-abortion bias in every case.'

'Mr. Finnegan, I will overlook your unprofessional outburst at this time, but please remember you have been warned several times, and you may try the patience of this court once too often. Your case against the newspaper and the publisher is dismissed.'

'Will you remove yourself from my cases?'

'No. This court is impartial and unbiased. I take umbrage at your accusations I am not fair. When you are wrong on the law and a decision goes against you, have the good grace to accept it. You may take this where you wish.' Dockendorff was confident the Court of Appeals would uphold his judgment.

'Why do you want to preside at all the abortion cases?'

'I only handle whatever case is assigned to me. I don't know how to get through to you Mr. Finnegan. You just do not understand how the law and courts work.'

'Your Honor,' Jessica Sterne said, one of the three lawyers on the legal team for the newspaper, 'I apologize for Mr. Finnegan's embarrassing display here today. I would remind the court legal proceedings are very expensive. We are asking the court to order Mr. Finnegan to pay our court costs for defending against his frivolous case. My client has been victimized by Mr. Finnegan throughout. Since it was so inappropriate, we request double costs as a punitive measure to prevent the waste of the court's resources, as well as the newspaper's finances. For Mr. Finnegan to learn a smattering of law, how to file a claim and drag everyone into court for a hearing, is an abuse of process. And he keeps doing it.'

'So ordered.'

'Your Honor, am I not entitled to make submissions to the court on this issue of costs?'

'You wish to say something Mr. Finnegan?'

'Your Honor, with all due respect, there was nothing frivolous about my claim. The news media are not unbiased. In fact, they are so biased they function as the Ministry of Propaganda for abortion. Unless no one can see the obvious bias through denial, as it seems this court cannot see it. My friend's application fails to meet the test of frivolity for double costs.'

Mickey watched Dockendorff grow visibly agitated as he openly contradicted his decision.

'Who are you to question my judgment? A professional lawyer would know better than to argue with the judge. I have already found your motion frivolous without merit, so your repetitious argument is another waste of the court's precious time. Ms. Sterne is correct. Triple costs are hereby ordered. You cannot expect to come to court Mr. Finnegan, without paying the price. Court is adjourned.'

Mickey eventually received a bill from the newspaper for $30,000 for the afternoon hearing. The Daily Record and Jeremiah Patrick never made any attempt to collect the costs. They knew Mickey did not have any money, and they only wanted the outstanding court debt so he could never sue the newspaper again, and they could continue to write whatever they wanted about him and pro-life. As Dolores predicted, none of the news media in Calgary accurately reported on Mickey's libel lawsuit against one of their own for defaming pro-life. They did report he lost the case, that the Daily Record was vindicated, but no one in the public ever heard what the case was really about, a woman who was rushed in an ambulance to the emergency hospital from the Craigenback Abortion Clinic. The Daily Record headlined its report of the newspaper's victory over Mickey as PRO-LIFER SHOUTS AT JUDGE. Dolores asked Mickey about the newspaper story the next day when she saw him at the Crisis Pregnancy Center.

'What happened in court yesterday?'

'Dockendorff threw a judicial tantrum. Then the newspaper

said I was rude and uncivil. What can you do?'

'You mean they just made it up?'

'Pure creative fiction. I never yelled at anyone.'

'The headline makes you sound so inappropriate.'

'The mere existence of pro-life is inappropriate to them. Dockendorff dismissed my libel case against the newspaper, but the Daily Record headline is more libel, thereby proving my case against the biased newspaper. It's a perfect circle.'

'I warned you. The reporters don't tell us the news, unless it suits them. The news media cover up the truth about abortion.'

'Freedom of the press belongs to those who have one. The ink-stained wretches of the press hide the truth, the doctors are killing people instead of healing them, the courts are executing the innocent, and the Pope, bishops and priests honor the pro-aborts and keep their distance from the pro-lifers. It's a crazy world.'

'Only God can judge it all in the end.'

'God help me, but I look forward to it.'

'You want people to be judged and punished?'

'It would give me some satisfaction.'

'You don't sound very Christian. Jesus wanted to save people.'

'So do I. But some people are reprobates beyond redemption, rejecting God until their choice and decision is hardened into stone. Like the opinion makers in the media, the talking heads who believe their lofty tongues can dictate what reality is. What else can I do but hope for divine justice to set things right?'

'Divine justice, or your own thirst for vengeance?'

'I'm just saying they are all on the road to hell. Whether they get all the way there is not for me to say. I'll accept whatever God decides. It will be justice from Him.'

Dolores had to admit she felt the same way. 'Actually, I agree with you. They're all rotten. This is driving me crazy. I can't take it anymore.'

'Didn't you once tell me we have to take it, when I said I don't have to take it?'

'I can't take it anymore. That's all I know. Something has to happen. Something has to give.'

'You know what was strange? During the hearing, when I was reading out the terrible things Jeremiah Patrick wrote about me, he was shaken. He started crying, and his lawyers had to comfort him, putting their arms around his shoulders.'

'You never know what is in a person.'

'It didn't stop him from getting my case thrown out.'

'That's business. Pro-life always has to look bad. But you got to him personally.'

'I can appeal. I have a good case. I'm right on the law. Even Patrick knew he was in the wrong.'

'Mickey, there's no justice. Don't you know how the world works? It's only the abortion system using the law to legitimize themselves, keeping power and control. A court decision settles everything, even right and wrong. Or the appearance of right and wrong.'

'But the law–'

She turned around and walked away from him into her own office, not letting him finish, not wanting to argue about it anymore. She hated the law, and courts and judges. Mickey watched her go without saying anything more. The pain in his head hammered at his pulsing temples. He could not stand it anymore either, the falsity of it all, the way pro-life was always made to look so bad. His morning headache was a lousy way to start the day, but a few more of the white powder pills would make him functional again, ready to begin writing his notice of appeal.

37

After the mass Bishop Blair removed his vestments in the sacristy of St. Mary's Cathedral. He rested his shepherd's staff in the rack so it would not fall, with the crook facing upwards. The last of the Sunday masses was over, and now he could relax, enjoying a restful afternoon. He walked from the church to the rectory next door where he lived, and went to his private rooms. There he removed his white clerical collar, and his priestly black shirt, pants and shoes, putting on a pair of tan corduroy slacks, and a blue open necked shirt, the one with the white palm tree pattern. The shirt barely covered his pudgy body; he would have to get some new ones on his next visit. The sedentary life of a priest was catching up with him, and he was getting fat and soft. He was invited to too many dinners he could not decline, and he was not getting enough exercise in his golf games, when the sport was in season. He did not like the long walks when golfing anyway, preferring the motorized carts. Getting older was another reason for packing on the pounds. He bent over with difficulty to adjust his comfortable pair of open sandals, his stomach getting in the way.

As his clerical clothes came off he felt the unburdening of his strenuous duties as a Catholic bishop. The Bishop had to deal with so many people; everyone wanted to speak with the Bishop, with all of their problems and petitions. They expected him to solve everything. Now he could be alone for a while. He began to hum as he settled into his squishy chair in front of his computer and booted up the system.

The desktop appeared on the screen of his monitor, and his plump fingers typed his secret password on the keyboard. The bishop was known for his limp handshake, so delicate it was as if no one was there behind it. Many of the parishioners did not like shaking the bishop's hand, even though a handshake with the bishop was usually regarded as an honor among Catholics. With Bishop Blair, the experience of shaking his limp, cool hand felt a bit creepy. People put his weak handshake down to his aristocratic status as the Bishop, giving the peasants only the faintest of royal gestures during a greeting. As he used those same effeminate fingers to type his password, Blair looked around to double check he was alone. He had taken the extra precaution of increasing his computer's security with the password ENIGMA, rather than any religious allusions. No one would ever guess it. Nor would they realize his password was his own ironic self-commentary on a secret life no one suspected, one he did not want to analyze, or confess. Or stop.

The pictures of the young boys he had taken on his last vacation to Thailand filled the screen. He took pleasure in seeing them again. He remembered how free and open he could be in Asia. With enough money no questions were ever asked, and there were always plenty of young boys willing to satisfy him. The cost of each boy was only a few coins for him, the rich white tourist, dollars taken from the Sunday collection plate with the loose bills unaccounted for, but a fortune for the children with their poor families needing to eat. He smiled at the thought he was helping the families. It was an act of charity; he was their rice-bowl. He knew the boys enjoyed their relationships with him, loved him for his gifts and jokes, liked their loving times together as much as he did. When a relationship was one of mutual consent, what did age matter, and where was the harm?

He looked forward to his sex vacations all year, relived through his photo collection the rest of the time back in Canada when he was waiting to go back to Asia again. No one knew him there, and no one would ever know back home. As the picture gallery automatically changed the photographs in front of his fixated eyes, he reflected on the recent settlement in the abuse case against the priests. Although the settlement cost the diocese millions of dollars, almost bankrupting it, some property could be sold. Appeals to the parishioners for more donations in the mass collections would make up the rest in time. Even a bankrupt Catholic diocese never really closed its doors and stopped offering the sacraments. Christ promised His Church would endure forever, and the gates of Hell would not prevail against it. The Bishop had faith. As Horace Blair clicked through the saved photographs in his pictures file he felt a growing excitement rising within him. The boys in their naked poses on the beds, their suggestive looks inviting him once again as he relived the delicious moments with them, all completely at the service of his desires, thrilled him.

His performance at the press conference announcing the settlement had been a fine one, deploring the actions of the priests who betrayed their vows, betrayed the Church, betrayed their people, betrayed God, and above all betrayed the innocent and vulnerable children. He thought he had struck all the right notes. The bishop was justly proud of his diplomacy and tact, his expression of sensitive caring and contrite humility of behalf of the Church and the offending priests. He announced the new zero tolerance policy, and the new programs of investigation of complaints and support for the victims, as he promised *Never Again*. He did not take any questions from the reporters at the press conference, not wanting to be grilled on his own responsibility for transferring the priests from parish to parish when their sexual activity became known, protecting them. They were good, sincere men, part of the priestly brotherhood above the lay people, and only needed some treatment. And there was the reputation of the Church to consider. As the Catholic Bishop he did not have to give interviews to the press and submit to questioning. He was the authority on high, and made his statements for the reporters to take down and disseminate to the public.

Continuing his virtual stroll down his vacation memory lane, his hand also went down, and he stroked himself through his pants without thinking about it, so natural was the gesture for him, comforting in its second nature. He unzipped his fly to feel the pleasure of the skin of his hand on the skin of his hardening penis. He stroked himself, humming happily, going through his photo collection of child porn, looking forward to his next vacation, only a few days away. The Christmas season was over now, and the winter would soon be over. He looked forward to his coming retirement, when he could live full time as an expatriate in Asia, warm and happy in the sun with all the willing boys. Only for a little time more would he have to settle for his annual vacation in the tropics. The people in Canada were not ready yet, did not understand the beauty of an intergenerational romance. The country still had its child abuse laws, and statutory rape, and he could hardly preach publicly what he really believed. He would be blindly persecuted for his love. The tight sweet bottoms of the boys were such an exquisite pleasure, their cries of pain so exciting. Who but an initiate could understand such secret mysteries, or love the little buggars the way he did?

God knew he deserved to get away. Mickey Finnegan the crazy nuisance even subpoenaed him to be a witness in his libel case against Jeremiah Patrick and the Daily Record, wanting him to testify no Catholic like Patrick should be running a pro-abortion newspaper, have him say in public court no Catholic should be involved in abortion in any way. Thank goodness the lawyers for the Diocese had quashed the subpoena. Dockendorff was a reliable man. He had known what to do. They could laugh about Finnegan at their next golf game in the spring. Mickey Finnegan was insane. What evidence did he as the Bishop have to give about the workings of the Daily Record? And it was Finnegan who organized the picketing of himself as Catholic Bishop when Catholic Charities was exposed for funding pro-abortion women's groups. What a nut. Who in his right mind pickets the Catholic Bishop?

His wandering thoughts riveted on the next pictures, the

boys licking one another from behind on their hands and knees. He liked that too, liked doing it, and liked it when they did it to him. It was exciting, the moist soft tongue of a young boy licking his anus, and the soft slick tissues of a boy's anus receiving his tongue. He could stay down there forever, enjoying the moans of pleasure from the boy letting him know how much he enjoyed it, how much he loved him. *'It's even better than a boy's young mouth sucking my cock,'* he thought, *'even better than sucking him off.'* The boys might bleed a little sometimes, but they were young and would quickly heal. Grooming the boys, bringing them along to be his sex partners made them willing in the end and was a delightful process in itself. Those know it all moralists who condemned man boy love, who were they to judge? He loved the glory hole. Who could resist that? Whenever he went soft just before penetrating one of the boys, he found masturbating while he knelt down on his knees and licked the boy's behind always made him come. It was his favorite and never failed him, the anal kiss, the holy of holies.

The dark allure of his perversion engulfed him; he was carried away on waves of forbidden desire. Bishop Blair's body stiffened as he watched and stroked himself; he shuddered, and he felt the paroxysm of his orgasm coming as he sat at his computer looking at the pictures of the boys, the sticky white semen coming out of his prick on his fingers. 'Fuck me!' the bishop cried out. 'Fuck me!' He was beside himself in sexual ecstasy, even though there was no young brown bum nicely lubricated with his saliva and its sweet darker brown hole in the centre to push himself into. His hand in his pants moved more quickly up and down at the secret pictures on his computer screen, rubbing his still erect and now wet and sticky penis, and he could hardly breathe. He was coming again. Another trip to the tropics, that was what he needed now. No one suspected he was a Catholic Bishop when he wore ordinary street clothes on his sex tourism jaunts, and he liked it that way, the anonymity so freeing from the attention and esteem usually accorded to him by the priests and laymen of the Church.

38

On January 22nd, the anniversary of Roe v. Wade, the Supreme Court case in 1973 that legalized abortion across all of the United States of America, the pro-lifers met in the basement hall of Sacred Heart church for the Pro-life Resistance Intergroup Strategy Meeting, PRISM. Abortion had been legalized around the same time in England in 1967 and Canada in 1969. The purpose of the meeting was to settle their differences so they could work together during the demonstrations at the Craigenback Abortion Clinic. The pro-lifers usually joined different kinds of groups working separately in different areas of the movement, like education, pregnancy counselling and politics, but the abortion clinic was the one place they all went to demonstrate, the focal point bringing them together, and tensions were rife among them. Nearly fifty years of legal abortion had marginalized the pro-lifers, leaving them frustrated and powerless to change the dominant acceptance of the status quo.

The Crisis Pregnancy Center was still open, but did not see many people anymore after the telephone line was disconnected, and after the signs placed on their front door and interior walls stating the center was pro-life and did not provide any birth control or abortion services. Sadie's disastrous abortion was over, and she was out of the hospital and home again waiting for her body to heal, living in the same apartment with Rick. Mickey was still hurting from the lost Christmas Eve lawsuit over the censorship of words on the pro-life protest signs, and his libel case against the Daily Record which Judge Dockendorff had tossed out. The previous lost case over the graphic pictures of aborted babies was still under appeal, and so was the libel case, and cases involving the signs on walls and the disconnected telephone injunction, and the buffer zone at Craigenback's.

Mickey always appealed everything, hoping he might win something someday, but appeals took a long time. After the judicial crippling of both the Crisis Pregnancy Center and the protests at Craigenback's, Mickey was losing his faith in the law. Dolores was right, the law was only an instrument of the abortion establishment. The law was a system of legitimized social control which no longer had any relation to true justice. Always a champion of the importance of the rule of law, he had now come to see there was no law, only the rules set by the abortionists. The law was only an extension of abortion politics, raw judicial power, some procedural rules for the appearance of fairness, and the killing of the unborn. It was not justice that must be done and seen to be done; it was injustice that must be done and seen as justice, a legal game of smoke and mirrors, accomplished with only the appearance of a high level of rationality in which the judicial decrees were pronounced, usually unintelligible to the ordinary person. The pro-lifers may not have understood all the complex legal jargon, but they felt and understood the power of the rulings of the pro-abortion courts if they transgressed them. The force behind legal abortion and freedom of choice was simple enough. The sad women who came for counselling in a personal crisis and wanting an abortion as the way out had no awareness they too were only pawns of powerful social forces which were controlling them for their own agendas of population control, eugenics and the elimination of the disabled.

He was ready for an active campaign of civil disobedience, for a stand of defiance to the unjust abortion laws, but without violence. He hoped he could build support for more direct action at the intergroup strategy meeting. The time had come for mass sit-ins at the Craigenback Abortion Clinic. When he acted before as a lone ranger locking the front door with a chain and padlock to symbolically close it down, Jessica Sterne accused Mickey of endangering life by blocking exit from the building in case of a fire. The pro-aborts and the news media and courts were so good at turning everything around and making pro-life look bad, just the same as the time they accused him of disturbing children in the neighborhood with offensive signs when the abortion clinic was killing children. Mickey marveled at the way everything could be twisted in human disputes. But if he could get more people to join him in civil disobedience Calgary would see there was something wrong with abortion simply through the strong opposition of so many people. He prayed silently for the strength to speak with clear and persuasive reason at the meeting on the crucial need for non-violent civil disobedience in pro-life.

Mickey, sitting at the head of the table in the church basement, called the Pro-life Intergroup Strategy Session to order. 'Let us all rise and say the Lord's Prayer together for unity:

'Our Father, who art in heaven-'

The whole mixed bag of pro-lifers joined in saying the prayer.

The Pro-life Resistance Intergroup Strategy Meeting PRISM was an informal gathering which rarely met. They were all Christians, but of different denominations, mostly Catholics and Evangelicals who were active in pro-life. Some Pentecostals were there. The mainline churches were mostly supporting freedom of choice and abortion rights, and were not present at the meeting. When people asked why there were so many different groups in pro-life, Mickey could only say pro-life was like a mosaic. Pro-life was one big picture made out of many small pieces. Dolores and Mickey were attending from the Crisis Pregnancy Center CPC, and Dora and Sara represented their own new organization, Women United For Families, WUFF. Julie attended the meetings, but always remained silent, letting Mickey and Dolores speak for the Center. Other group representatives sat around the simple meeting tables and hard chairs in the church basement. Charlie Kelly, the maverick pro-lifer who loved baiting the feminists was also there, representing no group but himself. Kelly was famous in Calgary for his incendiary quotes to the news reporters, the ones they loved replaying over and over to destroy the credibility of pro-life, such as his oft played quote: 'If we knew women were going to change the law to kill their babies, we should never have given them the vote.' No one could control Charlie, and no one among the pro-lifers had the authority to ban him from the Craigenback protests. His misogyny was a trial for the pro-lifers. They wanted people to understand pro-life was pro-woman, not pro-child in opposition to women. Women were hurt by abortion too. Charlie was a public relations disaster for them. Cantankerous old Sara with her inappropriate comments was another embarrassment.

Mickey was feeling good, no headache this night. Yet. He took four of his pills before the meeting even began, so no headache could ambush him during the discussion. He lost no time in stating his agenda after the end of the Lord's Prayer. 'I think rescue missions with civil disobedience should begin at Craigenback's, and we should encourage new recruits to get involved. The rescue missions are non-violent, but they are real resistance, like Gandhi and Martin Luther King. Gandhi called it soul-force.'

'What we really need,' Charlie said, 'is the violent overthrow of the Canadian government.'

No one paid his sedition any attention. They knew him. Dora and Sara immediately disagreed with Mickey. 'Gandhi was a Hindu,' Sara said.

'Gandhi said it was clear as daylight abortion is a crime,' Mickey answered her. 'Martin Luther King was a Baptist reverend.'

'Martin Luther King was black.'

Dolores jumped in. This kind of talk from Sara could not be allowed. 'This ugly talk must stop now. Pro-life isn't racist. Planned Parenthood are the racists. They set up their abortion mills in black and Hispanic neighborhoods to get rid of the unwanted minorities.'

'Dolores is right," Mickey said. 'Just read Margaret Sanger, the founder of Planned Parenthood, writing about getting rid of human weeds, wanting more children from the fit and less from those who were unfit in her opinion, and saying people should have a license to have children. Scary stuff, and all of it coming true in some countries. Just look at China's coercive abortion policy. The government controls the reproductive lives of its citizens.'

All of this is over Sara's head. She is old now, a lonely widow, and no one pays her much attention. She just knows as a fundamentalist Christian abortion is wrong. 'When I was growing up, my parents taught me the DPs were going to be a big problem. We see them all around us in Canada now. All the races and immigrants.'

'DPs?' Julie asked.

'Displaced Persons,' Mickey explained, 'the term for refugee immigrants from Europe after World War 11.'

'Canada is multicultural,' Dolores said. 'We need immigrants because we aren't reproducing ourselves with all the contraception and abortion and lack of marriages and divorces among those who do get married for a while. Canada is an elderly dying country. I'm a brown skinned Filipina myself. How can you say those things in front of me?'

'Right again,' Mickey said. 'A nation killing its own children has no future. We are living through a long demographic winter, with no springtime on the horizon.'

'It's so multicultural now, it's becoming illegal to call

Canada a Christian country,' Sara said, 'which leads to more abortions, the farther we get away from God.'

'We absolutely are not racist in pro-life,' Mickey said. 'Please don't say those things ever again Sara, either publicly or privately. Don't even think it.'

Dora defended her friend Sara, changing the subject back to Mickey's proposal for civil disobedience. 'We should confine ourselves to peaceful picketing, prayer vigils, and sidewalk counselling at Craigenback's. Your illegal actions are going to get us all completely removed a mile away, and we won't be able to do anything. It's your fault we have to stay behind a buffer zone after you locked the doors, and now you're talking about recruiting more people to break the law.'

'Do you accept the abortion clinic has a legal right to exist, and we should obey the abortion laws?'

'Yes, Christians should obey the law.'

Mickey responded. 'The Bible is very clear we should obey God rather than men. The Bible says rescue those being led away to death. That's in Proverbs. The Popes of the Catholic Church have always taught there cannot be obedience to an unjust law. Let me show these photocopies I brought with me.' Mickey handed around the passage he copied for the night's meeting, Paragraph 73 from The Gospel of Life, by Pope John Paul 11:

> *73. Abortion and euthanasia are crimes which no human law can claim to legitimize. There is no obligation in conscience to obey such laws; instead there is a grave and clear obligation to oppose them by conscientious objection.*

Dora and Sara were not buying it. Looking at the sheet Mickey gave her to read, Dora said: 'This doesn't mean we should go out and deliberately break the law. It only means we should not be forced to cooperate with abortion, like a doctor or nurse saying they won't do abortions as part of their jobs.'

'All of us are forced to go along with abortion all the time,' Charlie said.

'The Bible says to obey the authorities Mickey,' Dora said. 'To be law abiding Christians.'

'Adolf Hitler had the authority to pass racial laws against the Jews. Should people have obeyed those laws? The Fugitive Slave Law in America required anyone who saw runaway slaves to return them to their owners. Should people have obeyed that law?' Mickey said.

'Don't confuse the issue. Christians should obey the law.'

'Operation Rescue did a lot of high member sit-ins at abortion clinics based on that Bible command to rescue people," Mickey said.

'But the whole Operation Rescue movement was crushed. No one does that anymore,' Dora said.

'The Bible remains the Bible,' Mickey said. 'The issues are the same. Wrong and unjust laws, even if passed by the legitimate authority. I can't seem to get through to you I am not saying anything new or radical. If we obey the unjust abortion laws, then we too are part of the abortion system.'

'Speak for yourself,' Dora said. 'I'm not part of the abortion system. I am pro-life. You also break the law with your fraudulent Crisis Pregnancy Center, lying to people.'

Mickey, Dolores and Julie exchanged glances, seeing Dora also had an agenda for the meeting, a personal agenda she had just suddenly revealed. Should they defend the Center, or let her comments go and not rise to the bait?

'You have to change the hearts of the people to change the abortion laws,' Dolores said.

'First you have to change the hearts of the Church leadership to change their people,' Charlie said. 'Everyone just goes along with abortion, with nary a peep against it, or sometimes a little peep against it. When do you ever hear a sermon against abortion by one of Bishop Blair's priests? You don't hear any sermons like that, while they all hobnob together at the top of society.'

'Your resentment of the leaders of society is well known Charlie,' Dora said.

'And rightly so. God is mocked by all these hypocrites,' Charlie said.

'God is not mocked, not in the end. The Bible promises God is not mocked,' Dolores said.

'Amen to that sister,' Charlie said

'Don't be facetious,' Dolores said. 'Now you're mocking me too.'

'Not really. I respect you. It's the elites everywhere, in the government, in the church, in the courts, in the news media, in big tech, in Hollywood, in the professions that control us all that I can't stand.'

'And it's getting worse,' Mickey said. 'They have the money, and their constant success emboldens them even more.'

'The problem with you Mickey, is that even your civil disobedience works within the abortion system. You accept arrest and punishment. What we need is a people's revolt, an insurrection,' Charlie said. 'We don't really have a democracy. We live under an oligarchy of the elites.'

'You shouldn't say violent things Charlie,' Mickey said. 'James Kopp nicknamed Atomic Dog took his pro-life activism to a terror campaign, shooting at abortionists in their homes with a long range rifle. He said he was only trying to wound them to prevent abortions, but he eventually killed someone, and finally got caught. We absolutely must renounce violence in pro-life.'

'Many weird things happen in the abortion wars. Tiller the Killer was assassinated by a psro-lifer while Tiller was volunteering as an usher in church, not doing any late term abortions that day, and Kermit Gosnell was convicted of murdering abortion children born alive after abortion by stabbing them in their spinal cords with scissors. The 'dreaded complication' of a baby born alive was an easy solution for him, but even the pro-abortion state charged him with murder,' Charlie said.

'Gosnell was an exception with his House of Horrors,' Mickey said. 'I hope he was the exception. Even the pro-aborts condemned him. But many others are advocating for infanticide now beyond abortion. More violence towards children. We don't know if Craigenback is doing it too. Gosnell got away with it for years.'

'And the pro-aborts make your non-violent civil disobedience look like violence towards them anyway,' Charlie said. 'Nice distinctions are lost on them. You can't win. We are all violent pro-lifers, by definition.'

'Of course,' Mickey said. 'The violence of abortion is projected onto us. The evil of abortion is projected onto us. We are the evil ones. They absolutely have to put us down. The best defense is a good offence. When they call us 'anti-abortionists' they even manage the reversal of hanging the word 'abortionist' around our necks. Neat trick. '

'You two are both impossible dreamers,' Dora said. 'Let's discuss what we can actually do, with the way things really are.'

'You mean how we can nibble around the edges,' Charlie said. 'If they let us do that.'

'I think we are talking about the way things really are,' Mickey said. 'We just don't agree on what we can do about it.'

39

On the same night the pro-lifers were meeting in the basement of Sacred Heart church, Sadie wanted to have a talk with Rick in their apartment. She wanted to talk about what happened during the abortion, but he didn't want to talk about it. He tipped his bottle of beer back for a long swallow. They had both avoided the subject, even though she was still in the recovery stage from her injuries. She confronted him as they sat in the living room, trying to break through his silence.

'Rick, don't you have anything to say?'

He finally looked at her. 'It's over and done with. Just get on with it.'

'I demand you say something to me.'

'I suffered too you know.'

'What do you mean?'

'How long's it going to be?'

'For what?'

'Til you're better. Til we can do it again.'

She couldn't stand him anymore. She said nothing all the rest of the evening, ignoring him. Rick became frustrated, and began to shake her in her withdrawn silence. He slapped her face. Sadie fell back against the wall and began to cry. Rick was even angrier, and slapped her again. 'Stupid bitch,' he said. Sadie collapsed on the floor, and began to beg him. 'Please don't hit me again.' In his fury he dragged her shrieking by the hair into the bedroom, and threw her on the bed. He left her alone in the bedroom, and sat down in the easy chair in the living room, opening another bottle of beer. Sadie rolled herself from her back onto her hands and knees on the bed, and from there was able to move off the bed and stand on the floor again. Her insides hurt. She did not say anything, just standing and staring through the open doorway at Rick sitting in the living room. He was watching her too. 'I'll beat that baby out of you yet, out of your mind.'

'I want out.'

Rick, guarding the door, shook his head no. '

'You can't go out.'

"I meant I want us to split.'

'You can't go out.'

'You're blocking the door, keeping me a prisoner here?'

Rick did not answer her. He took another swallow.

'Can I go to the bathroom? I need some of my painkiller pills.'

'Okay, you can go there.'

Sadie walked out of the bedroom, but instead of going to the bathroom she went into the tiny kitchen, got the long carving knife from the drawer, and stood above Rick sitting in his chair. She pointed the knife at his throat. Rick saw the look in her eyes, and he sat very still, not daring to move. Sadie breathed deeply, collecting herself. Something had snapped and changed in her. 'If you ever touch me again, there will be blood on the walls, and it won't be mine. I will cut your throat in your sleep. I will cut your balls off. I swear it. I've had it with your brutal control. Now get out.'

Rick was very careful not make any sudden moves. He stood up slowly, got his coat and left, saying nothing more. As he stumbled down the stairs, he felt remorseful he had attacked his wounded girlfriend, making things worse for her. He knew this time he had gone too far. The way Sadie was feeling, an apology and flowers and a promise never to do it again would not work to heal the rift between them, not this time. The murderous rage in her face and eyes, her voice so calm and yet so cold, had frightened him. He had never seen the deadly side of her before. He decided to stay away from her, at least for a while. She was too scary. He could not trust her after she threatened to attack him in his sleep. 'Stupid bitch,' he mumbled again on his way down the stairs, not knowing where he would spend the night.

Sadie was not a heavy drinker, but after Rick left she went to the refrigerator and took out one of his beers, and went to the bathroom for her painkillers. Glad to be alone, she poured a glass from the bottle, and washed down some pills, and settled into the comfort of the cushions on the couch. She did not want to think about her abortions. Or Rick. She did not want to think about anything; she wanted to forget. She sat in silence, sat in the pain, and did not think at all. She held a cold beer bottle on the bruises on her face. Her mind drifted back to the past with her father and mother and twin brother. Happy memories came back to her of their happy family life before her parents' divorce. She had forgotten, in the midst of the fighting and angry shouts between her parents, the happy times of a family she had known. Just the presence of a family, her family, troubled as it was, had been there for her.

Now she felt no sense of family, with her parents divorced, and Rick gone, and without any children of her own. She went to the refrigerator for another bottle of beer. She took some more painkillers. Her body ached from the roots of her pulled hair to her stomach, where they had taken out her insides, and where Rick kicked her. The loss of her womanhood was something else she did not want to remember. She was surprised at her desire to kill Rick. She had been ready to do it, She had felt the urge to kill. Was she getting harder as time went on? What was happening to her? Was it getting easier to kill?

She brought the glass to her lips, but it was empty. Sadie returned to the refrigerator, took out another bottle, did not pour it into a glass this time, and settled back deep in the cushions of the couch. She took a drink from the bottle. She was lost in her drunken dream of a home and family in the mists of memory of the past, drifting through the intoxicated haze of her mind as the alcohol and pills took possession of her. She was not thinking of the terrible present. She did not think of Rick at all. He was no good. He had not protected her. He left only a few hours ago, but as far as she was concerned he was ancient history, no longer part of her life. He was long gone.

The early memories of her mom and dad and her brother, those were the thoughts she dwelt on now, but seen through a rosy glow divorced from the old reality. She gave herself to the comforting waves of relaxation flowing through her battered body, drowning her sorrows, sinking downwards into the blackness of oblivion, forgetting everything. She felt a pleasant disconnection from both herself and the disappointing world around her, living in the private fantasy of her own mind. All the youthful happy promise of love had come only to this ultimate loneliness, and she took another drink, and some more pills, discovering the escape of drugs and alcohol.

40

At the PRISM meeting Mickey decided to defend the Crisis Pregnancy Center, wanting to explain the neutral image pro-life philosophy, and answer the false charges of immoral deception. He saw the meeting was going to turn into a long night of argument. He wished he could skip it, these pro-life meetings when they were all together was just another bureaucracy. Charlie and he agreed on that, if little else.

'We advertise to reach the abortion bound woman. We want to talk with her and give her the facts and truth about abortion. Who better to talk to than a woman who thinks she wants an abortion, but doesn't know much about it, or is reacting to a crisis in her life with no support. A woman who is being directed through the whole abortion system by false words like *Family Planning* and *Birth Control* and *Reproductive Health*. Don't concede those words belong to the pro-aborts. We are reclaiming the language. It's a very intelligent approach.'

'Dumb women led around by their noses to have abortions,' Charlie said.

'It's dishonest to deceive the women. Period.' Dora insisted.

Dolores supported Mickey. 'Working at the Center, I'm impressed how many women first think they want an abortion, and then change their minds when they get some true information and caring support. Mickey's right. Think how many women and abortions are routinely processed through the system, just like that? A lot of those women would have changed their minds too, and a lot of babies saved.'

'That's right,' Mickey said. 'Pro-life is not talking to the people who are aborting their children. We are trying to reach those women, and help them.'

'It's still dishonest,' Sara said, 'breaking the law.'

Mickey was not going to waste his time trying to instruct Dora and Sara on the moral theology of mental reservation. He had tried before, but they had their minds made up and did not want to listen to him. 'You always think like a moralist Dora. It's only manipulation of the system which manipulates us. We are surrounded by bureaucratic systems: political systems, legal systems, education systems, health care systems, government funding and income systems, and the birth control and abortion system. I am manipulating the abortion system for a good purpose, to throw a monkey wrench into it.'

'My husband Bill a pastor says it is never right to do evil for a good purpose. The end does not justify the means.'

'Satan is behind it all. We never talk about that reality.'

'I wish you would shut up about Satan,' Dora said. 'It's too much of an obsession with you.'

'Can we get back to rescue missions and civil disobedience?' Mickey said.

'Maisie Barstowe has been in jail a long time,' Dolores said, 'for refusing to sign bail conditions to stay away from Craigenback's. As soon as they release her she goes right back, and prays on the sidewalk and talks to the women inside the buffer zone, and they arrest her again. Someone has given up her life for the unborn.'

'Maisie is a good example,' Mickey said. 'She has sacrificed her freedom for the unborn, suffering along with them. Maisie Barstowe is the only pro-lifer in the country, the only one. The rest of us play at pro-life safely around the edges, going on with our own lives while the children die.'

'You cannot expect us to give everything up and go to jail,' Dora said. 'We have responsibilities. My husband would never allow it.'

'We would lose our charity number for WUFF,' Sara said. 'We need our charity number to get donations and keep operating as a pro-life group.'

'They are killing babies, and you are worried interfering with the murder would cost you your charity number?' Charlie said to her.

'Those numbers are hard to get. The government is biased against pro-life charities to begin with. We have to be careful.'

'My uncle is a Knight,' Julie said. 'Every year they sponsor the Hike for Life in Prince's Island Park to bring in donations. If we break the law we would lose the Knights' support too.'

'Do you think a walk in the park once a year is going to do anything to stop abortion in Canada?' Mickey asked her.

'Are you insulting the Knights of Columbus now? They're good Catholic men. They do a lot of charity work.'

'We need to educate people,' Sara said. 'The educational pro-life groups like ours are the best way to go.'

'Do you think making some presentations to a few student

classes, if the schools will let you in, will make much difference to abortion in Canada?' Mickey asked again.

'We need a new evangelization of the whole culture of death,' Charlie said. "Make people truly Christian again, and legal abortion is finished.'

'Sara is right,' Dora said. 'People need to be educated on the facts about abortion. They just don't know what is going on.'

'Sounds likes the Socratic and Platonic position,' Charlie said. 'Virtue stems from knowledge. To know the good is to do it.'

'Not necessarily,' Mickey said. 'Sin chooses the evil, knowingly and freely. But my question is: Do we really act like abortion is murder? If we really acted like abortion is murder, laying down our own lives and freedom to oppose it, it would be the most educational witness of all. If we knew a two year old toddler was being murdered next door, would we sit down and write a letter to the editor about it?'

'We have to obey the law,' Dora said. 'You can rationalize your illegal behavior, but it doesn't make it right.'

Dolores jumped in. 'What about the beautiful pictures of mothers and babies saved through the Crisis Pregnancy Center?'

'Still doesn't make it right,' Dora said.

Mickey and Dolores just looked at each other. If the babies didn't matter to Dora, what could they say to her?

'But we are educating people about abortion too. Just not in a classroom. We do it at the Crisis Pregnancy Center.'

'Not the same thing as our education when you mix it with lies to get people in,' Dora said.

'You idolize Maisie Barstowe,' Mickey said. 'And I agree she is doing something brave and sacrificial in breaking the law at the abortion clinic. She goes into the buffer zone, gets arrested, and spends months in jail. When they release her she goes right back. It's been going on for ten years now. How can you support Maisie, but object to me?'

Dora challenged him. 'If you think that way, why aren't you doing the same thing with her? You only break the law sometimes for a brief sentence in jail or small fine. Get your name and picture in the news.'

'You're right Dora.'

'I'm right?'

'Not right about my motives, but right I should be getting arrested with Maisie. I only disobey the abortion laws sometimes. The rest of the time I obey them, to my shame. I enjoy my life, I go out and do things while the children die all around me. I too am part of the culture of death.'

'So you're a hypocrite,' Sara said.

'Aren't we all?' Charlie said.

'It bothers me though,' Mickey said. 'It's on my mind.'

'Maisie Barstowe is the only free one,' Charlie agreed. 'She refuses to give up her freedom and goes into the buffer zone. They arrest her and put her in jail, but she is still free in her soul, even though she is a prisoner of conscience in a jail cell. If all us acted as Maisie does, the abortion laws would be defeated. But she acts alone, the only one. That's funny, the one in jail is the only free one. The rest of us are prisoners of the law and the buffer zone, self-imprisoned through our obedience.'

'I used to stress the importance of the rule of law,' Mickey said. 'Now I have come to see the moral imperative of disobeying the abortion laws. That's all I'm saying.'

'But Maisie's heroism has no impact,' Charlie said. 'The abortion system can absorb her pathetic protests, undisturbed like a dominant empire crushing a local revolt. And Satan just laughs.'

'Maisie feels called to do what she does,' Sara said. 'We can't all do it. She doesn't believe in a cookie cutter approach to pro-life. She knows we're all different. She doesn't expect us all to break the law and go to jail the way she does.'

'Maisie is playing politics too,' Mickey said. 'Don't you think it would mean a lot to her if people did join her, instead of standing safely across the street and cheering her on?'

'You're not one of us Mickey,' Sara said. 'You are always critical of all of us. You need a deep conversion.'

'Sara's right,' Dora said. 'You are a sick sick man. You should be in prison for your crimes.'

'Are you saved Mickey?' Sara asked him. 'Are you born again?'

'I thought pro-life cherished the unique dignity of every human being, from conception to natural death, and pro-life loved the unloved, and wanted the unwanted,' Mickey said. 'Except for me? Who points out we are all one way or another part of the culture of death, letting the babies die while we all comfortably live? And we are the adults and they are the children.'

'I'm not responsible for abortion,' Dora said again. "I am part of the pro-life movement.'

'There is no pro-life movement,' Charlie said. 'There is only Maisie Barstowe. And she's imperfect. She's a useful poster girl for the pro-life movement to point to as the pro-life heroine in jail, and she plays the politics of keeping their support.'

'Charlie, you are even more cynical than Mickey,' Dolores said.

'I see what I see.'

Dolores tried to be diplomatic. 'Maybe you are too hard on yourself Mickey. Too hard on everyone. You are asking a lot of people. Asking too much for most people.'

41

Charlie opened a new line of discussion. 'I got one of Smiling Jake Corcoran's begging letters today. He says send money now, right away. The fate of western civilization and life as we know it hang in the balance.'

Mickey said. 'I got the same letter. Smiling Jake's bank balance must be running low.'

'For shame,' Dora said. 'Pro-life has to raise money to do its important work. Grass roots direct mail fundraising is the only way. The government isn't helping us.'

'That's true,' Mickey said. 'I've used the same approach myself. But the doomsday scenarios seem a little contradictory coming from Smiling Jake.'

'The world as we know it is under attack,' Sara said. 'I got the letter too. Smiling Jake is warning us Craigenback is starting up another abortion mill.'

'Things are getting worse,' Mickey said. 'There isn't a thing Smiling Jake Corcoran can do stop it, even with his political contacts and his fundraising letters. Maisie Barstowe sitting alone in jail can't stop it all either. That's why we need civil disobedience and rescue missions. Direct action. The political approach has failed. The legal approach has failed. The education approach has failed. Our counselling work has failed. Nothing works. Smiling Jake says his role as political leader is just to pump sunshine, keep everyone's spirits up.

Except when he sends his dire warnings to raise money.'

'Your civil disobedience will fail too,' Dora said. "It's been tried before, had its vogue, then people drifted away when the abortion system started the drastic laws and punishments to stamp it out.'

'The police are only thugs when they arrest peaceful pro-lifers trying to save lives,' Charlie said. 'Your friend Sgt. Ryan is only one of the thugs when he arrests us.'

'Shame on you.' Sara said. 'Shame. Shame. David Ryan is a very good Catholic man, doing the best he can in an impossible situation. He is also a Knight. You can't expect him to give up his job as a policeman.

'Why not?' Mickey asked. 'That's my point, we are all part of the abortion system, the adults protecting ourselves while we let the children die. Why should it seem so far-fetched for a man to surrender his job rather than be part of the killing of the unborn? It should be a natural refusal for Police Sgt. David Ryan to participate, knowing as he does its wrong, just to save his job and his hefty police pension.'

'You and Charlie are judgmental men,' Dora said.

Mickey had to bite his tongue not to say 'Look who's talking,' but he did glance at silent Julie who suffered Dora's judgments at the Crisis Pregnancy Center. Julie did not reveal anything in her blank face.

'It's a long defeat in pro-life,' Mickey said. 'A long defeat.'

'It's the pro-lifers who will always have hope,' Dolores said, remembering her confession, and how Fr. MacIntyre inspired her to live again. 'We can always pray for an end to abortion.'

'Pray?' Charlie said. "That's your strategy? How pathetic.

The situation is so hopeless we can only pray about it?"

'Prayer is a tremendous power, even if we can't always see the results. We have to hold on to our faith in God. He is all-powerful, whatever the appearances. He lets himself look weak in this world. That's God's Christian way, letting his son Jesus be crucified, but winning through defeat.'

Mickey supported Dolores. 'Because of pro-life, abortion will always be controversial. Abortion will never be normalized as just an accepted way of life. People know its wrong deep down. We say it publicly so it can never be forgotten or denied. Abortion is wrong. We are a voice for life, even if it seems at times our voice is only a weakened whisper easily drowned out by the noisy shouts of freedom of choice and abortion rights.'

'You people involve yourself in a lot of activities opposing abortion,' Charlie said, 'but you never get anywhere. Satan is too powerful in this world, too smart for you.'

'Charlie,' Dolores said, 'keep the faith. God is watching, and the Bible says the man who gives voice to injustice will not go unheard by the Lord.'

"Let's take a bathroom break,' Mickey said. The meeting was a long one, and his headache had come back. He needed some place private to take some more pills.

42

During a break in the meeting, Mickey went to the bathroom, and took four more of his painkillers. He carried them with him in the pocket of his shirt in case one of his headaches attacked him, and this night was especially frustrating. When the meeting resumed, he tried once more to bring his agenda for rescue missions to a successful conclusion.

'If we saw a child endangered in traffic we would run into the street to protect the child. If we saw a child crying for help from the window of a burning house, we would rush into the house. But with the unborn children, we walk by the abortion clinic on the corner and go home and say 'What's for dinner?''

'I do what I can,' Sara said. 'I have to live too.'

'That's just it, we are all involved in our own lives, following the instinct for self-preservation, and we let the children die. If I'm wrong about this idea, please show me. It bothers me.'

'You are too extreme to expect us all to go and lay down our lives for the unborn,' Dora said. 'What do you expect, to have us all hanging from crosses outside Craigenback's?'

'Logically, isn't it true, the adults should not be living safely and let the children die all around us? We all accept abortion, and don't endanger ourselves over it. Isn't it true? Aren't we all accommodated to legal abortion? Am I wrong?'

'How could we do it Mickey, die with the unborn?' Dolores

asked. 'How would it work?'

'It doesn't make sense,' Charlie said. 'Are you going to be like a Muslim suicide bomber down at Craigenback's, explosives strapped under your clothes?'

'I don't mean committing violence ourselves.'

'What then? Be like a Buddhist monk, go down and sit in the lotus position, douse yourself with gasoline, light a match and immolate yourself in protest?'

'No,' Mickey said. 'Don't misunderstand me. Murder and suicide are not the Christian pro-life way. I don't know how it would work. All I'm saying is the unborn are children who are dying, and we adults are safely living. I can't get away from it.'

'We do die, Mickey,' Sara said. 'I die inside all the time. It's terrible to be down at the abortion clinic, holding my sign, and there is nothing I can do to stop the women going in.'

'Thank you Sara,' Mickey said. 'I know how you feel. Jesus said the greatest love was to lay down your life for your friends. We are the friends of the unborn children. Their only friends. No one else cares about them. So how can we lay down our lives for them, our unborn brothers and sisters, in solidarity and equality with them, in complete oneness with them? Dying together? That's my question.'

'We have to accept our human limitations,' Dora said. 'First you want to go down there and break the law, and now you talk about dying with the unborn. I worry about you. What's going to happen to you?'

'I'm just saying. It's just a question I think about. I like my life too. I admitted that before.'

'We are one with them Mickey,' Dolores said. 'The unborn children are of no account in this world and trampled on, and we pro-lifers are of no account and trampled on. They lose their rights, and we lose our rights.'

'Except for the most important right of all, the right to life. They are dying, and we are living.'

'We don't let them die alone,' Dolores said, revealing her heart for the unborn. 'We are down there with them. The children are not unloved, dying alone and unloved. We love them. Even when their own parents don't love them and don't want them. We are with them, as close as the authorities will allow us to get. We pray for them. We are there, giving our witness. Right at Craigenback's. That's why it's so important we can stay there.'

'But that's all we are,' Mickey said. 'Witnesses, bystanders, while they die.'

'Not if we suffer about it, not if hurts us. We are not indifferent witnesses. We care.'

Mickey looks at Dolores, and loves her love. He knows despite his extreme thoughts on the subject of dying with the unborn children he does not really want to be a martyr.

'We have a right to live our own lives,' Sara said, still justifying herself.

'Do you enjoy your life?'

'Yes of course, life is a wonderful gift of God.'

'Do you think the unborn children would enjoy their lives?'

'You know I want them to live.'

'So we get to enjoy our lives, and they don't. It's not fair.'

'Mickey,' Charlie said, shaking his head, 'the body politic

may be sick, but you can't even expect the courage of civic engagement from most pro-life people. Everyone is hunkered down, living their own lives and protecting themselves and their families. How can you expect martyrdom?'

'I'm just thinking out loud. Here, let me read you something I wrote recently. It's short. I call it A Parable.' Mickey took out another sheet of paper to share with the group.

"Let me read you this story. It's not long. I call it a parable.

A PARABLE

There was a man who went to church early one morning on his birthday to pray, and he congratulated himself and said to the Lord: 'I thank you Lord I am not as other men, involved in or indifferent to abortion. I pray for the unborn, I send donations to the pro-life education group, and I write letters to the editor. I walk in the park once a year with my fellow Knights of Columbus to raise funds for pro-life, and this year we brought in enough money to donate an ultra sound machine to the crisis pregnancy center, where my wife is a volunteer counselor. I pray at the abortion mill once a week behind the buffer zone, on Tuesdays, from two to three in the afternoon. I was even arrested once for a sit-in at the abortion clinic, and spent a night in jail.'

The man left the church very pleased with himself, passing by the abortion clinic on the way to breakfast as it was not his day to protest, and he shook his head in disapproval at the sinners who stood in front of the abortuary holding their signs supporting a woman's right to choose. He pitied them for their ignorant involvement in the culture of death. He hurried past as he had a very busy day planned with many interesting activities of work and play ahead of him; he was late for his birthday breakfast, and his wife and children and friends were waiting for him at home.

A pregnant young woman walked past him going into the abortion mill with her head lowered, her face obscured by a hat drawn down to cover herself, and the man looked away. He disapproved of the woman who was going to kill her unwanted child, and he congratulated himself once again he was not part of the culture of death and not responsible for all the abortions. The man safely lived, and enjoyed his birthday breakfast, and his wife and friends and life at home that day, but the child died alone in the abortion mill with no one to protect him, and without a birthday or a home.

The group was silent. 'That's beautiful,' Dolores said.
Then Sara said, 'You stole that from the Bible.'
'I adapted the parable of the Publican and the Pharisee from the Bible to the modern abortion situation. It fits. It expresses what I was trying to say to you.'
'No,' Dora said. "We don't need you Mickey as our new Messiah. Jesus will do. You're no prophet, no saint. Sounds like you have a bad case of survivor guilt. You're alive and the children are dead. I get it.'
Mickey's parable was quickly ignored. But Dolores was moved to share something of her own experience.
"Can I share a poem with you all?" she asked. 'I have it here. I wrote it after some years after my abortion. It just came to

me one night when I was walking in the winter.' She did not wait for the group's permission, but reached in her purse and took out the poem she kept folded there, next to the letter to her daughter, and read it to the people sitting around the table:

aborted woman

a cry of sorrow,
rising in the night cold air–
quiet doves asleep.

trees black in moonlight
listen to her private grief–
leafy branches are heaped.

'where are my children?'
she asks the sky–no reply–
stars above are steep.
heaven is closed,
is silent–yet love is deep–
winds blow as she weeps.

'That's lovely,' Julie said. The rest of the group were silent. Then the mood quickly changed, getting back to the business of the meeting.

'Why not,' Charlie said, 'if you want to try new tactics, use butyric acid inside the abortion mill? It stinks for months. Or we can put superglue in the door locks, prevent them from opening?'

'Not the kind of image we want Charlie. We are not vandals. Pro-life vandals. Vandalism seems immature to me.'

'Law breaking isn't the image we want either,' Dora said.

'Why does God allow it?' Sara asked out loud. 'Why does God allow all the babies to be killed? He has the power to stop it. Why doesn't He?'

Mickey felt Sara's anguish. She might be a stubborn problem at times, but she was an elderly Christian woman, and it was a good question, a trial of faith for all of them. But now was not the time to get into a deep discussion on the mystery of evil and God's silence. The pro-lifers were meeting to plan their practical strategy at the Craigenback Abortion Clinic. The meeting had been sidetracked several times already. 'Let's get back to our agenda.'

Sara ignored him and spoke again. 'The killers of the babies dishonor the Creator. They belong to the devil's party. They oppose the truth, they oppose the good. Abortion is satanic. Satan is the chief of the fallen angels, the leader of all the other devils. Satan is the head abortionist.'

Charlie was glad to find some support.

'You're right Sara,' Charlie said. 'It's Satan we are fighting.' He too thought the pro-lifers were reluctant to face the real spiritual battle in abortion. 'The Church of Satan even has abortion rituals in its worship services. Unbelievable.'

'Satan hates God creating new lives in His own image and likeness,' Sara said.

'Sara, I'm impressed,' Charlie said. 'You have read your Bible.'

Dolores intervened. She tried once again to be a peacemaker

and smooth things over.

'The sidewalk counselling is very important Mickey. Sidewalk counselling is our very last chance to help a woman change her mind just before she walks into the abortion clinic. We should try and remain on the sidewalk close to Craigenback's, not get ourselves removed even further away by Judge Dockendorff.'

Mickey was disappointed even Dolores would not support his desire for more civil disobedience. Dora smiled. She was delighted to have Dolores as an ally in her objections to more of Mickey's law breaking.

'He's a wicked wicked judge' Sara said. 'Dockendorff is a reptile, a little toad of a man.'

'Dockendorff is one of the minor demons,' Charlie agreed.'

'The Bible warns unjust judges. I don't envy him, when he faces his own judgment in the end,' Dolores said.

Mickey's headache was killing him. He leaned forward placing his head in both his hands, his elbows supported on the table. The meeting was going nowhere. The public would not understand talk about Satan. Much of the Church too no longer believed in the Devil and Hell anymore and never talked about it. He believed it, but he wanted to keep the focus on abortion in pro-life, and not the Evil One.

'Satan be gone!' Sara said. 'In the name of Christ I command you: Be gone!'

'Stop the killing,' Dora said. 'Stop the killing.'

43

'We absolutely must continue the sidewalk counselling,' Dolores repeated. 'It's what Maisie is fighting for when goes into the buffer zone, the right to freely talk to the women going into the clinic about abortion.

Dolores remembered the day of her own abortion. She ignored the protesters when she was going in the clinic, and ignored them again when she came out, walking past them with her head down, staring at the sidewalk. She felt ashamed the moment she walked out of the abortion clinic. She did not know she would be standing on the sidewalk in front of an abortion mill herself holding a protest sign, standing up for life, wanting a chance to talk to the other women going inside. People sometimes told her she should mind her own business. She used to think the same way, that she should not interfere with the privacy of other people and their personal freedom of choice. But now she knew the victim children had no choice. It was her business to care about them, not to stand idly by and let them be killed. The unborn children were her brothers and sisters in the human family. Now Dolores had tears in her eyes at the dissension in this rancorous meeting of the pro-life movement she had joined, and her voice quavered.

'Why do we always have such friction in pro-life? This saddens me. In such a noble cause. Why can't we show each other civility, and mutual respect?'

'Because we don't respect each other,' Charlie said. 'We don't really like each other. Don't be naïve. It's fallen human nature all around. In a fallen world, even great causes are always crippled by pride, and tragedies and failures, and treachery and betrayals. Just look at the history of the world. Look at the history of the Catholic Church.'

'Look at the life and death of Jesus,' Mickey said. 'With friends like these, who needs enemies?'

Dora and Sara had trouble accepting Dolores. She had an abortion before. She worked with Mickey. But now they were glad to see her support their objections to civil disobedience. Dora saw her chance. 'Will you promise Mickey, not to have any more rescue missions at Craigenback's? Will you give us your word not to padlock the front doors again? Will you not come and picket anymore, so the rest of us can do it our way?'

Mickey just looked at her. How had he lost control of the meeting so badly that the resolutions coming out of the discussion were the exact opposite of his intentions going in? There was no support for his rescue mission at all. 'I don't know, I'll have to think about it. I can't promise away a matter of moral principle. I can agree not to do it again right away, until we get a clearer picture of how things are going to develop with all the appeals in the courts.'

'You agree then, no breaking of the law for the time being. Will you let us know if you are planning to do it again? We don't want to be picketing there at the same time. We don't want to be associated with it.'

"Sure, I can let you know.' Mickey said, wanting to be cooperative. He wondered if the lack of support for civil disobedience was a genuinely different opinion on tactics, or if he was right and the adults were keeping themselves safe while the children died. Dora smiled in triumph at Mickey's capitulation. She was expecting he would soon be removed from pro-life with her complaints to the authorities, and would never be able to launch any rescue missions anyway.

Dolores summed up the consensus. 'If we are still present at Craigenback's, the unborn children are not dying alone. We are there in solidarity with them. Somebody loves them. We can sidewalk counsel the mothers. We can love them both.'

Everyone nodded in agreement. Except Mickey. He remained silent, aware the outcome of the meeting was the exact opposite of what he had intended and argued for, the necessity of civil disobedience.

44

'There's one more thing,' Dora said. She wanted to press the rest of her agenda for the meeting. 'I don't agree with showing gory pictures of aborted babies at the protests. We should be positive and show beautiful pictures of healthy babies and unborn children still alive.'

'Judge Dockendorff already banned the photos and pictures of aborted baby parts,' Mickey said.

'I mean if you break the law and do sit-ins at Craigenback's. If you can find anyone to join you in doing it, please don't have people standing around with the gruesome photos on their signs. That too would be breaking the law.'

'The grisly pictures telling the truth about abortion are powerful and effective. They show abortion for what it really is. The silent screams of the unborn can't be heard, but their broken bodies can be seen. Are you part of the mass denial too Dora?'

'Those ghastly pictures are offensive. Bishop Blair disapproves of them. He says the photographs of aborted babies fail to respect the human remains of the dead. He says its exploitation of their deaths.'

'A subtle point,' Charlie said. 'I didn't know Blair had it in him.'

'Blair always has refined sensibilities above the rest of us poor peasants,' Mickey said. 'He should come down in the trenches on the front lines and get his hands dirty like the rest of us.'

'We make ourselves look like weirdos, standing on public street corners holding horrible pictures,' Dora said. 'Like the man in Bowness Park who sits all day covered in signs saying THE END IS NEAR.'

'Maybe it is,' Charlie said.

'It's late,' Dolores said. 'Let's not argue tonight about what kind of pictures to use when Mickey has already agreed not to have any rescue missions right now.'

'It is a hypothetical question,' Mickey said.

Charlie questioned Dora who had taken over the meeting. 'What do you hope to achieve in the meantime, with your law abiding mainstream methods?'

'We will gradually win support for incremental limits on abortion, with laws like parental notification, Twenty four hour waiting periods, mandatory counseling and ultrasounds before abortion.'

'And leave abortion access fundamentally undisturbed?'

'For now. All we can hope for realistically in step by step change.'

'Baby steps. I don't agree with the incremental approach. We can never compromise on completely banning abortion. I could never vote for a partial law while accepting abortion goes on as usual.'

'You will never get an outright ban on abortion in today's climate Charlie,' Dora said. 'It's totally unrealistic.'

'It's a matter of principle. No compromises. No exceptions.'

'We have to dialogue with people, reach out to people

with respect and good will, find common ground. You are dreaming if you think you outlaw abortion just like that.'

'Dialogue? Are you nuts? Do you think the pro-aborts have any real interest in dialogue? It just makes them look reasonable, while they ram abortion through. They have no good faith or good will to have an honest dialogue. You're dreaming if you think you can change anything that way.'

'I'm not going to argue with you Charlie. You're being judgmental again. We have to build bridges, not burn them. Working for gradual change in the law is realistic. Dialoguing with people of different beliefs and opinions is civilized and professional.'

'You can't dialogue with the deaf. They can't hear you. You can't make the blind see. No wonder the pro-aborts always win when the pro-lifers are so naïve.'

'We can change the system from within.'

Charlie was becoming visibly agitated to the others. Would the woman never shut up he wondered. 'Then you become part of the abortion system. Partial laws won't stop a single abortion. People will get around them.'

'I wish you weren't part of this system,' Sara said.

'Too bad I wasn't aborted, Sara?'

'I didn't say that ever. It's all lies.'

'But the cellphone video shows it. It was on the six o'clock news. The whole city saw and heard it.'

'It never happened. They doctored the tape.'

Charlie suddenly stood up, noisily pushing his chair back on the tiled basement floor. 'I've had enough of you idiots for one night. I'm leaving. You're all useless. Mouthy women who love to talk.'

'Women are insuppressible Charlie' Mickey said. 'Don't you know women will be heard?'

45

'One last thing,' Dora said. Mickey sighed. The woman was completely in charge and control of the meeting now, the way she liked it. 'What is it now?'

'We should not be telling people we are against birth control in pro-life. Contraception is a separate issue. Pro-life is about abortion.'

'Contraception leads to abortion as a backup to birth control failure,' Mickey said. 'And what is called birth control is abortion, early chemical abortions. Contraception and birth control are connected. All the birth control has not brought down the number of abortions. What does that tell you?'

'No, birth control is a separate issue. It's futile if you think you can ever stop birth control in the modern world now.'

'It's futile to think you can ever stop abortion if you don't.'

'If you want to oppose contraception and abortion, making yourself a right wing minority of the Catholic Church, you will never get anywhere.'

'I'm afraid ignoring and accepting contraception will never get anywhere.'

'There's still a chance stopping abortion. Most people are somewhere in the middle, but not on contraception. Birth Control is normal life now.'

'Many people say 'I'm not against birth control, but I draw the line at abortion.' But it's too late by then, they have already opened the door to all of it.'

'If you want to define pro-life so narrowly, we are doomed to ever getting anywhere with the public. You are as rigid as Charlie.'

'Contraception, sex without children, lies at the heart of the culture of death.'

'If you feel that way, you should be a Catholic priest and preach the Vatican's line to the people. You wouldn't last long here in Bishop Blair's Diocese in Calgary. Catholics here don't accept the Church's teaching on birth control. They won't follow it, and they won't hear of it, and the priests know that, and won't speak of it. No one expects them to believe that anymore.'

"It's not Bishop Blair's Diocese.'

'Pro-life is about abortion,' Sara said, supporting her friend Dora. 'I know, let's sign a petition. Write a letter to the editor. Have a conference. With a banquet and a speaker. There's lots we can still do in pro-life about abortion.'

'There's more to it Sara,' Mickey said. 'Much more. There's embryonic stem cell research, killing embryos which is destruction of human beings. Cloning, assisted suicide, and euthanasia. Do you realize there are millions of embryos frozen in liquid nitrogen tanks stored in in vitro clinics all over the world, and not even the Church knows what to do about it? It is an insoluble problem. You can't morally dispose of the embryos, you can't morally use them for research, and you can't adopt them and put them in another woman's womb. Those embryos are human beings in an impossible situation, frozen for years in suspended animation. It's mind boggling what is going on in the name of science. Pro-life must speak out on all of it, restore respect for life and the right to life.'

'Mickey,' Dora said, 'contraception is another insoluble problem. Can't you see that? We might touch the hearts and minds of people about killing already conceived babies, but birth control is here to stay. I'm being realistic and pragmatic. You're too idealistic and unrealistic.'

'Dora has a point,' Dolores said. 'I try to show the women at the Crisis Pregnancy Center what's wrong with all the birth control junk, but contraception is conventional wisdom now.'

'The teaching of the Church has never changed on birth control. And never will. It is the natural law. It has just been ignored and set aside.'

'The Church cannot dictate everything we think and believe,' Dora said. 'We have intellectual freedom now. We can disagree with what the Cqtholic Church says, and still be good Christians. Even Catholics don't believe what their church says about birth control.'

'Your Pope even speaks out against capital punishment,' Sara said. 'That's got nothing to do with pro-life. Murderers should be executed.'

'The Pope wants the state to respect even the right to life of convicted criminals,' Dolores said. 'That's inspiring. What an example of respect for life.'

'Some terrible criminals deserve capital punishment,' Charlie said. 'Bleeding heart pro-lifers make me sick.'

Mickey wanted to defend Dolores from any attack on her: 'Let's find something we can all agree on. How about there should be burial or cremation for aborted children, instead of throwing them in the dumpster or selling their body parts and tissues for many uses. Can we all agree on that?'

Everyone nodded agreement. Dora said:

'Yes, we can take that stand for humanity.'

'Pro-aborts oppose that. They say it causes distress to the women who have abortions and tramples on their beliefs to have laws requiring humane disposal of an aborted fetus,' Charlie said.

'No surprise they oppose burial or cremation for aborted children,' Dolores said. 'They can't allow any recognition the unborn children are human beings.'

Encouraged by the agreement, Mickey tried another non-contentious issue.

'And are we all as pro-lifers agreed euthanasia and assisted suicide are against human life created by God?'

'Yes again,' Dora said. 'No argument there. Life belongs to God. Euthanasia and suicide are pro-life issues. The killing is expanding from the unborn children to the sick and elderly. Every life is valuable.'

'Good,' Mickey said. 'We don't have to fight about everything.'

'But I don't agree with your stand against vaccines derived from aborted fetuses a long time ago. Using the vaccines is moral now, it isn't cooperation with abortion.'

'Using products including vaccines that come from abortion is horrendous. What does it matter if the abortion was a long time ago? Using those vaccines gives credibility to abortion.'

'I disagree,' Sara said, 'you're always too extreme Mickey. If there is an epidemic and no other vaccines available you can use the ones involved remotely with abortion.'

'It creeps me out to think of injecting cells from aborted babies into my body.'

'It's a form of cannibalism, it you think about it,' Charlie said.

'Don't be so over the tope about everything you two.. It's really a form of organ donation from the dying.' Dora said.

'It's nothing of the kind,' Charlie objected.

'Let's not solve everything tonight,' Dolores said,

'The state is the biggest killer of all these days,' Charlie said. 'State protected abortion, and state subsidized abortion, and in countries like China, state enforced abortion.'

'It's enforced here too,' Mickey said. "Just see what happens if you try to interfere with it.'

'Yeah,' said Charlie, 'but at least here there are no laws restricting how many children you can have, and state authorities stepping in with enforced abortion.'

'Here it's all controlled by social stigma. Just have a large family and see what people feel free to say about it. Even the new Pope said Catholics don't have to breed like rabbits but should practice responsible parenthood.'

'Who cares what he says?' Charlie said. 'Just another left wing globalist one world United Nations lover controlling the freedom of people, spreading birth control and abortion over all the countries of the earth. He doesn't even believe people should have their own countries with borders. It's selfish populism to him, not his one world fraternity.'

'And he approved vaccines that come from aborted babies,'

Mickey said. 'He said it must be done. The right to life is opposed to legalized killing. That is what we are up against, legalized killing.. Think of it. That is the crux of it. Legalized killing. And then we even make use of their dead bodies.'

Dolores jumped in again. 'Please Dora, Sara, Mickey, these are big questions you're debating. We have accomplished all we can tonight I think. It's late.'

'This is important,' Mickey said. 'The babies are born alive by caesarean section, and the cells are harvested within five minutes or they are useless. The baby is alive, the heart is beating, they don't use any anesthetic as that would impact the cells, and the baby is in great pain. People just don't know what is really going on in using aborted baby cell lines to develop vaccines, and other medical research. Then the baby finally dies after birth and their body parts have been harvested.'

'The truth is ghastly,' Dolores said. 'We are all mostly in the dark.'

'I can only say one last thing. It sums up everything I have been trying to say tonight. All of our pro-life activities within the structure of the controls of a pro-abortion society are only made possible by the authorities' repressive tolerance. They tolerate some minimal non-threatening protests only to protect smooth functioning of the machine of most of it. We cannot succeed in changing things in this situation where we are controlled even in our objections, totally controlled even in our opposition. We have lost our freedoms.'

'Well said Mickey,' Charlie said. 'But you can't expect the people here at this meeting to have an interest in or understand the Marcusian principle of repressive tolerance.'

'We do what we can,' Dora said.

'We do plenty,' Sara said.

'I have one last thing too,' Dora said. 'We need a unified pro-life message. If we ever get a law against abortion again, it should only punish abortionists, not the women who have abortions. Charlie has been saying to the news reporters the women should be punished too.'

'That's right,' Charlie said. 'Women used to be punished in the abortion laws. Now you want to give them a pass. I think you are only pandering to the public, to avoid criticism pro-life is against women.'

'Women are punished already by the very act of abortion,' Dolores said. 'Heavily punished.'

'You can't eliminate the responsibility women have for abortion, even if they are victims,' Charlie said.

'We are a long way from any kind of restrictive abortion law at all,' Mickey said.

'So where do you stand on including or excluding women from charges and punishment in an abortion law?' Dora asked Mickey.

Mickey sighed.

'I don't know. I'm tired right now. I can't think. My head hurts.'

'We can still pray. We can always do that. They can't take that away from us,' Dolores said 'Again, I find that kind of talk defeatist. We can't do anything, so let's pray,' Charlie said.

'We're not going to argue about that,' Mickey said. 'The

power of prayer is great. Prayer is like entering the cave where the tiger dwells.'

'This new Pope also said the Church is obsessed with abortion, and doesn't have to talk about it all the time,' Charlie said. 'After that Bishop Blair said abortion wasn't a priority anymore.'

'I know,' Mickey said. 'How much worse and depressing could things be?'

'Weren't you leaving Charlie?' Dora said. 'You are still here arguing standing up behind your chair.'

'You want me gone?'

'I find you a negative influence.'

'I say the truth. The truth must be said.'

'The other Pope was inspiring,' Mickey said. 'John Paul 11. He said we exist in a culture of death and must work to build a civilization of love. Now that was a pro-life rallying cry: to build a whole new civilization.'

'Yet he created the College of Cardinals that voted in this undermining Pope. Just like the pro-life American presidents always appoint pro-abortion judges to the Supreme Court. You would think it was important enough to get that right.'

'That is also depressing,' Mickey said.

'The pro-life movement is incompetent and inadequate from top to bottom,' Charlie said.

'We are ordinary people up against a monumental and overwhelming problem Charlie,' Dolores said.

'An unspeakable evil,' Mickey said. 'An abominable crime.'

'What about you Charlie?' Dora said. 'Are you incompetent and inadequate?'

'Are you an emasculating bitch?' Charlie said.

Mickey didn't like Dora but he had to intervene.

'Charlie we can't talk to the women like that. That's a long way from the civilization of love.'

'High sounding phrases and rhetoric,' Charlie said, 'when we can't even have a civil discourse at a pro-life strategy meeting.'

'Let's end the meeting with a prayer,' Dolores said. 'How about the Serenity Prayer. I think it fits everything.'

And she led it:

> **God grant us the serenity**
> **To accept the things we cannot change,**
> **The courage to change the things we can,**
> **And the wisdom to know the difference,**
> **Amen.**

The meeting ended. Mickey walked home alone in the cold winter air to help his headache, walking in the dark night back to his home in the Crisis Pregnancy Center. He thought about all the disagreements. It was a wonder to him how the pro-lifers all knew abortion was wrong, something the whole world was confused about, yet they could not agree on anything else. Dora and Sara weren't so bad, they meant well, they loved the unborn. He would have to try and be patient with them. Their obnoxious hearts were in the right place. Maybe he could heal the breach and work with the. But he did not know how busy Dora and Sara were in their campaign to discredit him, to remove him from pro-life, and take over the Crisis Pregnancy Center.

46

The next day Charlie's cell phone rang.

'Charlie, the Warriors of God are calling you.'

'Oh boy, the circus has come to town.'

'What do you mean?'

'Why are you calling me?' Charlie was still sick with anger at the pro-lifers from the night before.

'We heard about the meeting last night. We think you may be one of us.'

'How did you hear about the meeting? Did you have someone there?'

'We have our sources. We heard Dora and Sara gave you all a hard time.'

'I can't stand those self-righteous old biddies. They just drip with a superiority complex they can't hide.'

'You should respect the elderly Charlie.'

'You're all the same. Willful mouthy women never know what a pain they are with their nagging and incessant chatter. Much better you should all remain seen and not heard, silent and sweet, ready to love, honor and obey. Maybe the Taliban know what they're doing.'

'Are you referring to me, or Dora and Sara?'

'Take your pick. All you women are emotional children. You only think you're logical, and then go out justified in your irrational acts. A deadly combination, stubborn pigheaded women who think they are acting with common sense. Women are stupid, even the smart ones.'

'We are nothing like those two.'

'What do you want?'

'You really shouldn't disrespect old people as a pro-lifer.'

Charlie was still fuming at all the pro-life craziness from last night. Now this one. 'So you're morally pure, you just blow people away?'

'We understand we are in a war. A culture war.'

'What's on your mind sweetheart?'

'Will you join the Warriors?'

'I'm not one of you.'

'Let's talk about it. We heard you spoke out strongly to the pro-life wimps. We feel the same way.'

'I don't join groups. Any groups.'

'We can work together for more effective direct action.'

'Groups are bureaucracies, even terrorist groups.'

'We aren't terrorists. And we have a minimum amount of structure. It's called leaderless resistance. The small cells don't know of each other. One person can even be a cell in the resistance, acting alone unknown to the others.'

'I like that idea. Consider me a cell of one, unknown to everyone else. A lone wolf.'

'You mean it? Or are you just being sarcastic?'

'You want me to be a triggerman for you?'

'We can talk about possible targets.'

'I refuse to be a pawn of the judges and politicians, the whole abortion system. Why should I be a pawn for you to move around?'

'Who said anything about using you as a pawn? We feel the same way, no one uses us either.'

'Are you a mother?'

'Yes, I have my own children.'

'Are you Catholic?'

'Yes, very much so.'

'You have a strange mind as a Catholic pro-life woman, willing to kill other mothers' sons and daughters in your holy war on abortion.'

'Abortion is the war on children and mothers. What we do in killing the killers is justifiable homicide. It's in the law.'

'I'm thinking about things, but I don't really need anyone's help.'

The voice at the other end of the line was now inquisitive. Typical woman, Charlie thought, curious, wanting to know about him. 'What are you thinking of doing?'

'Things. Nobody's business.'

'Maybe we can help you with our experience.'

'I don't need any help, and I don't join groups.'

'Don't disrespect us Charlie. I called you precisely because I respect your independent spirit. We put ourselves on the line for the unborn children. We're not like the milk and water pro-lifers, the pacifists who keep themselves safe.'

'What are you planning to do next? The Warriors have been quiet lately.'

'We will watch and wait, and then strike, as need arises. I can't tell you our plans.'

Charlie laughed again. 'But I should tell you mine?'

'You can trust us Charlie.'

'How do I know you're who you say you are? How can I know this phone call is not some undercover sting?'

'We can meet and talk.'

'A meeting could be a set up too. Filmed and recorded. You might be an undercover cop wearing a wire, with a backup crew filming from a car parked across the street.'

'You've seen too many movies. We don't meet with many people Charlie.'

'I'm honored. How many people do you have in your organization?'

'We can't talk now.'

'You know, it doesn't matter to me if it's one or a thousand. I don't join groups.'

'If you're a loose cannon Charlie, maybe you're right, maybe there is no place for you in the Warriors, acting in our name. We believe in discipline.'

'Discipline? In pro-life? Don't make me laugh.'

'It was a mistake calling you. You're not one of us.'

'Pro-life wouldn't know discipline if it came up to bite them.'

'Goodbye Charlie.'

'I'm not one or you and I'm not one of them. I'm starting to feel there's no place for me anywhere,' Charlie said, hanging up to end the unexpected and unwelcome overture from the Warriors of God. No one was going to recruit him. He was Charlie Kelly. The Warriors were just like the head bangers at the meeting last night, those futile fools who wanted to try and do something to stop it all. Might as well ban the tides of the ocean from rising, stop the waves from beating on the shore, as stop the flood of abortions sweeping the world.

I don't see any point being involved with the pro-aborts and pro-lifers fighting it out anymore, thought Charlie. *There is nothing I can do about it, and it only makes me angry all the time. Time for me to retire.*

47

In the months after Sadie ended her relationship with Rick she drifted from man to man, not caring who it was as long as she had company to get through the night. She only wanted a drinking buddy, and someone who accepted going to bed with no ties. She became known in certain drinking circles as an easy lay. Sometimes a man would grow serious and exclusive with her, but then she knew it was time to move on. Her drinking grew continually worse, and after a few months the men were not so interested in her anymore. She gained weight, and her once pretty face showed the increasing the signs of her lifestyle, her dull eyes lifeless, with no spark of life, not attracting anyone. She rarely smiled, and if she did, it was a tight smile devoid of warmth and joy, Sadie's knowing street smart smile letting people know she understood the transactions going on around her. A certain kind of man was still attracted to her easy hardness, despite her thickening face and body, the kind of man who knew what he could get from her and what it would cost, knowing it would not be much. Toxic shame was driving her now, guilt and anger, but she did not know herself, the mental obsession in her mind thought all was well.

She began to see things during her drinking, snakes crawling over her, and she huddled under the blankets wanting the awful creatures to leave her alone. The snakes pursued her beneath the blankets and she screamed, the sounds of her voice muffled under the bedclothes. She tried to shake the snakes off, scratching at herself: 'Get them off. Get them off.' But there was no one to hear her frantic fear. Then the voices started, telling her to kill herself. She could not walk over the Center Street Bridge without the voices commanding her: 'Throw yourself over,' and she held on tight to herself to make it across the bridge. Other times when she was using a knife to spread butter on the bread the voices urged her: 'Cut your throat, make an end of it, cut your throat now.'

Sadie stopped using knives, but the commanding voices still ordered her to kill herself, and she was afraid her own body was turning on her, and she resisted the voices because she did not want to be driven into madness and suicide, she did not want to kill herself against her will. At night she lay in bed with her right hand clenched around her neck protecting herself from the voices commanding her to cut her throat. She never told anyone about the voices. She was afraid they would think she was crazy and lock her up. But she did not think she was schizophrenic hearing the voices; she thought it must be the alcohol making her see snakes and hear voices, and she swore to stop drinking.

After a few days sober she felt better, and the strange sights went away, and the voices fell silent, and she felt well enough to drink again. Then the snakes and the voices returned, and she heard new voices, the small voices of children whispering 'Mom.' She looked around but no one was there. Then she heard the child voices again, both of her twins saying: 'Mom, Mom.' She did not know what to say to them, but she did answer the voices in the night, just as low and soft: 'I'm sorry. I'm sorry,' she said. Then the voices went away again.

She wasn't working anymore, living on welfare, her medical records supporting her claim for disability. When the check came in at the end of the month she joined the other regulars down at the Cecil, the cheap hotel, a rundown building in the east end of Calgary, the cement block façade painted a faded green color over the chipped walls. The lines of the blocks showed through the paint, and a large neon sign blinked on the roof, the pink letters spelling out CEC L, with the I letter burned out. The sign had not been repaired for years. Drunks sat on the outside doorstep of the Cecil Hotel in the warm summer months, sometimes wobbling to their unsteady feet to engage in pathetic fistfights when the intoxicated angry words went too far. The Beer Store was just behind the Cecil, selling cases of the precious golden liquid for the derelicts to take to the shabby places they called home.

Beside the Cecil and the Beer Store stood the Calgary Hostel for the Homeless shelter. The whole city block catering both to the drinking habits of the destitute clientele and their housing needs was an area shunned by the rest of the prosperous city. Many of the drunks and homeless did not like the city hostel with is rules and supervision, choosing to live instead under the nearby bridge across the Bow River and river pathway, all their worldly possessions in their wire shopping carts, free from bureaucratic regulations. The police were often called to the area to intervene in the drunkenness, the drug dealing, the fights, the sexual assaults and the prostitution, or to remove the people sleeping under the bridge.

She needed the feeling of people around her, as long as they did not get too close, and there she could meet a man for the night. The drink made sure no one got too close, all the drinkers at the Cecil soon losing touch with any sober talk. Sadie did not mind there was no real communication in all the drunken shouting at the tables of the cheap hotel. She did not want to talk about anything real herself. She was only there to forget. As the month went on and her welfare check was quickly spent, when she ran out of money for cigarettes, she took the discarded butts from the ashtray on the burned green tablecloth of the hotel table, and smoked them. Soon she developed gingivitis, her gums bleeding from the germs of the unknown mouths smoking the cigarettes before. To keep paying for her draft beer at the Cecil she gave herself to the men who still wanted her, going outside for a quickie in the alley behind the Cecil, standing up against the wall so the man could enter her, or going down on her knees to take him into her mouth. Sometimes she would turn around to face the wall and let the man take her from behind, but that cost him extra.

She began playing a dangerous game with herself when she was home alone, cutting her wrists, just deep enough to feel the sharp steel of the razor blade slicing her soft, warm, pulsing flesh, and watch the ooze of red blood seeping outside of her body onto her skin. She bandaged herself, and wiped off the knife, feeling in control as she cleaned up. Sometimes she mixed alcohol and pills and cutting her wrists all together, wondering how far she could go, enjoying the self-punishment, feeling the pain she thought she deserved, the pain better than the numbness of feeling nothing anymore. She had thoughts of going all the way and seeing her dead babies again, joining them on the other side. Once she filled the bathtub with warm water and lay in it, wanting to make the blood from her cut wrists flow freely under the water, hoping she might never wake up again. But she always lived; release did not come for her in her dance with death.

She hated going to bed now, dreading the nightly ghostly visits of her dead children, and wanting to avoid her other recurrent nightmare. In that dream there was a glass house, and inside a baby. The interior of the house was on fire, and there was no way in, and the baby would surely die. Sadie would bang on the glass walls, but they would not shatter, and she had to watch the baby burn. She stopped going to bed at night and went out to the Cecil every evening as long as she could, staying until the late last call when everyone had to leave the closing hotel. When she finally fell into bed she could not help crying herself to sleep, remembering them.

My children are ghosting me, Sadie thought. *Children, please stop ghosting your mother.*

The voices attacked her again as she staggered home from the Cecil, telling her to throw herself into the middle of the road in front of the oncoming cars. Sadie held on tight and refused to kill herself and somehow made it home, walking on automatic in an alcoholic blackout. When she woke up the next afternoon she could not remember how she had got back to her room. Sgt. Ryan arrested her one night as she stumbled home with her right hand clutched around her throat in the middle of the road with the traffic coming at her honking their horns and swerving around her. He took her to the drunk tank for her own protection, so she could sleep it off. Sadie woke up on the floor of the graffiti scrawled cell with no bed. Some other people arrested the night before for public intoxication were also up, hollering obscenities, demanding someone come to see them. She was confused at first, waking to find herself in a cell at the drunk tank, but after a few moments she understood she must have been arrested the night before. She could not remember why.

Sadie was relieved to find out she had not committed any crime the night before, and was being released now that she was sober again, hung-over as she was. The kindly policeman Sgt. Ryan suggested she should go to the detox unit at social services, and offered to drive her there, but Sadie said no, she just wanted to get back to her apartment. She never expected getting arrested would ever happen to her, but she was actually well known by sight to the policemen who patrolled down by the Cecil. This was the first time they had stopped her, when they saw her wandering through the dangerous traffic in the middle of the road. When Sadie saw Sgt. Ryan coming towards her she held out her wrists in front of her and said:

'Cuff me officer. Arrest me.'

'Why?'

'I want to confess.'

'What have you done?'

'It was me who killed my babies.'

'How?'

'I had two abortions.'

'That's not illegal, not a crime.'

'I should be punished. I want to be punished. It's only right. Arrest me.'

Sgt. Ryan did arrest her, but for her public drunkenness. Sadie swore off drinking after her arrest, and managed to keep her vow never to drink again for three weeks. Then the cravings started, the need for a drink, and the memory of the disgrace of her arrest was forgotten, overtaken by the stronger memories of the warm pleasure of a drink going down into her stomach and rising through her bloodstream to her brain. She promised herself she would control her drinking this time. She was a grown woman and had learned her lesson. She could drink socially and normally like everyone else, if she set her mind to it. It was only a matter of will power, and she knew she was strong willed.

Besides, she needed the drink to sleep. The terrible dreams still came every night even without any drink in her, the nightmares when the two tiny visitors came to her, reaching out to her. In one of her dreams the child was looking at her imploringly, the child crying and asking her, 'Mommy can you save me?' When she reached out to the child he faded into the distance, unreachable. And she feared the other ghostly visitor who came to her in her dreams every night, the man in the white gown, and the mask over his face, and the cap over his hair, coming at her with sharp hooked knives, and she woke up screaming. One night the ghostly man in white loomed over her, staring at her with only one eye, and she ran out into the street and grabbed a stranger and begged for help: 'He's looking at me, He's looking at me,' she tried to explain, but the stranger shrugged the mad woman off and went on his way.

Sadie returned home to bed, and crawled under the covers and slept fitfully again, tossing and turning from side to side. 'Where are my children?' she said, when she awoke in the afternoon again, and consciousness gradually returned to her in the midday light, and she discovered herself lying in bed in her cheap room in the boarding house. 'Where are my children?' Then she remembered, and it hit her again. 'My babies are dead,' she shouted, alone in the empty room, no crib in the corner. 'My babies are dead.' Racking sobs of grief convulsed her alone on the bed, with no one to hear.

48

Nearly a year after the meeting of all the pro-life groups back in January, nothing much was happening in the pro-life movement anymore. Abortion was a dead issue in Calgary. Another winter was coming, the November days darkening early in the evening dusk, the air colder and the clouds grayer. Autumn was over; all the leaves had fallen from the trees and blown away, leaving the bare branches etched against the somber sky. The agreement reached at the Pro-life Intergroup Strategy Session was also dead, collapsing over the year. The pro-lifers in the different groups no longer spoke to one another. Judge Dockendorff had removed old Sara one mile away from the Craigenback Abortion Clinic, and Mickey did not defend her in court, agreeing she was an inappropriate protester better not seen or heard.

Dora and Sara did not forgive this latest disloyalty, his betrayal of pro-life in their eyes, and were more committed than ever to his own removal from pro-life completely. If any new volunteers or financial donors arrived to support Mickey, they were soon turned away by the angry women, who told them he was a renegade not supported by the other pro-lifers, the legitimate pro-life movement in Calgary. The Crisis Pregnancy Center found it difficult to continue operating under the attacks from both outside and within pro-life. Because of the injunction on the telephone line, and the court ordered signs on the front door and inside office walls, hardly any women came to the Center for counseling anymore, only a handful referred by local churches for help. The silent telephone calls watching the Center were still coming in every day, conveying an eerie hostility in the atmosphere making the volunteers uncomfortable before they quit. Some few loyal counselors remained, including Dolores and Julie.

Abortion was entrenched in Calgary as an accepted way of normal life, all the efforts of the pro-lifers ineffective to stop it. Dora's strategy of gradual progressive change brought no positive results. Mickey felt he was released from his promise, and decided he must begin his campaign of civil resistance at Craigenback's, even if no one joined him. At least he could be one person who was a sign of contradiction to the abortion system, someone who did not accept it. Early one morning, he padlocked the front door of the Craigenback Abortion Clinic once more in protest of the continuing legal abortion in Calgary. If the law and authorities would not defend the right to life of the unborn children, he would close down the abortion mill himself, but without violence.

After locking the door, he stood within the buffer zone the pro-lifers were not permitted to enter on the sidewalk in front of Craigenback's, and held a protest sign with a picture of Jesus, and the mangled body of an aborted child, with the words in large bold letters ABORTION KILLS CHILDREN. In those simple actions, locking the door, and holding an illegal sign with prohibited words and pictures in the buffer zone his right to life rebellion was complete, violating all four of Judge Dockendorff's injunctions at Craigenback's. He did not challenge the fifth and sixth injunctions, the ones blocking the Crisis Pregnancy Center's phones, nor did he take down the signs on the walls at the Center. He could not do anything about the telephone company, and if he took the signs on his office down he ran the risk of losing the house. The pro-lifers still needed the house as their basis of operations, and he was reluctantly forced to accept the situation.

He held a press conference standing in front of the locked doors while holding his restricted sign, saying to the reporters his actions were in the tradition of non-violent civil disobedience, making the symbolic statement the abortion clinic should be closed by the whole community, and calling for people to join him and support his actions. He did not get far in his speech before Sgt. Ryan and three other policemen arrested him. As the four policemen carried the limp body of Mickey by his arms and legs to the waiting paddy wagon, the reporters from the Daily Record and the television stations filming him continued interviewing him with their microphones stuck close to his face, the reporters walking along beside the policemen who ignored them.

'Why are you making this public defiance of the law, and why did you call us?' one of the reporters asked him. 'Isn't this just a publicity stunt? Aren't you orchestrating your own arrest?'

Mickey turned his head to speak into the microphone the reporter was holding close to face as the police carried him away. 'I am expressing my political, religious, free speech, peaceful assembly and all constitutional rights to be a dissenting minority in a free democracy. It's not a stunt. It they left me alone, I would still be there in front of the clinic, doing my part to stop abortion, the killing of the innocent. I represent true law and order.'

The reporter laughed. 'Quite a speech, under the circumstances.' The reporter started to ask him another question, but the mid arrest interview was interrupted when Mickey was thrown into the open back doors of the waiting police van, and the doors were closed sealing him off from sight. A policeman now carried the sign of Jesus Mickey had been holding. His sign of Jesus and the aborted child had been seized as evidence to be produced against him at the coming trial. He was taken in the arrest van to the local police station, and when he was led inside the front door the officer on duty behind the counter smiled and greeted him. 'The abortion clinic must be open.'

Mickey was searched and all of his belongings taken away, including his belt and shoelaces, his watch, and even his pocket sized New Testament he had hoped to read while imprisoned in the holding cell. He thought they might leave him his Bible, that he had constitutional rights to religious consolation even in jail. When he was photographed and fingerprinted, the police technician said to him softly, so no one else could hear: 'You have some good points Mickey, but you go too far.'

Mickey just as quietly responded: 'They went too far the first time they ever legally killed an unwanted child. Killing the first one opened the floodgates for all the slaughter now.' The police technician continued fingerprinting him in silence, smearing the black ink on his fingers and pressing his fingers and thumb on the identification cards used for the criminals. Then he was thrown into a dormitory cell with other prisoners, to await his arraignment when Judge Dockendorff was available.

He lay on a bunk between two thieves. One of the thieves berated him: 'You're a jerk,' the thief said. 'We take care of jerks in here.' The other thief defended him: 'Leave him alone. He shouldn't even be in here.' Mickey was worried a fight might break out over him, but the two prisoners were only talking tough. 'Those are fancy clothes you're wearing,' the first prisoner said, looking Mickey over and noticing his dress clothes. "And nice shoes. I bet you eat the best foods.'

'You got me wrong," Mickey said. 'I'm not a big shot.'

The prisoner laughed at him, and Mickey wondered at how the dispute over abortion went on everywhere, even among the inmates in jails.

A guard came to the dormitory cell and called out through the bars "Finnegan!', and he was marched to the courtroom to face the judge. The guards shackled him in handcuffs and leg irons for the walk, and two uniformed policemen wearing holstered guns walked on each side of him, escorting him as if he was the most dangerous of criminals, and might make a desperate attempt to escape. In the courtroom he stood in the prisoner's box in the center of the room, and four uniformed policemen also armed stood around the four walls. One of the policemen was a woman, and she looked straight into his eyes, staring at him with undisguised hatred. Mickey had a sense she would be pleased to shoot him if he gave her the slightest excuse. He wondered why the abortion system took so many precautions for one lone, non-violent and powerless pro-lifer. What was it they were all so afraid of? He noticed Sgt. Ryan standing in his place against the back wall.

49

'Ms. Summers?'

The nurse at the Free Clinic called Sadie in from the waiting room. Sadie got up from her chair and followed her to the inside room. The results of her tests last week were back. The lumps in her breasts worried her. They hurt, putting pressure on her outer skin, causing her to break out in spider veins pushed out from below. Only eleven months had passed after her abortion last Christmas, so she had gone for the tests, as much as she hated doctors now. She took another seat in the inner counseling room. A few minutes later a new doctor doing his weekly volunteer work at the welfare clinic opened the door, walked into the room, and sat behind the desk. He was not the same doctor she saw last week-the doctors always changed at the Free Clinic for the poor people. He smiled at her. 'I'm Dr. Crawford. How are you today?'

'Fine, thank you.'

The doctor grew serious. 'I'm afraid you're not fine. The tests are positive. They confirm you have stage three breast cancer. In both breasts.'

'How can that be. I'm still so young. Only twenty-two.'
'Could be many factors. Genetics, lifestyle, trauma.'
'I nearly died from an abortion last Christmas.'
'I see it all here in your file.'
'It's a bad memory. I don't like to talk about it.'

'I understand. You have had two abortions, and you were also on the birth control pill since you were an adolescent, and you have never had a child. A woman's first childbirth helps transform her breast tissue to stabilize if from the carcinogenic effects of the Pill and abortion.'

'Why would the doctors give me cancer causing pills?'

'All I can tell you is the birth control pill is a class one carcinogen according to the World Health Organization. Patients are generally warned about the possible risks. Didn't your doctor talk to you? Did you read the warnings that come with the pill packages?'

'Everyone downplayed any risks.' But Sadie remembered the woman Dolores at the Crisis Pregnancy Center who had tried to warn her, and she had not listened. 'What are my chances?'

'You have an aggressive cancer that is inoperable. Chemotherapy and radiation may buy you a little time. With a double mastectomy done immediately you might live longer. Otherwise, you only have a few months to live.

'Aren't there side effects with chemotherapy?'

'Yes, fatigue, immune system weakening, hair loss.'

'First you butchers took out all my insides, everything that made me a woman, and now you want to cut off both my breasts? Make all my hair fall out?'

Dr. Crawford retained his smooth professional poise in front of the angry street person patient with her crude ways of speaking. He could understand she was distressed at the bad news of the tests. 'I'm sorry. You've had some tough breaks. But as a doctor, I am not personally responsible for what happened to you. I have never seen you before.'

Sadie jumped out of her chair. 'And you won't see me again, you smug little prick,' she shouted at him, and she stormed out of the office, slamming the door against the wall, and stalking through the waiting room to reach the front doors and get out.

50

The court clerk called out: 'All Stand.' Judge Dockendorff entered the courtroom from the door behind his elevated judge's desk. He took his seat, and looked at Mickey standing in the prisoner's box. 'Well Mr. Finnegan, what do you have to say for yourself this time?'

Mickey had lost his access to his painkiller pills in jail, and his head was aching as he faced Judge Dockendorff yet again, but he talked through his pain.

'Your Honor, for a law properly to be a law, it must satisfy four tests according to St. Thomas Aquinas—'

'What on earth are you talking about? This is a court, not a schoolroom.'

Mickey shrugged. 'You asked me what I have to say for myself. This is what I want to say.'

'It's all irrelevant. You should get a lawyer. You are in serious trouble.'

'I am explaining my mental state to you, my thoughts and motivations. That's all relevant to crime and punishment.'

'You have been warned to get a lawyer. Whatever you say now will only seal your fate.'

'Nevertheless, I wish to explain myself to the court.'

'Proceed, but I warn you I will cut you off if necessary. You will do no grandstanding here in my courtroom.'

'Thank you, Your Honor. As I was saying, St. Thomas sets

out four tests for a just law. It must be an ordinance of right reason, promulgated by the proper authority for the common good. Those are the four tests: right reason, promulgated, proper authority, the common good.'

Judge Dockendorff glanced to the side, looking through the courthouse windows. He was bored already. Mickey was not going to let himself be demeaned by the judge's obvious show of indifference. He continued his philosophical argument. 'Your injunction does not meet all of the four tests for a just law. You are the proper authority, and your orders have been publicly proclaimed by you, but they are not according to right reason, and they are not for common good. Your court orders protect the killing of innocent children and harm women. Therefore, they are not binding laws.'

Judge Dockendorff turned his attention away from the windows and back to Mickey. He had heard him.

'St. Thomas Aquinas is not before me. He is beyond my jurisdiction. This is not a schoolroom to argue the philosophy of law. This is a practical courtroom.'

'I have just explained to you why I disobeyed the court orders.'

'Then you admit your guilt.'

'No, I am not guilty of breaking the law when it is an unjust law.'

'Your reasoning is vague, not legally precise. What, pray tell, is the common good? And who makes that determination?'

'St. Thomas defines the common good as a set of conditions in which people can find their human fulfillment.'

'By that definition, abortion is part of the common good,

giving women freedom and increased options to fulfill their life's ambitions.'

'You make an incorrect judgment on the common good. When abortion comes first, women come last, and unborn children come in dead last. Women deserve better than abortion. There's no good in abortion. It damages all of society and everyone in it. Far from the common good, abortion leads to the common harm.'

'Well, Mr. Finnegan, it seems the common good is subject to interpretation, is a debatable notion, and society disagrees with you about what is best for women. I don't see why that is any business of yours at all.'

'Because-'

'Mister Finnegan, I have given you some leeway, but for the life of me I cannot understand what abortion and St. Thomas Aquinas have to do with disobeying a court order. I have already ruled St. Thomas Aquinas is not before me. You are before me, before this court, brought here for breaking the law. You are in contempt of court. You have just confessed you do not respect the law and deliberately broke it.'

'Confessed? I have not-'

'Court is recessed until tomorrow morning while I consider the appropriate sanction for you. Clearly, fines and imprisonment do not deter you. You use the court as a public platform to advance publicity for your cause. You enjoy the martyrdom. I order you to appear before me tomorrow morning at ten o'clock for your sentence. You will remain in custody until that time.'

'I haven't even had a trial. No evidence has been presented

against me. My protest sign, my press release are all in the possession of the police. Don't they even have to prove the case against me, if you want to be legally specific?'

Judge Dockendorff ignored him. 'Court is adjourned,' he said, arose and left.

51

Sadie went directly from the Free Clinic to take her usual seat at the Cecil Hotel. She wanted nothing to do with doctors anymore, preferring to dull the pain from her cancer with alcohol and the street drugs floating around the Cecil. The codeine painkillers, the Percocet and Oxycontin, were always available if you had the right connections, and had the price. When her welfare check ran out before the end of the month and she was broke, her body would be the price. Sadie was just waiting to die. She did not care anymore; in her deep depression she had given up on life. She was dying of self-loathing as much as the cancer, and there was no doctor for that.

In her drunken reverie she idly burned herself again on her arms with cigarettes as she sat in the Cecil, making herself feel the pain. No one paid any attention to her bizarre actions. The acrid smell of her burning hair and skin was nauseating, but it made her feel something. Sitting lost in her intoxicated brooding in the Cecil, a new idea gradually came to her. It would be her last mission in life, the one thing she could do. Sadie did not tell anyone about her idea for her last mission, but the more she sat over her glasses of draft beer in the cheap hotel, and the more she thought about it, the clearer her new idea seemed. She would need a little assistance, but she could keep most of it to herself.

Bernie joined her at her table, and she took the first step in her plan. She knew Bernie liked her, and knew she could get him to help her. He was a regular down at the Cecil, and knew many people. His matted hair and beard, the tattoos on his bare arms beneath his dirty black T-shirt fit right in with the other regulars. They trusted him as one of their own. He was skinny, his biceps slack in his muscle T-shirt, his skin of his face bleached white from lack of exposure to the sunlight and from his use of crack cocaine, which he sold to his customers at the Cecil.

'Hi Babe,' Bernie said to Sadie, sitting down opposite her at the small round table, covered with green terry cloth to soak up spilled beer. 'What can I do you for?'

Sadie gave Bernie one of her most welcoming smiles, feigning human emotions she could no longer feel, a cracked smile showing her yellowing teeth from her smoking, her front tooth chipped from a fall on her face one night. Bernie was enchanted, and Sadie saw it. 'Maybe there is something you can do for me.'

Bernie was hopeful. Sadie never showed any interest in him before, usually rebuffing his advances.

Sadie was known in the Cecil to get up and walk away without a word to sit at another table alone if anyone tried to talk to her. She did not even bother making any excuses to suddenly get up and move to her own separate space in silence. The denizens of the Cecil accepted her quirks. and Bernie was very surprised she spoke to him.

'Name it Babe.'

'It's a secret. If I tell you, how do I know I can trust you not to say anything?'

Bernie leered. 'Trust me. You know I want to do something for you.' He licked his lips, wondering if she got it.

Sadie leaned over to Bernie to whisper, the bar room noisy from blaring music from the jukebox, and people talking over the noise, making it hard to hear one another. 'Can you get me a gun?'

Bernie was startled at the unexpected request. Sadie was not part of the criminal circle down at the Cecil. She was known as a juicehead, and an easy lay, but she had always refused him before. He resented her treating him as unworthy. Who did she think she was, the Queen of Sheba?

'Why do you need one?'

Sadie continued her flirtatious innocence. 'A girl has to look after herself.'

'From who? Tell me. I'll take care of him.'

Sadie saw she could manipulate the tough male hero. 'No, don't get involved. I'd just feel safer if I had a gun at my boardinghouse. People keep moving in and out, and strangers are always knocking on my door. The place is a zoo. It's dangerous.'

'Move.'

'The place suits me. It's cheap. It's close to here. I'll probably never use the gun, but I'd feel better if I had some protection.'

'Have you ever used one?'

Sadie widened her smile. 'No. But you can teach me.'

'Guns are expensive.'

'Maybe you can help me,' Sadie said, 'looking straight into Bernie's befuddled eyes, 'and I can help you.'

He had always tried to impress her he was a tough man, and now he was being put to her feminine test. He wanted to pass the test. 'I can get you one, but you don't know how to shoot.'

'We can go somewhere, take that camping trip you mentioned, and you can teach me. And I can teach you what I know.' Sadie laughed teasingly, and raised her glass of beer to take a drink, looking at Bernie over the top of the glass, staring deep into his eyes.

Bernie was delighted with Sadie's unmistakable offer of herself, the chance to be alone with her. He knew a secluded wilderness spot not too far from the city. He had tried to get Sadie there before. He was one of the few men at the Cecil who had his own car, an older Ford pickup truck with a cracked windshield and noisy muffler. The two regular denizens of the dark and smoky hotel barroom talked about their planned trip to the country over their drinks.

'Sure, in Wolf Creek,' Bernie said, thinking of the conservation area just outside the city limits. 'It's private there, except on the long weekends.'

Sadie lit another cigarette from her smoldering butt. 'We can go during the week. I'm free if you are. The change would be good. Fresh air and blue skies.' She took a drag on her new cigarette.

Sadie dangled the dream of a day in the country with her, and the even better promise of a long night with her. Bernie ordered another round of draft beer for both of them, and they talked some more, planning their nice trip to the outdoors, their first date, both of them enjoying the fantasy.

52

The next morning Mickey was brought to court from the jail cells again, and again guarded by four armed policemen stationed around the walls of the courtroom. He had the book he wanted for his statement before sentencing, using his one phone call to ask Dolores to bring it to him. She handed the book up to him in the prisoner's box where he was again standing, facing Judge Dockendorff.

'Mr. Finnegan, I have deliberated carefully over an appropriate sentence for you—'

'Your Honor, I believe a man about to be sentenced is allowed to make a statement to the court, is he not?'

Dockendorff sighed at Mickey's interruption, but since the whole city of Calgary was watching through the news media present, he allowed it. 'Proceed. But I warn you again, any speeches will be curtailed if necessary.'

'Isn't this one time a prisoner is allowed to say something personal, even if it is not legally professional?'

'Proceed.'

'Yesterday during my trial in which I confessed I was guilty of not recognizing an unjust law as binding upon me, such as laws which enforce abortion rights, I quoted St. Thomas Aquinas. Today at my sentencing I wish to quote to you the words of Pope John Paul 11 from his encyclical *The Gospel of Life*—'

'The Pope has no authority inside this courtroom Mr. Finnegan.'

'Bear with me Judge. It's only one short quote which goes to my state of mind and motivation, why I did what I did, and how I feel about it now. Every defendant has the right to say something before sentencing.'

'Defendants usually apologize to mitigate the coming sentence. I have a feeling Mr. Finnegan, you are impenitent and will only compound your situation. I advise you to be careful.'

'Thank you, Your Honor.' Mickey read from the Pope's letter to the world, the same passage he read to the assembled pro-lifers at the Pro-life Intergroup Strategy Session back in January:

> *Paragraph 73. Abortion and euthanasia are crimes which no human law can claim to legitimize. There is no obligation in conscience to obey such laws; instead there is a grave and clear obligation to oppose them by conscientious objection.'*

Mickey handed the Pope's book up to Judge Dockendorff so he could read the paragraph himself. Dockendorff read it briefly, handing the book back to the court clerk to return to Mickey. The Judge did not want the Pope's encyclical to part of the court record. St. Thomas Aquinas, the Pope, and Mickey Finnegan were a threat to established law and order. If all the Catholics started following the obligation to oppose legal abortion the whole system would fall apart.

Anarchy would result. Hard won freedom of choice and abortion rights would be lost. Judge Dockendorff himself as a Catholic would have to resign, or even more inconceivable, rule in Mickey's favor. This problem must be dealt with.

Mickey remained adamant he had nothing to apologize for in his sentencing statement to the court: 'Your Honor, I have no choice. I must in conscience as a Catholic, as a man, before God, disobey your wrong and unjust court orders enforcing the killing of innocent children.'

Judge Dockendorff was incensed at Mickey's direct accusations against him.

'Mr. Finnegan, God is not before me. The Pope is not before me. St. Thomas Aquinas is not before me. Your conscience is not before me. You are before me, brought here by the police. Your deliberate actions in defiance of the law are before me. That is all that is before me. If you refuse obedience to the law, then I too have no choice. I sentence you to a lump sum fine and court costs of two hundred and fifty thousand dollars, that is two, five, zero, zero, zero dollars, payable to the Craigenback Abortion Clinic. Failure to pay the fine and court costs will result, not in imprisonment, but a ban on you from bringing any more legal actions in the court. The ban from court is a just remedy for your contempt of court disobeying a court order.'

'I do confess one thing Judge. Since we are all mostly Catholics here, I wanted to get down to the Christian sources of law, and Catholic beliefs and teaching about the law, in the great traditions of western civilization.'

'So you think it is your place to teach me the law, Mr.

Finnegan?'

'I believe it is the Church's place to teach us the law, from God's commandments down, and our place as Catholics to obey those laws.'

'Have you never heard of separation of Church and State? That is our system now, not the theocracy you apparently would prefer, but which no longer exists. We have religious freedom now.'

'And where has it led? To legalized killing of the innocent. That can't be true purpose of the rule of law. That's just license.'

'You must obey the law.'

'I do obey the law, the higher law, God's law higher than your human law. Your law protects abortion. God's law forbids it.'

'These higher law philosophies are quite dangerous.'

'Dangerous to what?'

'The day's matters have been concluded. This court is now adjourned.'

Judge Dockendorff stood up. The court clerk said: 'All rise.' Then the judge exited the court through the door in the wall behind his giant elevated desk.

53

The next day Mickey made his arguments in a follow up hearing in the court about his penalties.

'Your Honor, you know I don't have any money. And you know I have taken a stand on principle pro-lifers do not pay money to support abortion. Now you have ordered me to pay a fine directly to the abortion clinic, something you know I can never do.'

'Mr. Finnegan, how you choose to accept the sentence of the court is entirely up to you. It is well established in law that an appropriate sanction for contempt of court orders is a ban on the offender bringing actions in the court.'

'The right of free access to the courts is fundamental in a democracy, including the right to self-defense against any charges. You leave me stripped of any legal rights, and crippled in my pro-life work. I now have no legal rights at all, just like the poor unborn children.'

'You call breaking the law pro-life work? It's simple. If you will refuse to recognize the authority of the court, you are banned from the court. Your conscience is not supreme. This court is supreme, and will be obeyed.'

'I cannot and will not pay the fine to Craigenback.'

'That is your choice. You will not be appearing in my court again except as a bound and gagged prisoner if you break the law and are arrested for harassing the abortion clinic again.'

Jessica Sterne stood up, representing Craigenback. 'Your Honor, we have done a title search on the house used for the Crisis Pregnancy Center where Mr. Finnegan both lives and works. He is the registered owner. We ask your court order today for fines and costs awarded to us also be enforced against the house for non-payment.'

'Granted. I see no reason to change standard procedure in this case. Mr. Finnegan, you will find your vigilante justice is extremely expensive if you go against the law and the court. So ordered. The house can be seized to satisfy any unpaid court judgments.'

'But I have the right to the appeal period before any actions are taken,' Mickey said. "Isn't that right.'

'I'm sure the Craigenback Abortion Clinic will act properly,' Mr. Finnegan.

'Yes, Your Honor,' Jessica Sterne said. 'We believe in the rule of law.'

Judge Dockendorff decided to make a speech of his own:

'The matters before me are concluded. Let me clearly warn you Mr. Finnegan. If you ever break the law again, the full weight of the law will fall upon you and crush you, I promise you. You are the leader of this rabble of lawbreakers calling itself pro-life. You will find the authority of this court is strong, Mr. Finnegan. This court will do its duty and discharge its responsibilities. This court will be obeyed. You have been warned, If you disagree with the law, you have the appropriate democratic means to change it. Break the law again, and there will be a judgment coming. Court is adjourned.'

Dockendorff was speaking to the whole city through the assembled news media in court. He would turn Mickey Finnegan the greatest rebel into the greatest example not to interfere with the abortion system. Dockendorff was satisfied his message had triumphed and rose to leave. The court clerk called out 'All Stand', but Mickey sat down in the prisoner's box, ignoring him. Judge Dockendorff hesitated a moment at this latest contempt of court, but decided he had Mickey under control and the judge exited through the door behind his desk.

The next day the pro-life groups in the city distributed a press release dissociating themselves from the outlaw activities of Mickey Finnegan. Smiling Jake Corcoran, Dora Wood, Sara Allgood, and Bishop Horace Blair all the signed the press release:

> We are law-abiding citizens in pro-life. We obey the abortion laws, and when the law is changed to once again protect the right to life of unborn children, we expect people to obey those laws as we obey the laws now. Mickey Finnegan and the Crisis Pregnancy Center do not represent or speak for the majority of the pro-life citizens of Calgary. Despite the large amounts of publicity he receives for his radical activity, he really has no support. Mickey Finnegan is a minority fringe element of the true pro-life movement in Calgary.

Mickey's blinding headache was paralyzing him when he read the Daily Record and saw the press release. He had to lie down and take some more painkillers to cope with this demanding ordeal. He needed to think, and he needed to act in the limited time remaining to him during the appeal period. At least he was released from custody, and could plan his next moves. The delays caused by Dockendorff's insistence on procedural correctness had given him some time. He might lose his beloved house to Craigenback, and the new owner could do whatever he liked with it, even turn it into another abortion mill. Mickey would never let that happen. He would burn the house down first.

Everything he had done to try to establish true law and order had been twisted and used against him, but he could still use some legal rules to his advantage, even if he no longer had access to the courts. Like the unborn children, he could not come to court and be recognized, could not claim the law applied to him. He had no standing. He was a nonperson without legal rights. They owned him now, owned his house, owned anything else that once was his. He had to think, had to find a way out.

54

Mid-November, a week later on a Wednesday Bernie and Sadie drove in his truck to the Wolf Creek conservation area. They set up their small pup tent in one of the interior campsites and started a fire. Sadie thought it was lovely, sitting around the campfire, drinking some beers, cooking hotdogs on sticks held over the open nighttime flames, warmed by the blazing red-blue yellow flames of the burning logs in the chilly November air and smoking a joint, even if Bernie was boring. They did some lines of coke off the wooden picnic table at the campsite. Later they slept together in the tent and Sadie gave herself to Bernie, trading he sexual favors for the gun he said he had but would not show her yet. Bernie thought it was odd she insisted on keeping her blouse on, and climbed on top, and would not let him touch her breasts.

The next morning he showed her how the gun worked, a semi-automatic nine millimeter Beretta. 'It's lightweight with great stopping power. You can cock the hammer and set if for a short pull of the trigger instead of a long pull. That'll be easier for you with your woman's hands.'

Sadie fastened her interest on the gun. She loved the feel of it in her hands. 'Will it kill someone?'

'If you're close to your target it'll stop him permanent. Best to aim for the upper body area, that's the biggest target.'

Bernie showed her how the safety and automatic magazine

worked to load the Beretta, how to rack the slide to load the first bullet into the firing chamber, how to use her thumb to manually cock the hammer for the first shot for the short trigger pull. All the automatic shots would be a short pull after the first one.

'You might be surprised at first how noisy it is,' Bernie said. 'Have you ever handled a gun before?'

'No, never. Guns have always scared me.'

'You might get comfortable with this one after some practice. It will be yours.'

They used empty beer cans set up on rocks for target practice. Sadie was surprised how tight the trigger was, how hard it was to pull it. Her shooting was wildly off from hitting any cans when she started shooting, and she kept moving closer and closer to try and hit something. Finally she was three feet away, and still had troubled hitting any of the cans. Bernie showed her how to use a two-handed grip, steadying the wrist of her shooting hand to make it easier for herself.

'Don't look at the can. Look down the barrel of the gun towards the target. It will help your aim. You're pulling your shots down to the right a little bit. That's why you're missing.'

Sadie thought she would have to get very close to her target to make sure of a direct hit. A shotgun would be better, but would be impossible to smuggle in. She would have to make do with the Beretta hidden in her purse. If she handled things rights she might be able to get really close and have the time to fire more than one shot. She fired again at the beer cans, steadying the gun with both hands, her feet firmly planted, squinting down the barrel of the gun with her eyes, and the can in front of her went flying away from her, tumbling through the air. Bernie praised her.

Sadie flushed with excitement at her triumph. She enjoyed the feeling of power flooding through her; she had fired a gun and hit the target. She practiced some more, and she hit the cans again, and from further away. She loved the feeling of shooting and hitting the cans again and again. Her confidence in her mission began to build.

Bernie saw her excitement. 'Do you think you could really shoot someone Sadie?'

She smiled at Bernie, a private smile meant just for him in their new intimacy, and held her finger to her pursed lips, and blew on her finger as if she had just fired it and was blowing away the smoke. She could drop him now she had the gun. Bernie was surprised at the answer she acted out with her finger. He had expected her to say something like she didn't know if she could shoot someone. She lightly touched her finger on Bernie's lips:

'Secret.'

55

In the afternoon of Christmas Eve, Dolores and Mickey sat in the waiting room of the Crisis Pregnancy Center, discussing Judge Dockendorff's penalties against him and what Mickey was going to do next. Both Mickey and Dolores had something to say to each other that would change their lives forever. They did not know of Sadie's preparations for her secret mission, an event which would also change their lives. Dolores sat behind Julie's reception desk facing the front door, and Mickey sat in one of the chairs for the clients in the waiting room. On the desk lay the remains of an informal Christmas party they had just shared with Julie, and some other last volunteers at the Center: sandwiches and pizza slices, Cokes, and a crumbled Christmas fruitcake. Mickey leaned over the desk, and picked up a slice of the cake, trying to keep the pieces from falling into his lap. Dolores handed him a paper napkin. It was their last meal together.

'Do you remember today is the anniversary of Judge Dockendorff's order to put pro-life signs on our front door and office walls?' Mickey asked her. 'It was one year ago today, right on Christmas Eve.'

Dolores looked at the hated sign on the reception room wall, placed there by the Sheriff at Judge Dockendorff's direction.

This Crisis Pregnancy Center does not offer or refer for Abortion or Birth Control Services

'Not much of an anniversary to celebrate.'

The time had come; he had to tell her now when they were alone. 'Dolores, this is hard to say, but I have been thinking of moving.'

Dolores was surprised, especially since she too was soon leaving. 'Moving? Where?'

'Somewhere in Asia. I will be an expatriate, a refugee from the Canadian abortion system, an exile.'

Dolores laughed. 'Are you kidding?' She saw he wasn't. 'What? You mean leaving Canada?' Mickey nodded.

'What will you do?' Dolores asked.

'Live in some Catholic country where abortion is illegal. I'm sick of being arrested, sick of being under the control of Catholic mediocrities like Lester Dockendorff who go along with the abortion system, become the system.'

'The pro-aborts are in control here.'

'I won't take it anymore.'

'I never thought you would quit, and run away.'

'I tried and failed. I wasted all those years, all my time and work, studying the law and going to court. All futile from the start, a pro-lifer going for justice to the pro-abortion courts.'

Mickey looked out the front window at the sidewalk, as if he hoped someone would come walking to the door for an appointment. All he saw was poor Ethel, walking back and forth to burn off her manic energy so she would not have to go back to the hospital.

'I can't imagine Calgary without you,' Dolores said. 'You'll leave quite a hole.'

'We all come and go. I'll soon be forgotten. I was never an

important person, only a fringe pro-life activist.

Dolores turned her mind to practical considerations. 'What about the house? If you don't appeal and don't pay the fines, won't you lose it to Craigenback?'

'I sold the house.'

Dolores stood, and walked back and forth behind the desk a few paces before she could speak. 'You sold the house?'

'Yeah, I couldn't let Craigenback get it.'

'Speaking of that, how did Dora and Sara seize Center's bank account?'

'Sgt. Ryan told them they could take the bank account if they had a good reason and a witness.'

'Doesn't sound right.'

'Shows how much he knows about the law. You need a court order to seize a bank account.'

'You should have taken Dora's name off the bank records.'

'I messed up. Too much trust in human goodness.'

'Wasn't the bank suspicious when she cleaned out the account?'

'I asked them about it the next day. They said four women came in at ten minutes before closing time. They never saw Dora before, but her name and signature was on the bank records with signing authority, so they gave her everything. They said it was noticeable how the four women clustered about the teller's counter, watching everything closely, like good witnesses. They gave her a bank draft and then she gave it to the government.'

'Remember when she came back to the office after you fired her, and hung around for a long visit, and when we were all busy and our backs were turned, she photocopied some of our documents to take to the government?'

'Another mistake I made, letting her come back for a visit. I didn't want to be mean to her.'

'When big companies fire people, they have security escort them to the door.'

'I escorted Dora to the door before, but I let her come back again. We always try to be Christians, but she just wanted to drop the dime on us.'

'They gave the money from our bank account to the government?'

'Yeah. They said it was money we obtained for a fraudulent crisis pregnancy center. We don't have any money any more.'

'What happened to the rest of our volunteers. This place is empty now.'

'Most of them quit right away. They got scared off with all the pressure on the Center. Friends of Dora and Sara watching us come and go. The silent telephone calls. Dockendorff's court orders against me. Now talk about police investigations and charges and raids. Dora called them all at home and scared them She called Julie too. Dora even threatened Julie she would lose her baby Jeffrey to social services after she went to jail for working here.'

'Can you get the money back from the government?'

'It will take a long time to get it back, if ever.'

'Can you put out an emergency fundraising letter to our mailing list?'

'And tell them what exactly? Some disgruntled pro-life volunteers raided our bank account, and their donations were all taken, and could they please send us some more money to make up for the shortfall? You can't tell people when crazy stuff goes on. Right now, it's all behind the scenes, nothing in the news. I'm leaving anyway. Let them have their victory.'

'Are there any police investigations?'

'Of us, or Dora and Sara and Sgt. Ryan?'

Dolores could not believe what was happening. 'Anyone. Everyone.'

'No investigations. I called the police chief, and his spokesman said if I had a complaint against Sgt. Ryan and Dora and Sara I should sue them all in civil court to get the money back.'

'So our bank account is stolen, and the police were involved in the theft, and now they want to stay out of it?'

'I don't care about the police. I hate it I have to suffer because of Dora and Sara and their personality problems. I just want to do my own suffering, not their's"

'Do you think they are suffering? They seem well pleased with themselves.'

'They are inherently suffering. As the Poet said:

'Their curse is as mine is, To be their sweating selves, but worse.'

'Sgt. Ryan is responsible. Dora called me too, really stressed his police authority.'

'He's just a policeman she knows. Goes to mass at the same parish, Sacred Heart, the same one we do. His wife works with them at Women United For Families. Nothing official about it.'

'So the house and the money are all gone.'

'I'm sure Dora and Sara felt quite justified and moral.'

'This makes me mad. Those women are crazy. Why can't they put their efforts into closing down Craigenback, instead of destroying a crisis pregnancy center?'

'I'm afraid the people in pro-life are often a great disappointment.'

'Not all of them.'

'Julie knew what they were planning, but she kept silent.'

'I understand her. She was afraid she could get in trouble and lose her baby.'

'Pro-lifers are timid scaredy-cats.'

'Dora and Sara need their heads read.'

'They have run amuck. I usually have no interest in the squabbles among the women, the pecking order, the infighting, but the consequences this time were serious.'

'It's always serious, the hurts that go on among women.'

'Then I should have taken it all more seriously.'

Dolores was still outraged. 'I can't believe they could be so cold and hard, so vicious.'

'Pride, politics, infighting turf wars and ego. It's the same human story everywhere in this fallen world, even in pro-life. Everyone wants the donations, the volunteers and the press coverage for their own groups.'

Dolores was still upset. 'How could Dave Ryan aid and abet the theft of our bank account. He knows us too. He's a policeman for God's sake.'

Mickey smiled at her, a knowing smile but not a happy one. 'There is no justice Dolores. Remember? No rule of law. And there is no pro-life movement. There is only raw judicial power, and the killing of the unborn. I know that now. I have been a fool. When it comes to freedom of abortion, all the rules go out the window.'

Dolores could not bear to see her hero such a beaten man. 'Maybe you never had any children of your own Mickey, but you are a father. Many children are alive because of you.'

' Okay. What will you do, now that the Center is finished?' Mickey asked her.

'I don't know. I have to think.'

'I'm sorry it turned out this way.'

'You're not to blame.'

'Maybe I am.'

56

'What are you going to do Dolores, now that the Crisis Pregnancy Center is closing?'

'I don't know. I'm kind of burnt out, to tell you the truth. I need a break for a while, this is all too much. I'm sure I will do something for pro-life in the future.'

'I'm sure you will.'

Dolores put her coat on, but sat down again to talk to Mickey one last time. Her curiosity was unsatisfied, and she hoped to get some answers to questions she had always wondered about.

'Mickey will you tell me something about yourself?'

'What do you mean?'

'You don't say much about yourself. We have gone through so much together, and I really don't know much about you. It has always been pro-life business between us.'

'What do you want to know?'

'You seem nervous sometimes. What was your childhood like?'

'I had a good childhood. Good parents. I remember lots of playing with the other boys in the neighborhood schoolyard, all the seasonal games. Summer was baseball, fall was football, and winter was hockey.'

'No bad experiences?'

'There were some problems. I remember when I was very

young, only eight or something like that, I was left alone at night to babysit my younger brothers and sisters asleep in bed when my parents went out. I used to get scared up alone late at night. Our house was old and creaked. I heard noises, especially in the cellar. I remember I would stand at the top of the basement stairs, holding the door partly open, and calling down the steps, 'Is anybody there"

'You must have been terrified.'

'I was used to it. It was our life. We lived surrounded by factories down by the Bay in the North End of Hamilton. In the daytime we played on the train tracks, climbing the ladders on the sides of the railway cars, running along the narrow tops of the boxcars, playing tag, shouting 'You can't catch me."

'That sounds dangerous.'

'I suppose if anyone saw us we would have been told to get down.'

'So you weren't scared to do that?'

It was fun. I was only scared at night, calling down the cellar steps at the noises, imagining some bad men were down there getting ready to attack us upstairs. But there was never any answer to my calls. I would lock the cellar door, and sit with my back against it, holding a big carving, ready to battle the bad men down in the basement if they came upstairs and tried to break through the door and get in the house.'

'You had a vivid imagination.'

'Don't all children? I remember one night I opened the door, switched on the light, and crept down two of the top stairs, and craned my neck to look around. "I know you're there,' I called out, bluffing them. There was no answer except the loud creaking noises, and I quickly jumped back, and slammed the door shut and locked it again. Some of the children in the bedrooms heard the noises and shouted to me 'Mickey we want to come out with you.' 'No, I said, you have to stay in bed.' 'We're scared' they said.' 'Go to sleep I told them'

'Maybe you could have used the company.'

'I guess I felt my responsibility as a babysitter. But I was always glad to hear my parents' footsteps at the front door when they came home, and I could go to bed myself. You know, I never told my parents I was scared to be left alone at night. I always kept my feelings to myself, even as a child.'

'How many times were you left alone?'

'Two or three times a week.'

'And you always had these imaginary fights with the bad men in the cellar?'

'Yeah.'

'That's horrible. You should have told someone. The Children Aid's Society might have investigated.'

'I don't want to give you the wrong impression. We weren't abused or neglected children. Our parents took good care of us. They both worked hard. They just liked to go out and drink some nights. It was all part of the working class world in the factories.'

'The big kids go out and neglect the little kids. I get sick of it. Are there any responsible, mature, adult parents of a happy family?'

'I'm sure there must be.'

'And you turned out to be a nervous type of person ever since. It really affected you.'

'I don't know. Did my early experiences make me nervous, or was I a high strung wound up person to begin with? I don't blame my parents. They did the best they could.'

'What happened to your parents?'

'They're both dead.'

'How did they die?'

'My mother had a sudden aneurysm. I wasn't there. I was told she said she had a terrible headache, and collapsed and died. Just like that she was gone. I never saw her again except laid out in her casket at the funeral.'

'And your father?'

'That was much different. I saw him the last week of his life dying in the hospital, tied to his hospital bed because he was thrashing around so much. He was dying from cancer and could hardly speak anymore. He went through a progression of raving, repeating the same things over and over again. First he was saying, 'Why? Why?', and then that changed to, 'I don't understand, I don't understand.' At the end he was saying only: 'I'm sorry, I'm sorry', but he wasn't looking at any of us there.'

'My father died horribly too, drowning in front of me on my eighth birthday at a party in the park.'

'Must have been traumatic for you.'

'I still don't like my birthdays. I felt so guilty he died at my birthday party. Otherwise wew would not have been there.'

'I'm sorry for what happened to him, and to you.'

Dolores started scratching her arm again. 'What do you think your father was talking about at the end of his life?'

'I think he went through some kind of death bed conversion. When he died I was the first to find him, he died alone. God took him just the two of them. He looked beautiful when I saw him. I can't explain how he could look beautiful after the last terrible week of suffering, after his last agonies of the death rattle, his body shrinking before us, a man diminished, as if he was a burnt sacrifice offered up, totally consumed, but after his death I saw a light of peace on his face in the dimmed hospital room. Some luminous change had come over him in death.'

'That's awesome.'

'I wish I had been there and he did not have to die alone, but whatever incredible thing happened between him and God was meant to be private between them I guess.'

'He died alone but not alone.'

'My mother came into the hospital room soon after. She put her hand on his cheek and said 'He's still warm, he's still here.' I never expected that from her.'

'People are surprising sometimes, what's inside them.'

Mickey turned his head to look at her, having recited his memory of his father's death staring ahead as if he was seeing it again. 'I hated him. He was a failed and disappointed man working in the local factory, who dreamed of being something more. He was frustrated, and tried to live out his ambitions for higher education through me. His failures made him bitter, and he resented his youth impacted by the Great Depression and World War 11. Our home was always full of secondhand books from the salvage store, fine hardbound collections of the novels of Charles Dickens, Mark Twain, you name it, and all the leading writers of English Literature. He read them all, laughing in his bed at night something they had written. l Imagine the potential he had that he could never develop in a time of survival in a broken social world.

'Sounds like you admired him, not hated him.'

'I resented the pressure to fulfill his life.'

'He wanted the best for you, save you from his mistakes.'

'He did use to say a lot I was wasting time, not applying myself to what I could learn and do.'

'Fathers and sons, mothers and daughters, they all have their difficult relationships, their rebellions and identifications, but everything gets worked out in the end.'

'We didn't have the time. He died young, when I was only 17.'

'But you recognized his goodness at the end.'

'Yeah, I thought of that great line: Nothing in his life became him like the leaving it. I learned later I think he received many spiritual graces in his final struggle, what the Church calls the gift of perseverance, and the gift of final penitence. He never gave up trying to find the meaning of life, even on his deathbed, this ordinary man who worked in a factory, married and raised a family, liked to read books, but never read the Bible or went to church, and liked to drink.'

'An amazing destiny for an ordinary man unregarded by the world, to come to God in the end.'

'My father's death led to my conversion to God, as I grieved and mourned and also tried to make sense of it all. I eventually came to see the Resurrection of Christ was the only answer giving any comfort or hope to death.'

'Mickey, that's beautiful. Your father gave you a great inheritance, a legacy undreamed of. You were your father's son, you kept questioning too what is the meaning of life and found God.'

'I was an atheist before. I could never understand how a spiritual God without any body and without any beginning or end could create this physical universe out of nothing. That's the doctrine of Divine Creation, *ex nihilo*. I still don't understand how that is all possible and true.'

'The only answer is that God is omnipotent. He is all powerful, including powerful enough to make creation out of nothing.'

'Yes, I know now I can only live with faith in what I don't see and don't understand fully.' 'So your father as he lay dying received his spiritual gifts and later on his son received the gift of faith. It is all so beautiful.'

'Beautiful? I don't understand why Christianity contains so much suffering either, why it all has to be this way.'

'It's the evil in the world. The cross, the cross of Christ is the only answer. Cling to that.'

'I do. When my father died everything the whole world was shattered, and seemed hopeless and meaningless. The whole world felt closed to me, as if I was confined within the prison walls of death. Only then did I understand the message of the Risen Christ, only then did it speak to me of hope in eternal life without death, a life beyond this world.'

'Tell me some more about your mother.'

'One thing sticks out in my mind. She never liked my father's mother very much, her mother in law. We all called her Granny. Mom looked after her when she was bedridden and lived at our house, but Granny used to complain to Dad about her treatment from Mom. Dad would say to Mom 'What did you do to her,' and Mom would be angry and offended, saying, 'I didn't do anything. I'm just taking care of her.'

'A touchy situation.'

'Yeah. Eventually Granny had to be placed in an institution, it was too much to nurse her at home. Dad would visit her every Sunday, but Mom never did. After Dad died Mom felt she had to go at least once and tell her. Granny was in a coma, just lying silent in her bed. Even when Dad visited her she just lay there and he would sit in a chair beside the bed just being with her. When Mom finally went to see her she too just sat silent in the chair beside her bed. But then something unexpected happened. After Mom was sitting there for a while, Granny turned her head, and looked at her, and said, 'Fred's gone.'

'She knew.'

'Yeah, she knew if Mom was there that Dad had died. Uncanny.'

'What happened after that?'

'Mom began to visit her once a week too, until Granny died, although she never spoke again.'

'Your family was so human, in its brokenness and in its special moments.'

'We were cursed and blest in our lives.'

'Speaking of life, how did you become a pro-life activist?'

'That came later. Some people think I must have been personally involved and hurt by abortion. It was really simpler than that. I saw a film that showed two actual abortions, and I was stunned to see two babies torn apart and killed. One of the dead babies lay with his broken body on a stainless steel clinic table with his arm bent back, and it seemed to me he was waving to me, calling to me, to come and help.'

'Another conversion for you. God speaks to you through others, your father's deathbed fight, that baby's death.'

'I'm always amazed now people don't see it, the truth of God and the truth about abortion.'

'No, they just don't see.'

She has a lot of questions, Mickey thought. He felt uncomfortable. He didn't like these personal talks about feelings. The confessionals. Yet Dolores had been such a good friend and co-worker he felt she deserved what she was asking from him now.

'Have you ever been in love?'

'I thought I was a few times, but I guess I wasn't in the end.'

'A few times? How many times?'

'Doesn't matter. It was a long time ago.'

Dolores could see Mickey was not going to talk about himself anymore. He was closing up again.

'I have to go now Mickey.'

'Merry Christmas,' he said, and not ironically. He meant it. He extended his hand to shake hers.

'Merry Christmas Mickey. Take care of yourself.'

'Sure.'

'I mean it Mickey. I've noticed your eyes are bloodshot many mornings, and I've seen the extra-large bottles of Tylenol with codeine in the medicine cabinet. I don't know what's happening with you, and I know you don't like to zy much about yourself. But maybe you should talk things over with a doctor. Don't let abortion destroy you.'

Mickey was surprised and ashamed at Dolores's quick and deft confrontation, but he only responded with his practiced smoothness. 'Okay.'

There was nothing more to say. But Dolores could not just leave him like that. She stepped forward inside his outstretched arm to shake her hand and gave him a final hug, a quick kiss on the cheek to say goodbye, and she was gone.

He was alone. One of his headaches began, the agony gripping his entire skull all around from front to back, squeezing his head. Sharp insistent stabs of soreness beat in his temples, while at the back of his head, at the base where it joined his neck, he felt a dull throbbing ache, as if a pool of pain had collected and overflowed its shores. An unholy crown of thorns pierced every part of his head. He went into the bathroom, opened the door of the medicine cabinet above the sink, and took six of his painkiller pills. He knew he had a problem, but soon, very soon, he would be out of the country, away from all the tension of abortion and pro-life. He would go through his withdrawal then.

57

Sadie downed her last straight vodka, drinking at home alone. The date was December 27th, the first business day after the Christmas holidays, and it would be open again. Christmas had meant nothing to her, only a longer wait. The time for her last mission had come. She swallowed a handful of her painkiller pills, washing them down with the vodka. She would wear sunglasses to hide her eyes, and chew mint gum. The nine-millimeter automatic lay in her lap, her right hand clenching the handle and trigger. She kept the pistol with her over Christmas, liking the feel of it. Now she pulled back the bolt to load the first bullet into the firing chamber, but had the presence of mind to check the safety was on. She did not want to be the victim of some stupid accident with the gun. There would be no dignity in that. She wanted to accomplish her mission. He had it coming. She placed the Beretta in her large woven bag.

She thought again how it was the only solution. What he had done to her was unforgiveable, and there was no other way to punish him, no authorities to turn to. The authorities were all on his side, protecting him. She wondered how he would face death, he who had brought death to so many. The rage she felt, the fury at a lifetime of abuse from men had to have this final reckoning. People might think she was insane, but she had thought it through, and it made perfect sense to her. It would sanest statement she could make before the cancer made her too weak to act. She would kill Craigenback, the abortionist who had maimed her, and stolen her womanhood, killing her in both body and soul. It was too late for her now, and too late for Craigenback. She could do this one good thing in the time she had left, and rid the world of an abortionist. They had killed her feminity and maternal warmth, and now she was in fierce rebellion after a lifetime of passivity, of doing what she was always told. Always pleasing people. But they only wanted to use her. The thought of it all disgusted her.

In her fractured mind she considered also shooting Sincerity Burstall, who had pushed abortion on her, telling her so many lies, but she didn't know if she would get the opportunity. The important thing was to get Craigenback first. She realized many abortionists were also women, but whatever their agendas were in aborting other women the man who helped destroy her would have to pay for his deeds. *Would she have wanted to shoot a woman abortionist?* she wondered. Yes, they too should pay for their misdeeds, such as the nurse Burstall. No one was justified in performing abortions. Killing a woman abortionist might have made even more of a statement on the craziness of it all, but it was Craigenback behind his spectacles and white mask looming over her with his hands and knives inside her who remained the focus of her hatred.

Sadie prepared herself, seeing in the mirror she was not pretty anymore, absurdly wanting to look her best for her meeting with him. Her face was sallow, her eyes dull, and large black circles hung under her eyes. Thin spider veins colored red and blue lay broken on her cheeks. She used some powder to try to hide the ugly blotches on her face. She had put on rolls of fat on her once trim figure, and her voice had become harsh and grating. Her darkened gaze looked out with deep resentment at a hostile world, hating the woman she saw in the mirror. She would have to try to smile, be pleasant. Otherwise they would surely see through her, guess at her mission and frustrate her. How could she ever get away with it?

She was angry with him, and angry at herself for letting it all happen. Angry at her own weakness. And she was haunted. She did not want to be tormented by her abortions anymore. The thoughts would never leave her alone, of her two children she had lost through her own fault. And the fault of those who made it possible. She hoped when she killed Craigenback the nightmares would stop at last. Maybe when Craigenback was dead her babies could rest in peace, and she could be at peace. Last night had been the most terrible dream of all. She had been happy in her dream, holding a lovely laughing baby boy in her arms, the beautiful baby reaching up to touch her face with his tiny fingers. The she woke, and realized there was no baby boy, no son, and she was alone in the long dark night.

She made the appointment to see Dr. Craigenback again with Sincerity Burstall over the telephone. At first they did not want to permit the unusual request to meet with the doctor, but they decided allowances had to be made for Sadie, who nearly died but did not sue them. Best to keep on good terms with her, be compassionate doctors and nurses. Sincerity mentioned to Dr. Craigenback that Sadie seemed to be a quiet woman. This time they made an exception. Sincerity's personal reference made the difference. Sadie hoped she would not have to shoot Sincerity too. Burstall had lied to her when she told her abortion would not hurt her, but Sincerity was only doing what she was trained to do. Like her. She hoped she could get close to Craigenback, have a clean shot at him. Security was tight at the abortion clinic, but they did not metal detectors or body searches. They knew her and accepted her as a returning patient. He would have to look her in the eye before she pulled out the Beretta and shot him.

The only other time she had seen him, she had not seen him. She had only seen a white surgical gown, and a white mask over his lower face, and a surgical cap over his hair, and thick eyeglasses covering his eyes. He was the faceless technician who invaded her body with his cold impersonal instruments of death. He was the butcher who carved her up and mutilated her. Killed her babies. Nearly killed her. Had killed her in the end. He was the one who put her babies down the garbage disposal, flushing them down the drain of the sink. He was the criminal she could not go to the police for help to stop him. The police guarded him and his clinic. She could not sue him because she had signed the consent form and accepted the risks. They had lied to her about the risks. She couldn't afford to sue him anyway.

She was not irrational; it all made perfect sense. It was not revenge; it was simply a matter of justice to even the score for what he had done to her. Sincerity Burstall she knew and recognized as a fellow human being she had talked with. Craigenback in his doctor's costume was just a thing, who had treated her as a thing. But things don't think and feel, things don't have nightmares, and things don't practice in the woods learning how to shoot semi-automatic Berettas. She had learned well. She had thought about her mission for a long time, and she had prepared herself for it. She did not even feel nervous. She had planned it and today she would carry it out.

Sadie swallowed the last drops of vodka in the bottle, called for a taxi, and directed the driver to take her to the Craigenback Abortion Clinic. A year had passed since her abortion. Tomorrow, December 28th, would be the one year anniversary of the day he destroyed her life. As she thought of the anniversary date of her abortion a deep and terrifying darkness descended upon her sitting in the back seat of the taxicab. The radio was still playing Christmas carols;

> **Silent night, Holy night,**
> **All is calm, all is bright,**
> **Holy infant, tender and mild–**

'Can you turn that off?' Sadie said to the driver. She did not want to hear about mothers and children anymore. The driver turned off the radio. He knew where he was taking this passenger. Her self-hatred had been paralyzing. She could barely remember the Christmas holidays, dark days she had drifted through alone in her drug and alcohol induced haze, silently moving lost in her own world. Now she was glad to be on the move, carrying out her purpose. She yawned. She had been sleepless for nights, but she willed to keep herself awake and complete her task. Her long journey of suffering would soon come to an end.

When the taxi finally arrived at Craigenback's the security guard buzzed her through the steel plated outside door. Sincerity Burstall was sitting at the reception desk behind the bullet proof Plexiglas, just like before. She smiled at Sadie and waved her to a seat in the waiting room, just like before. She spoke through the opening in the glass: 'Dr. Craigenback will be with you soon Sadie. He is expecting you, and wants to see you. He is just finishing up with a patient.' Sadie thanked her and took a seat. The armed security guard stood by the front door, just like before. He did not seem to suspect her. The same soothing music was piped through the waiting room, no Christmas carols, only relaxing zithers and ocean waves.

Doctor's office. Procedure rooms. The clinic. Sadie knew what lies all those words were now. How horrible being in this place again. She wished she had noticed before what a fortress the building was. Craigenback's was not a medical clinic, it was an abortion mill, a factory churning out abortions, as assembly line of dead babies processed with all the latest quick and efficient technology. Craigenback was a medical prostitute; he sold his medical skills if you had the money. The waiting room was empty; it was nearly lunchtime, the women who sat there in the morning now lying inside on recovery room beds.

A simple procedure, no problems they had told her. Like being an outpatient to get your eyes fixed with lasers. Sadie recalled now ever more clearly how it had been for her, torn apart and carried into the ambulance, the paramedics working frantically over her to keep her alive until they reached the emergency ward of the hospital. The technology was not so efficient with her. He would have to pay for it, the creep. She tried to remain looking calm as she waited, but she was screaming inside the moment she walked back into Craigenback's. He was a serial killer, his victims in the thousands. She was in the abortionist's lair, surrounded by death, and he would never be prosecuted for his crimes. It was all up to her.

58

Sincerity buzzed the inner steel door open leading into the back hallway. Sadie was led down the hall past several closed doors towards Craigenback's office. The inner death chambers were silent now, no whirring of the suction machine she could still hear whining in her mind. She wondered which door hid the garbage disposal and drains. Sincerity led her into the office, and directed her to take a chair in front of his desk. Sadie placed her large handbag on the doctor's desk directly in front of her, between herself and Craigenback's chair.

The nurse left her alone again to wait. Looking around the office she saw a full size stainless steel refrigerator in one corner. She walked quietly over and opened it for a quick look. Sealed jars filled the shelves, each jar containing parts of aborted babies. In the larger jars nearly fully formed little corpses floated suspended in preservative fluid. In the smaller jars she saw dismembered floating hands, and little legs and feet. Beside the jars were some sandwiches wrapped in wax paper, and cans of Coke. Lunch for the busy abortionist. Sadie could not bear to look at the horrifying jars, softly closed the refrigerator door, and ran back to her chair, hoping Craigenback would not come in and discover her snooping. She sat perched on the very edge of the chair, her clenched right hand lying in her lap tightly enclosing her thumb, her knuckles white. She wished he would come soon, her nerves electrified with the interminable waiting.

Moments later Dr. Craigenback came into the office from a side door, dressed again in the hated white medical scrubs. This time his surgical mask was loosened, lying on his chest. She did not know he had such a thick beard. Without the surgical gloves she could see his fingernails were chipped. The man was repulsive. Sadie shuddered to think those hands were once inside her, executing her babies. Dr. Craigenback smiled at Sadie in welcome. But first before sitting down he went to the wall safe behind a photograph, and opened it to check on his gold. He put his hand in the safe, and caressed the small but valuable bars, enjoying the feel of the heavy yellow metal, solid and dependable. Amazing something so tiny could be so substantial and valuable, so powerful. The gold bars clinked as he counted them in his safe. Having a client in his inner office alone with his gold was unusual, but everything was still secure.

Things were going well. Business was good. With the opening of his second clinic across town profits were doubling. He was contemplating franchising his abortion clinics as a national chain operating across Canada. His business advisors thought it was a feasible goal, providing he was patient and willing to expand his business gradually, without taking undue risks, and if he could get good people to operate under the Craigenback brand. Staffing was always a problem. He did not want disreputable characters operating under his good name. He locked the wall safe again, and replaced the covering picture frame of the photograph recording his award as Abortionist of the Year from the College of Physicians and Surgeons. The honor, and his recent induction into membership in the Order of Canada, had assured his prestigious success as a distinguished Canadian. The anti-abortionists could vilify him, but they were only a fringe minority of religious zealots, not representative of the real Canada, the establishment in power, the ones who mattered and who recognized his contributions to the health care of Canadian women. He felt justly proud. He walked over to his desk and sat in the chair behind it. Finally he turned his attention to Sadie sitting waiting for him, watching his every move, but he did not look carefully enough at her to see her fixated stare, did not see the hunter's glint in her eyes sizing up the movements of her prey.

'I'm very sorry what happened to you, Miss Summers. The accident, something went terribly wrong, and your artery was nicked. A rare complication. Nobody's fault. Abortion is a safe procedure. I am so glad everything turned out okay for you.'

'It hasn't turned out okay for me. Just look at me.'

'None of us could know of your pre-existing condition.'

'What pre-existing condition?'

'A weak artery maybe. Or scarring on the wall of the uterus from your previous abortion, which weakened the tissue at that point and led to the rupture.'

'Are you blaming me?'

'I am a very good doctor. I help women in need. I do my best at all times, to a high standard of medical excellence. Termination of pregnancy is my medical specialty. I am well known for it, an expert in mypage numberss. I get up every morning motivated by the knowledge there are patients who need me.'

'You hurt me.'

'I am a Catholic, Miss Summers. I like peace and serenity. The anti-choice protesters that day were very disturbing–'

'So it was their fault?'

'My clinic is under constant siege by them. I try to help women as a good doctor, and they are making my life hell.'

'What happened to me wasn't my fault with a pre-existing condition, and it wasn't their fault. Coming here was the worst mistake I ever made in my life.'

'You need to go back and visit the woman you were then, and tell her she made the best possible choice under the circumstances.'

'I never want to see that woman again. She was weak, pressured, scared. A woman who was the victim of men.'

'I certainly did not pressure you.'

Sadie could not believe what the doctor was saying, his attitude all for himself. He had shamed her enough. A mirthless laugh cracked her face. Craigenback was ridiculous. Her mood changed again. She stopped laughing, and her lifeless stare at the abortionist hardened. The evil one crouched beside her, whispering in her ear, like a squatting toad.

'You forced me when I wanted to stop.'

'It was too late. It would have been dangerous to stop. I did the best I could. I saved your life. With twins one of the twins often dies anyway. I did very well under the difficult circumstances the day you came here.'

'You killed my babies.'

'Your vagina was already opened by the speculum. Your cervix was clamped with the tenaculum, and frozen with anesthetic. It was impossible to stop. The procedure had already begun.'

'You could have stopped. My cervix wasn't open yet.'

'It would not have been safe. It was too late in my medical judgment to interrupt a procedure already begun. No one stops in the middle of an operation because of an emotional reaction of the patient.'

'What happened to me was safe?'

'Miss Summers, I am the doctor. It was not safe to stop at that point.'

'You ruined me for life.'

'I am not personally responsible for abortion, whatever happens. I am the best doctor–'

'Are you saying I am responsible for what happened to me?'

'Abortion is elective surgery. You made a free choice. As I recall, you really wanted it.'

'Tell me doctor, when did you first decide the Hippocratic Oath no longer applied to you?'

'What are you talking about?'

'First do no harm. Never procure a miscarriage.'

'I must tell you I find doing abortions extremely gratifying as a physician helping women. The procedure is self-evidently moral.'

Sadie shook her head. 'How can you do it? Day after day? Woman after woman? I'm baffled.'

'I do abortions precisely because I am a Catholic. As a Christian I have a moral duty to respect human freedom and conscience, and to help women in need, to relieve their suffering. Abortion is not about babies like they preach. I'm the doctor. Abortion is about survival for women. People have a need, and I have the ability to fill that need, so I could not in good conscience say no.'

'I'm not surviving. And you a Christian? You sent me to hell. I live in hell. Is that on your conscience at all?'

'I am the best doctor you could have had. I feel the moral obligation of this work. If I quit what I do, then the terrorists will win.'

Sadie finally saw through all the rationalizations of Craigenback, even in her own confused state. 'You're in denial of reality. Here I am. Reality. Sitting right in front of you. Can you not even see me now?'

'I see you Sadie, and I'm sorry for what happened to you.'

Sadie stood up then. *'Nothing happened to me. You did something to me.'*

'I was trying to help you. Any doctor specializing in pregnancy termination is going to sometimes perforate a uterus. It is inevitable and unavoidable, inherent in the procedure.'

'No one said that in my counselling.'

'I believe you were informed of possible risks, and signed the consent. As a good doctor I make that essential in my practice.'

'You're not a doctor at all. You're an evil, stupid, wretched man. An abortionist.'

Craigenback realized seeing Sadie again was a mistake. She was an angry woman he should have avoided, with communication only through his lawyers. He asserted his authority and dignity as her physician.

'I think you better leave.'

Standing, Sadie looked down at him sitting in his chair, looking so self-satisfied. 'We're done here,' she said. Craigenback should have reacted a second sooner before Sadie shoved her hand inside her oversized bag. The gun was in her hand. She withdrew her hand holding the Beretta from her handbag, and in one fluid, practiced motion slipped off the safety, cocked the hammer with her thumb, assumed her two handed shooting stance with her left hand steadying her right wrist, and shot him twice in the chest sitting in his chair behind the desk. The bulletproof vest beneath his shirt protected him, but the force of the shots at such close range knocked him out of the chair onto the floor behind his desk. The fallen doctor reached his hand under his shirt fumbling for his snub nosed .38 Special. He felt the handle, and pulled his gun out the shoulder holster. He got off one shot at Sadie, but he was in an awkward position sprawled on the floor. The bullet went wide, missing her. Sadie ducked, crouching low behind the desk for cover. She ran over to his side of the desk, and kicked the .38 out of his hand.

'Now you're mine.'

'No, don't. Please stop. I want to live' He tried to crawl away from her, but Sadie was upon him, looming over him. He begged for his life. 'Please, let me live.'

'Why should I?'

'I'm a human being. I don't want to be hurt. I don't want to die. I want to live.'

Sadie hated him the more he spoke. 'So did my babies. So did I.'

Surprising tears wet her cheeks.

Craigenback cursed and shouted: 'I'm a doctor for Christ's sake!'

The merciless avenger was very close to him now, bending over him, whispering in his ear:

'You're no doctor.'

'You don't want to be a murderer.'

'I already am. So are you.'

'This is wrong.'

Sadie smiled. 'Wrong? I'm wrong? You all made me this way. No one protected me at all. Now I'm bad as I can be.'

A crafty glimmer came into his eyes. 'Take the gold. I have more I can give you, lots more.'

'What good is your money to me now?'

'Not like this. I don't want to die like this.'

She shot him three times in the head to make sure, twice for her twins, and once for herself. The closed door to the office flung open. The security guard burst into the room. Sadie turned towards him. The guard held his gun in his hand, and shot at her. The bullet hit her in the left shoulder near her heart. The force of the impact spun her around, and she fell on top of Craigenback lying on the floor behind the desk, dropping her gun. Sadie gathered the last of her strength. She reached over Craigenback's dead body, and picked up the Beretta. Raising her right hand, she clenched the handle as tightly as she could. She pointed the gun barrel at the side of her forehead lying on Craigenback's chest, and squeezed the trigger.

59

On the same day December 27th Mickey walked through the heavy oak doors of Sacred Heart Church, dipped his fingers in the font of holy water standing at the entrance, and blessed himself, making the threefold sign of the cross over his face and chest. He knelt on one knee, genuflecting before the real presence of Christ in the golden tabernacle at the front of the church beside the altar. He took his place in the line outside the confessional box along the side wall. This would be his last confession before leaving Calgary and Canada for good, and his last evening mass. The annual Feast of the Holy Innocents demonstration early tomorrow morning at the Craigenback Abortion Clinic, and his plane flight scheduled later that night, meant he would not have the opportunity to go to church again before he left. His turn came, and Mickey stepped through the heavy purple curtain, and knelt in the dark anonymity of the confessional.

Fr. MacIntyre, slid the small door open covering the grill between the priest and penitent. 'Welcome my son.'

'Bless me Father, for I have sinned. It has been two weeks since my last confession.'

'May the Lord be in your heart and on your lips to make a good confession.'

'I have been in conflict with my opponents. I became angry with them. I have failed to love my enemies. I really don't like them at all.'

'Anything else?'

'I have spread strong criticisms of the Catholic Church. I am not satisfied with our leaders on abortion and pro-life.'

'I know who you are. I have seen the newspapers, and the television news and heard the radio broadcasts. It's everywhere, all over Calgary, your fight with abortion.'

'Yes Father, I am referring to those conflicts.'

'They even use your last name in the headlines: Finnegan Trial Continues. You have attained a high level of public recognition in our city. You may be the most famous Catholic in the Diocese, next to the Bishop. With such a position comes great responsibility.'

'I never thought of myself as an important person. I'm too disadvantaged as a pro-lifer.'

'You may be the only Catholic many people see.'

'I admit I failed to keep Christian love while standing for my principles. I understand we must speak the truth in love, but the heat of battle brings out my Irish combative spirit.'

'It wasn't just you. The rancor takes two sides.'

'Why is everyone in the Church so silent? I had little public support, so it was easy to make me the issue. How can there be pro-abortion Catholics, and the Church does nothing about them?'

'Your open conflict is not the Catholic way. We prefer to work quietly behind the scenes. Discreetly. With prudence. To protect the reputation of the Church. We work from within the system. Diplomatically.'

'I can't go along with that.'

'It looks divisive and disloyal, the open battle. As you said, we are a church of charity, of Christian love.'

'I don't regret the open conflict. I am not confessing for that. I do regret my anger at times.'

'I understand. There was hostility on both sides. Do you hate your enemies?'

'Sometimes, yes, I hate them.'

'Do you wish them harm?'

'I would take satisfaction to hear something bad happened to make them suffer.'

'Do you realize that is malice towards others? Do you see yourself as a malicious person?'

'Doesn't everyone secretly enjoy to hear how others are having problems?'

'If we love someone we are happy for them when good things happen to them.'

'Then I guess I don't really love them, my enemies, like Jesus said.'

'Do you wish them moderate or extreme harms?'

'Yes, sometimes. They should all burn in hell. I would cheerily consign them all to hell.'

'You cannot wish harm on anyone. You can't wish someone in hell. That's inhuman. It's certainly not Christ's way. You must pray for them?'

'Even Craigenback, the unrepentant abortionist?'

'Yes, even him. Leave judgment to God. Don't soil your soul with it. I'm sure none of them will get away with it in the end, no matter successful they are here on earth.'

'I'm just being honest Father, how I feel.'

'You lack spirituality if you hate people. And charity. And spiritual grace. And emotional self-control.'

'I know emotional self-control is essential for a pro-lifer. I am always warning our volunteers about it. But I struggle myself.'

'Self-control does not come easily. It is actually a gift of grace from the Holy Spirit. Our natures are fallen, our minds darkened, our wills weakened, we are divided within ourselves and all our impulses are in inner conflict. Self-control is something you must not only strive for but pray for.'

'I will Father. I know I need it.'

'You must repent of this negative hatred. You could lose your own soul. You could go down to hell.'

'I do repent Father. I am leaving pro-life. Fighting abortion has damaged me. I need some time to myself.'

'It's good you recognize the need for charity towards your opponents. Are you sorry for your sins? Do you wish to try and do better?'

'Yes Father. So I need to pray for emotional balance and love as a pro-lifer.'

'You need to do it as a human being.'

'But I can't get over how poor the Catholic leadership is. Bishop Blair is useless. The Pope shakes the hand of the pro-abortion American President in a smiling photo op. It all makes me sick.'

'It's not for you to judge. You stand in need of forgiveness yourself.'

'I can't help feeling someone else has to forgive us our

failures Father.'

'What do you mean?'

'The unborn children, Father. They have to forgive us all. We have failed them as a church.'

'All right. Anything else?'

'Not about anger.'

'You said you were getting damaged inside yourself by your fight against abortion. God does not want to see you hurt. Do you need counseling, some kind of help?'

'I need help fighting abortion.'

'I suggest you get some help. I can't force it on you, even as a penance, to go for help. Anything else?'

'Yes Father. I have sinned by obeying the abortion laws. I did not disobey and break the laws to save the lives of babies as I should have.'

'No one has ever confessed anything like this to me before.'

'It bothers my conscience. I only engaged in civil disobedience of the abortion laws a few times. Most of the time I obey the laws like everyone else. I did not interfere with the abortions going on. And now I am running away.'

'It is not a sin to obey the law. It is a sin to break the law.'

'It is a sin to obey unjust laws which kill the innocent. I just go along with the abortion system and preserve my own life, most of the time'

'We have to prudent on disobeying unjust laws, and suffering the consequences, or complying and trying to work around them. It is not an easy question.

'Are you complying to work around abortion?'

'I'm not going to argue with you. This is the Holy Sacrament of Confession.'

Mickey decided he had to speak the truth. 'I heard you told Sgt. Dave Ryan he was only doing his job when he confessed about guarding the abortion clinic. You confirmed him in his sin, instead of helping him out of it. How are we ever going to stop abortion that way?'

'I am bound by the inviolate seal of the confessional. I cannot possibly discuss anyone else's confession with you.'

'He's talking about it, what you said to him. He's justified now, the next time he arrests us trying to stop abortion.'

Kindly Fr. MacIntyre felt his own anger rising. 'This is a completely inappropriate use of the confessional on your part.'

'That's what I'm getting at, the inappropriate use of the confessional to continue the sin of abortion.'

'I think you better leave.'

'Are you refusing me absolution?'

'You may complete your confession, but no more of this.'

'Do you see why I say the unborn children have to forgive us all?'

'Enough! I am ready to absolve you. For your penance I want you to sit in the Church after mass, and pray for your enemies. And pray for the Catholic Church. And pray for me. Will you do that?'

'Yes Father, but you said something else wrong to me today. Fr. MacIntyre sighed. 'What was that?'

'You said God doesn't want to see me hurt. God allows people to be hurt all the time, including His Christians.'

'He has his Divine reasons unknown to us.'

'But the reality is quite different from the empty bromides you hear preached in the New Church these days, that God loves everybody, and we should love God and should love everybody too. Carefully crafted generalities calculated to disturb no one. The sermons are empty, never addressing any of the issues really going on.'

"I absolve you in the name of the Father, and the Son, and the Holy Spirit. Go in peace.' Fr. MacIntyre slid the grill covering closed again, ending the confession.

Mickey did as Fr. MacIntyre directed him, kneeling in the darkened pews of the church after mass, praying before the nativity scene, the replica of the Christmas stable set up at the foot of the altar. The statues of the shepherds and sheep, the figures of Mary and Joseph kneeling by the manger with the baby Jesus were all in place since Christmas Eve. Yellow straw was spread on the miniature stable floor, and pots of red poinsettia flowers surrounded the Christmas display. The statue of an angel was fixed above the stable roof, bearing a banner proclaiming Glory to God in the Highest.

He thought of all the pro-abortion Catholics: Craigenback the Catholic abortionist, and Lester Dockendorff the Catholic pro-abortion judge, Jeremiah Patrick the Catholic publisher of the pro-abortion newspaper, David Ryan the Catholic policeman who arrested him, Jessica Sterne the Catholic lawyer who prosecuted him, the Catholic mayor Wanda Winters who supported abortion, and the Catholic Bishop Blair who remained silent and aloof from it all, keeping himself and his church safe and respectable. He tried to pray for them, he tried to forgive them, he tried to love them. He prayed they would repent and not go to Hell.

As he knelt and prayed he felt his burdens lifting from him. He had done all he could and had failed. No one could do more than their best, even if it was not very good. He hoped some good might come out of it all, but he would never know. He was leaving Calgary, and it was not his world anymore, leaving a failure in the eyes of the city, but leaving to go into a new life. He looked at the statue of the Christ child in the crib in the stable. There was no room for Him in the inn, and no room for himself anymore in Canada. He would attend the annual demonstration at Craigenback's the next day on the Feast of the Holy Innocents murdered by King Herod, and it would be his last pro-life witness in Calgary. After that, he would be gone, shaking the dust of the city from off of his feet.

He prayed for the souls of Sadie Summers and Nathan Craigenback. The news had been full of the murder/suicide all day, the phones busy among the pro-lifers. He had only seen Sadie briefly at the very end of her long counseling session with Dolores, when her boyfriend Rick was practically dragging her out of the Crisis Pregnancy Center. Whether Nathan Craigenback could be saved he personally doubted, but it was not for him to judge his soul, only his actions. The power to judge Craigenback belonged only to the Lord. At the end of his prayer he asked the unborn children to forgive him his failure, and for leaving them to die alone. He did not feel anything, no love, no hope, and he did not hear any reply to his doubts and anguish as he knelt in prayer in inner silence. But he rose from his knees with the wonderful new lightness of being confession and penance always brought him. He was free to go now. He would not be arrested at the demonstration tomorrow. He would only go for a little while, and slip away and be an anonymous face in the crowd. Dolores was coming to the protest rally too, and he would see her one last time.

60

The day was still December 27th, in the evening. Julie alone with her son Jeffrey at home in her apartment, and after hearing the news about Craigenback and Sadie, logged on to her secret email account she shared with the Warriors of God. Julie never met her Commander in the Warriors, who operated in small cells independent from one another to escape detection. None of the soldiers knew the structure of the whole organization, but only had knowledge of their own small part. Sometimes the independent cells would even act on their own in individual actions, following the principle of a leaderless movement. But Julie as a young woman had her Commander. The email message waiting for her was simple and direct:

> Hail Purity:
> Season's Greetings. The time has come to strike the deathblow at Craigenback's. He is thankfully gone, but his house of horrors remains. During the annual demonstration tomorrow on December 28th, you are to leave a backpack at the front doors of Craigenback's in the early morning. You will find the backpack outside your apartment door right now. Do not open or tamper with it. Someone else will detonate the package at the appropriate time. Merry Christmas.
> Silent Avenger

Julie was concerned at the message. This kind of violence was going too far. Mickey, Dolores and some of the other pro-lifers had been kind to her and Jeffrey. They were her friends, and Jeffrey's friends, when he had no father. They would be at the demonstration tomorrow, and people could get hurt. She hated the mean, self-righteous women like Dora and Sara who gave her so much trouble, and caused Mickey and the Center so many problems, but she did not want anyone hurt. She too believed pro-life was inadequate and ineffectual, and she was willing to work in secret for damage to the abortionists, but she had never before been asked to participate in such an overt and dangerous mission. What if the Craigenback Abortion Clinic was being watched and guarded, even in the very early morning hours? What if the police stopped her, and searched her, and found she was carrying a backpack full of explosives? Her Commander was asking too much. Julie thought a moment, absorbing the email, and then typed in her reply:

> Silent Avenger:
> I cannot be part of this mission. I am leaving tonight, and will be away from Calgary for the rest of the Christmas holidays with my parents. I no longer work at the Crisis Pregnancy Center. Please reconsider this action, as some pro-life people, and other innocent people, might get hurt. I recommend damaging the abortion clinic when it is deserted, not during a public demonstration with many people present.
> Merry Christmas of the Christ Child,
> Purity

Julie saved her message in the drafts folder without sending it, and signed out of the shared email account. She called Jeffrey to her and dressed him warmly. Then she turned out the lights and locked the door of her apartment. She saw a backpack leaning against the wall beside her door, but was afraid to touch it. She hoped nothing would happen, but she could not warn anyone without exposing herself. Maybe her email reply would not be received by her Commander in this late evening, and the backpack would remain untouched until the demonstration tomorrow was finished. She hoped no one else would find it in the meantime. The backpack leaning against the wall beside the front door of her apartment was suddenly an enormous problem she could not face or deal with. She did not know what to do. She only knew she was now heading to the bus station.

Before she wanted to do something for pro-life, for the unborn children, but these new developments changed everything. She could no longer be involved. Her private life with her family came first, and above all, she had to protect her son. She was all he had.

61

Not the Church, Not the State,
Women Must Decide Their Fate

The rhythmic chants of the pro-abortion counter protesters, their insistent drumbeat slogans, filled the early morning air as they faced the crowd of pro-lifers blocking the front doors outside the Craigenback Abortion Clinic.

Not the Church, Not the State,
Women Must Decide Their Fate.

The pro-aborts chanted over and over. They were working themselves into a frenzy for the coming assault to re-open the doors. Mostly young women, supported by some idealistic young male friends who believed in freedom of choice and abortion rights, their outrage at the pro-life interference with their personal freedoms was reaching fever pitch. The throng was angry now. First, Dr. Craigenback's assassination, and now this blockade of the abortion clinic the very next day. When they heard the news they came streaming to the Craigenback Abortion Clinic to prevent the end of their rights. As the crowd grew the intensity intensified.

Mickey with the small band of pro-life protesters had arrived earlier in the pre-dawn darkness, taking their position in front of the doors. Some were standing, some sitting down on the cold sidewalk, linking arms to block the doors with their bodies, the physical sacrifice their only weapon to save the lives of the babies. Some of the sitting protesters were linked together with bicycle chains looped around their necks, making it more difficult and time consuming for the policemen to remove them. Every minute longer it took the authorities to carry the pro-lifers away was another minute of life for the unborn children. The delay of the opening of the abortion mill would give the sidewalk counselors more time to approach the women coming for abortions. Some of the women might change their minds, go away after the long wait for the police to clear the protesters, or go away touched by their witness to life. It had happened before.

Yesterday Calgary heard the shocking news of Craigenback's murder by one of his former patients. Some of the pro-lifers wanted to cancel the annual Christmas Season Feast of the Holy Innocents demonstration, so soon after Craigenback's death. They did not want the association with such recent violence. Others argued it was the perfect time to shut down the abortion mill for good. The combination of a woman driven to violence by the abortion done to her, and peaceful, non-violent protesting at the abortion clinic, might be the end of Craigenback's. The cluster of protesters was smaller than usual, because of those who did not want to participate after the shooting. Many of the pro-lifers disliked any kind of negative confrontation, wanting a more positive image for their cause.

Dora and Sara were absent this morning, but Charlie Kelly

was there, despite his avowed retirement from pro-life. The protesters who came this morning decided to take the big step of civil disobedience this time and block the doors. They were emboldened by the dramatic turn of events. A strong public protest might ruin the image of the abortion clinic forever, even if the authorities did not shut it down completely. They did not want poor Sadie Summers written off as a lone lunatic, and hoped Calgarians would come to see it was the Craigenback Abortion Clinic that was the problem.

Mickey was one of those who believed a follow-up demonstration was necessary. He had his plane ticket and his passport to leave Canada in his coat pocket, but he could not pass up this one last chance to do something about abortion in his city. His suitcase was already stored in the trunk of a friend's car. The Crisis Pregnancy Center across the street was closed, the house darkened, Mickey locking the door for the last time as he left. His final walk through the house that was such a big part of his life left him feeling the sadness of last partings, but he knew he had no other choice and had made the right decision to go away.

He was defeated for now, but someday the right to life of unborn children would be restored, protected by the law. Pregnant women would be supported instead of abandoned to abortion on their own. Abortionists would be arrested and tried and imprisoned for their crimes. Society would be returned to sanity. He might not live to see it in his own lifetime, but it had to come sometime because it was the truth. Human beings could not live forever with the lie of legalized abortion; society could not function with such an evil at its heart. Violence was everywhere now, breaking out at any time in the most unexpected places. But people did not see the connection yet between the rampant violence in society and legal abortion,

The Daily Record and the television stations were full of the murder/suicide. The settled issue of abortion had reared its ugly head again and become news once more, as it always seemed to do. Mickey was interviewed, and he appealed again for non-violence in pro-life. The other owners of the Craigenback Abortion Clinic, the silent partners who hid behind the numbered company, decided to keep the abortion mill open after his death. One of the other owners, also a doctor, was willing to take Craigenback's place. Abortion must continue on, and be seen to continue. The pro-lifers also decided their peaceful protests must continue. Neither side in the conflict was going to allow the public to see them defeated, each side seizing the moral high ground of life versus choice, and each side spin-doctoring every event to their own favor whenever possible. Mayor Kathy Winters was quoted in the Record deploring the violence. Bishop Blair called for civility and decency among people of different beliefs and opinions, the Bishop calling for unity and peace among the Catholic people.

Mickey had been nervous in the pre-dawn darkness when the pro-lifers first gathered in front of the abortion clinic doors before it opened for the day, taking the critical ground blocking the entrance. The butterflies in his stomach were always in the anticipation, just like in court, or when a client walked through the doorway of the Crisis Pregnancy Center.

Once the protesters were in position for the demonstration and the conflict engaged he felt at peace. He knew in the early morning darkness the pro-abortion forces would soon be coming, and now they were here with their loud shouts:

> ***Not the Church, Not the State***
> ***Women Must Decide Their Fate.***

He wished he was a braver man, did not always feel anxious whenever he had to step out in public for pro-life. His nerves had always plagued him. Soon the police would arrive, and the news reporters, and the abortion clinic clients. But for now, when they were standing and sitting in front of the doors, the nerves left him. Now he was committed, the line was crossed and there was no turning back. Then the peace came, when he was surrendered, and accepted everything God would send that day. He always felt even more peaceful when the long waiting in the cold, pre-dawn darkness was over, and the day came, and the reports went out, and the people started arriving and the action was about to begin.

62

Not the Church, Not the State,
Women Must Decide Their Fate

Hymn singing and prayers strengthened the pro-lifers waiting for the crowd of counter-protesters chanting their slogans to make their move. Prayer was their first spiritual weapon in the battle to come; their surrendered bodies placed between the babies and the abortionists' knives their second defensive weapon..

Amazing grace, how sweet the sound
That saved a wretch like me–

The beauty of the Christian hymn written by the former captain of a slave ship filled Mickey with hope. People would one day come to see the evil of abortion, and want to stop it. All things were possible with God. Newton the slave trader had converted. The whole evil practice of legal human slavery, that peculiar institution once accepted as a pillar of normal society, supported even by the Supreme Court, had been abolished. Many abortionists were already changing, coming over to pro-life. That was amazing; imagine having thousands of deaths on your conscience, and still finding the grace of forgiveness from God.

Dr. Carl Lawrence, one of the converted abortionists, when he spoke to the pro-life rally earlier in the pre-dawn darkness, admitted he always knew he was taking a human life, the protesters holding their flickering candles in the darkness:

'I could feel the life at the other end of the suction hose like an electric shock when the vacuum touched the baby's body, and grabbed hold, and I could feel the resistance of the baby's body fighting back, the baby moving, fighting to live,' he said to the crowd. 'Why did I do it? To tell you the truth, it made me feel powerful, it felt like primordial power, like splitting the atom, to have that power of death over the unborn child at the first stirrings of the beginning of life. I'm ashamed of it now, but at the time it was a rush of power for me.'

His voice broke during his public confession, but after pausing for a moment to recover, he continued:

'I ask your forgiveness, and the forgiveness of the babies I deprived of life, and the forgiveness of the mothers and fathers I deprived of their children. I am so sorry. Instead of the healer I was meant to be, I became a death peddler. I profited from the grubby business of abortion. I can only thank God who writes straight with crooked lines for forgiving me, and giving me another chance. Now I stand with you, and give my witness for life. I hope there is hope even for me.'

Meredith Mcrae was there, Meredith whose mother was raped but who had her child. 'I'm so glad my mother let me live,' Meredith said to the assembled crowd. 'She was the victim of a crime of rage, My father, whoever he was, hit her over the head, and dragged her into an alley, and threatened to kill her, holding a knife at her throat. He made her pregnant, and after he raped her, he left her alone in the back alley to die. He was never caught. If I met the man now, I would punch him. But I am not nothing. I am something good. I am me. My mother's rape was not my fault. You should have met my mother. She passed away recently, but she was a wonderful woman. Not bitter at all. She chose life. What was done to my mom was a terrible crime, but I thank God she spared me. Mom told me once she didn't think I should be given the death penalty for my father's crime. She made a brave and generous, loving choice.'

Mickey saw Sandy standing beside him in the band of protesters. Little Sandy, only eleven years old, the abortion survivor whose crippled legs made her walk with a limping gait. She had survived a failed late term abortion and been born alive, but the forceps had maimed her. She was living proof abortion kills a human being, a little girl but a powerful witness to life. The doctor had wanted to drown her in the toilet when she survived the abortion, but the attending nurse had threatened to quit and report him if he did, so Sandy had lived. The nurse believed in abortion, but killing a baby born alive was too much for her once she saw her.

Sandy's friend Chrissie was standing with her, the two eleven years old girls holding hands. Chrissie said she could have been aborted, just like Sandy was almost aborted, like so many of the children who were killed when abortion was made legal in Canada 20 years ago. Chrissie's mother had loved her so much she had refused the chemotherapy for her liver cancer, and refused the doctors' advice to abort. Her mother risked her own life to protect her unborn child, and she both won and lost her gamble. She died soon after Chrissie was born, happy to see her healthy baby daughter for the little time they had together. Mickey said hello to the girls.

'Sandy, Chrissie, you're too young to be here this morning. But it's good of you to want to.'

'I want to be here for the babies,' Sandy said. 'I'm only alive today because of the grace of God, and one caring nurse.'

'Me too,' Chrissie said. 'I'm so glad my mom didn't abort me. We're all abortion survivors, our generation.'

Chrissie wiped a tear from her cheek.

'What's the matter?' Mickey asked.

'Mickey, they're killing babies,' the little girl said.

'Come here,' Mickey said. He held their hands, the two girls standing on each side of him in the midst of the crowd of pro-life protesters, waiting for the coming assault. Dennis Johnston stood behind them in the crowd. Heartbroken at the abortion of his child he could not prevent, he was active in pro-life ever since. Judge Dockendorff did not recognize any legal standing for Dennis and Mickey when they stood before him in the courtroom, but they stood together now on the sidewalk blocking the front doors of the abortion mill, where his girlfriend had gone to kill their baby. The law did not recognize the unborn child, or any rights for fathers when it came to abortion, but Dennis was real enough now standing on the sidewalk far from Judge Death's courtroom. Mickey mourned the loss of Manny Aquino, another man he had tried to help stop the abortion of his child. After Judge Dockendorff summarily dismissed them, Manny had gone home and put a bullet in his head. Mickey sadly wished Manny had not killed himself in his despair, wished Manny could be here with them now, fighting back.

Carol Conrad was there, standing in the pro-life crowd of witnesses for life, the aborted woman who was determined to be silent no more. Instead of hiding her abortion in shame, she had worked through her trauma and became a public speaker. She was free. Backed by the authority of her personal experience with abortion she became the founder of the Calgary chapter of Feminists for Life. Dolores too stood beside Mickey and the girls, a little impromptu family this morning. Dolores spoke to them:

'The Daily Record quoted Sincerity Burstall accusing us of being secretly glad Craigenback is dead, despite our saying we don't support killing abortionists. What do you think of it Mickey?'

'Sincerity is using the situation and spin-doctoring as usual. I havn't heard people say they are glad Nathan Craigenback is dead. Whatever happened between Craigenback and Sadie, their last moments must have been horrible for both of them.'

'Women who suffer from post abortion syndrome are in great pain on the anniversary dates of their abortions,' Dolores said. 'I remember Sadie had her abortion on this same day last year. We were right here, on this sidewalk, and I tried to stop her up the last moment.'

'Sadie Summers had it bad,' Carol Conrad said. 'It doesn't get any worse than that.'

'She never came back for help,' Dolores said. 'What a waste of a life. She could have learned how to grieve the loss of her babies. Find healing.'

'Dr. Craigenback was a wasted life too,' Carl Lawrence said. 'He could have been a real doctor.'

'I am glad he's dead,' Charlie said. 'I won't be a hypocrite about it.'

'Charlie, please please don't say that to any reporters,' Dolores said.

'I'm just saying.'

'Didn't you say you were retiring? Why are you here today?'

'Sadie Summers changed all that. I couldn't stay away today.'

No priests were there. Bishop Blair ordered all the priests of Calgary to avoid the annual Feast of the Holy Innocents demonstrations at the Craigenback Abortion Clinic. Any priest who disobeyed and involved the Diocese in controversial pro-life activism was transferred out of the city, exiled and kicking at clods of dirt in the fields of some small country parish far away. Smiling Jake Corcoran was also absent, saving himself as the legitimate mainstream pro-life spokesman for interviews afterwards, with carefully prepared remarks supporting the protesters while distancing from them if necessary. Dr. Stanley Egbert, the well-known moral philosopher in conservative pro-life circles, also preferred to skip the demonstrations, keeping his dignified status as a writer and professor in the academy.

Mickey turned his head from side to side, surveying the crowd, the people bundled up in heavy coats in the cold winter air in the early morning, some stamping their feet and blowing on their hands to keep warm during the long wait.

The snow was late this year, the sidewalks bare. He felt proud to be among them, the pro-lifers, for all their faults. They were the people of the light, keeping the right to life alive during the darkness of the abortion times. The flickering flames of their candles in the darkness illuminated the abortion mill looming behind them, shrouded in ominous shadows. When the first rays of dawn lightened the night dark sky, Mickey turned his face to the East, to watch the rising sun. The fire of the light came into him, warming his body and his soul. The Lord drew his heart, and Mickey lifted up his heart to the Lord. His heart was suddenly filled with happiness, with the fire and light of the love of the Lord. He felt he lived in a world of reason and purpose held in the loving hands of God, despite all the human madness. Life was full of meaning for him once more.

He shivered in the cold December air, standing in solidarity with the other pro-lifers, solidarity with the women, and solidarity with all the unborn children. They were not alone at all. The unseen presence of God was in their midst; the Lord God would fight for them against abortion. He could not help loving the fellowship of the tiny band of the apostles of life standing around him. Even with all the frictions in pro-life, he loved them. For a moment they stood united as one. His body was cold but his heart was on fire. Standing on the sidewalk in front of the abortion mill he stood on a tightrope over the abyss of heaven and hell. What they did in this life mattered. He tightened the hold of his hands on the hands of Sandy and Chrissie, and turned his head to smile at Dolores. The pro-life witnesses all joined hands, and since it was still the Christmas season, they sang another carol waiting for the conflict to come. Their tremulous voices rang out with the fire of love in the clear, cold, early morning air, on the Feast of the Holy Innocents:

**Away in a manger, no crib for a bed,
The little Lord Jesus lay down his sweet head–**

Even during the festival time of Christmas and family celebrations, the Church took care to remember when King Herod sent his soldiers to kill the Christ child, and all the boy children under two years of age to make sure they got him. The deaths of those Holy Innocents made the Christmas message something far darker than the pagan feasts now marking the midwinter time of merrymaking. Mickey felt the contradiction, but glad to be with the true meaning of Christmas.

After they finished singing the crowd became silent, some of the pro-lifers praying the rosary, the reassuring beads colored pink and blue for the babies passing through their cold fingers to calm their nervousness, waiting for what would happen to them. Mickey felt one of his headaches beginning, and reached in his pocket for the painkiller pills he always carried with him.

'What are you doing?' Carol asked him, seeing Mickey put three pills in his mouth. 'Why are you taking those?'

'I have a bad back. It's hurting this morning in the cold, standing here on the sidewalk without moving.'

Dolores was surprised to hear what Mickey said, but she

remained silent. Then the pro-lifers saw the first police car arrive. Sgt. Ryan stepped out of the driver's side, and stood on the sidewalk across the street, standing in front of the darkened and empty house of the Crisis Pregnancy Center, watching the two crowds of protesters and counter-protesters at Craigenack's, and deciding what he should do next. He heard the murmuring prayers of the pro-lifers, and the angry chants of the pro-aborts:

**Not The Church, Not the State,
Women Must Decide Their Fate.**

Ethel came walking by Sgt. Ryan, dressed in her orange coat, walking back and forth along the city block across the street from the crowd at Craigenback's. Ethel paid no attention to the noises of the people, intent on her own inner world, concentrating on her daily hours of walking to burn off her manic energy and keep her sanity. Cars still drove by on the roadway, people going to work in the early morning hours, the drivers glancing sideways at the large crowd of people standing on the steps of the house and on the sidewalk, wondering what it was about but without time to stop. Some of the drivers understood it was a pro-life demonstration and honked their horns in support. Sgt. Ryan had seen enough, went back to his police car and radioed in:

'Dispatch, we have a large crowd at the Craigenback Abortion Clinic, and it's still early. Things might get out of hand after what happened to Dr. Craigenback yesterday. I am monitoring the situation, but I suggest you send back-up.

I'm here alone.'

The police dispatcher responded over the airwaves: 'Are you in any danger?'

'Negative. So far.'

'Keep your position. Back up is on the way.'

63

Not the Church, Not the State, Women Must Decide Their Fate

The pro-abortion counter protesters had arrived soon after word was sent out from Craigenback's. Sincerity Burstall notified them as soon as she arrived for work, and saw Mickey and the other pro-lifers blocking the doors, despite the court order banning them. She was used to the annual Christmas protest, but the anti-abortionists had never blocked the doors before. She would see they were heavily punished this time. Dr. Craigenback had been murdered, and now this further outrageous defiance of the law. Women had a legal right to enter the abortion clinic. The time for minor fines was over. This time she would press for imprisonment. Judge Dockendorff had sternly warned Mickey the last time when he padlocked the clinic doors. The judge had clearly been serious when he fined him $250,000, and banned him from the courts. Sincerity remembered how Judge Dockendorff warned Mickey the law would crush him if ever broke it again. The two groups of protesters and counter-protesters were standing unusually close to each other at this demonstration, and were taunting each another.

'You have done it this time Mickey,' Sincerity shouted at him, seeing him in the crowd. 'You have gone too far this time. I'll see you go away for a long time.'

'I'd love to go away for a long time,' Mickey said back, Sincerity not understanding he was planning to soon disappear and leave the country.

'We love you Sincerity. God loves you,' some of the pro-lifers called back to her.

'God hates you,' Sincerity yelled.

'We still love you Sincerity.'

'Rot in hell, you are all anti-choice.'

'I am anti-choice,' Charlie yelled back, 'when the choice is killing babies.'

Not the Church, Not the State,
Women Must Decide Their Fate

the pro-aborts yelled back.

'My faith is my fate,' Dolores said, but quietly.

Sincerity mocked them: 'It's mommy or murder, is that it?'

'Mary should have aborted,' another voice in the abortion crowd shouted back.

Charlie was always willing to join a heated public debate. 'You're not feminists. What about gendercide? Do you kill little girls because the parents want a boy?'

'You're not pro-my-life,' Sincerity said. 'You holy-rollers, you're all hypocrites. A fetus doesn't have a soul. There's no killing.'

'God creates a new soul at every conception. It's awesome. It's His only new creation since the beginning, each new soul. The human parents only procreate, sharing in God's creative act,' Mickey said.

'It's always God with you people.' Sincerity said.

'We love you, Sincerity,' the pro-lifers called. 'We love all of you.'

Sincerity Burstall was not having any of this Christian love from people blocking her doorway, obstructing women's freedoms and rights. 'We don't judge why a woman wants an abortion. You people judge everything.'

'Repent of your sins. Obey God,' Charlie said.

'Long live abortion,' the counter-protesters chanted. 'Long live abortion.'

'That's my office,' Sincerity shouted. 'Let me in there. You have no right to keep me out of my own office.'

'Sorry Sincerity, not today.'

'You don't care about children. You don't give a damn about them after they're born.'

'That's a lie,' Dennis shouted back. 'You're the ones who say lives aren't worth living.'

'Your life isn't worth living.'

'There you go again.'

'No rape babies,' a young feminist yelled out across the two lines of protesters.

The gathering of pro-life protesters did not budge. Both sides wanted to seize the high ground of access to the clinic doors. The two sides of activists who often restrained themselves to verbal contests were today lined up like two opposing football teams, with only a few feet of distance between them. The pro-lifers were united in a massed crowd ready to make an impenetrable goal line stand, while the determined pro-aborts huddled together to push their way through the line of defense and reach the doors of the abortion mill and re-open them. The pro-aborts were ready to remove this last line of defense and score a victory for freedom of choice. The pro-lifers were just as determined to defend the right to life.

Not the Church, Not the State, Women Must Decide Their Fate

As the two lines of protesters and counter-protesters faced each other and waited, with their war chants and yelling, their songs and prayers, their arguments and insults back and forth filling the early morning air, Mickey saw the growing fury right in front of his face. The young women were livid at the pro-lifers for taking away their freedom of choice, blocking their access to their abortion rights. He sensed the spiritual warfare was nearing its peak, knew the battle at such close quarters would not be merciful.

'They're like a death squad,' Dennis Johnson said to Mickey. 'Murder for hire. Abortion's a cash cow for them. Are they worried they won't meet their quota of dead babies today?'

Mickey felt the festering pain of Dennis at the killing of his own child. 'Some of them are in it for the money. Some of them are misguided young idealists. They think they are in the right. Look at those young girls proudly wearing their T-Shirts printed with the slogan: I HAD AN ABORTION. How can we help such errors?'

'No one thinks they're a bad guy. They all do something good, the way they see it,' Charlie said. 'But they don't see it.

They are blind.'

'The scales will fall from their eyes someday,' Mickey said. 'There will be a judgment coming.'

'They make money out of abortion, that's a fact,' Dennis said. 'There's a charge for it. Blood money. Dockendorff was right. It's a business.'

'They don't want anything to stand in their way,' Charlie said.

'We stand in their way,' Dolores said. 'At least this morning, we stand in their way. And we stand in their way with everything else we do to defend the right to life.'

More people were arriving; the crowd of angry women growing larger, all of them chanting over and over:

Not the Church, Not the State
Women Must Decide Their Fate

Not the Church , Not the State
Women Must Decide Their Fate.

The crowd of counter-protesters was gradually inching even closer to the pro-life crowd blocking the doors.

'You two,' one of the teenage girls said pointing at Mickey and Dennis. 'What business of this is yours? If men could have babies abortion would be a sacrament.'

'Abortion is wrong and false,' Dennis said back to her. 'Don't be deceived by Satan and his lies.'

'You're the evil ones,' Sincerity said. 'Racketeers, corrupt organizations, breaking the law, conspiring to interfere with a woman's lawful rights, a heath clinic's legal rights. Primitive throwbacks with your ignorant opinions. Bullying people with brute force. You think your self-righteous religion justifies everything wrong you do, but it doesn't. You are so unenlightened. Don't you understand? WE HAVE RIGHTS TO SAFE AND LEGAL ABORTIONS. I demand you let me in my office.'

'I'm so sick of that lie abortion is safe. Abortion is never safe. at least one person dies in every abortion, the child dies.' Dolores said.

'You all have an agenda to control women. We are liberated from you now. We don't need you. We have the right to control our own bodies. We will fight forever for that,' Sincerity said.

'Radical feminism has enslaved women.' Carol Conrad objected, the feminist for life. 'The rejection of marriage has to led to hordes of single mothers, the lack of fathers, the breakdown of the family, a cycle of poverty for the mothers and children. Don't you understand? Everything you believe is false.'

'Everything you say is religious dogma,' a young activist shouted. 'Go talk to your imaginary friend God. Better yet, Fuck the Virgin Mary. Fuck the Church. Hail Satan.' and she started chanting again:

Women Must Decide Their Fate
Women Must Decide Their Fate.

'The time for talk is over,' Sincerity said, rallying her side. 'It's time to act. Let's open the doors.'

64

*Not the Church, Not the State,
Women Must Decide Their Fate-*

It's a Baby, It's a Baby

The pro-aborts were pumped up now for the hand to hand combat to come, and pushed forward with all of their group strength and war chants ramming against the huddled pro-lifers, everyone standing now, who pushed them back. The pro-life line held.

Sgt. Ryan could only watch, waiting for police reinforcements to arrive, so there was no law, only the people fighting each in the streets at the abortion mill. The pro-aborts regrouped, and made another thrust to clear a path through the pro-life barricade and get to the doors. This time one woman was raised high, and tossed onto the hands and backs of the massed crowd of both groups of protesters. They were crammed so tightly together against each other in the small space they formed one crowd, the young woman crawling over the heads of the people on her hands and knees trying to get to the abortion clinic doors. The pro-aborts tried to throw her forward, while the pro-lifers tried to block her progress and push her back. The woman kept crawling onward despite her precarious perch, determined to get to the doors.

Not the Church, Not the State,
Women Must Decide Their Fate

The pro-aborts kept chanting their drumbeat slogan in their fury. Keening high above the crowd was now heard the lone voice of a single pro-life woman at the back of the crowd, pressed against the doors of Craigenback's. She was not crying out for herself in pain crushed against the doors by the mass of struggling people, she was crying out over and over again:

It's a Baby, It's a Baby.

The troop of pro-lifers all took up her chant, and the two sides now fought and struggled with their cries and counter cries:

Women Must Decide Their Fate-
It's a Baby, It's a Baby.

Still the woman continued crawling over the top of the crowd, thrown forward by some hands, and pushed back by others.

65

*Not the Church, Not the State,
Women Must Decide Their Fate-
It's a Baby, It's a Baby*

Police Sgt. Ryan saw the pro-life and pro-choice counter demonstrations had turned into a riot, and called into headquarters again. This conflict would take more than a handful of police uniforms to re-establish law and order. 'Dispatch, we have a problem. Send more backup. Send everyone you've got.' Soon the police cars began arriving, lights flashing and sirens shrieking, and the police vans came to arrest the pro-lifers and clear them away, restoring the social order of abortion rights.

Mickey's foot slipped in the pandemonium of the tumultuous crowd. The woman crawling over the heads of the two groups of protesters jammed together dug her hands into his hair. Someone else was pushed into him and knocked him over and he began to fall. Someone knocked into him again, and he fell completely flattened beneath the mob. He could not breathe, fallen to the sidewalk beneath the trampling feet. He struggled to stand, pushing his hands against the sidewalk. Shuffling feet stepped on his hands, and pain shot up his arms to his excited brain. He did not want to crushed under the mass of people. The instinct for self-preservation drove him to his feet, to stand again, to breathe again.

Women Must Decide Their Fate-
It's a Baby, It's a Baby

Mickey tried to fight his way to the edge of the tightly packed throng so he could get away to freedom. Someone knocked into him again, and he was thrown down a second time, trodden beneath the battling protesters. His head cracked against the pavement of the sidewalk and bounced upwards. Searing pain wracked his brain, while the din of the shouting noise, the shouts and chanting of the crowd, the sirens of the police cars, assaulted his ringing ears.

Women Must Decide Their Fate-
It's a Baby, It's a Baby

Mickey fought again to his wobbly legs and feet. His head was dizzy, but still he felt the primal need to survive, to escape. He still tried to fight his way out, but someone knocked into hom yet again, and he fell a third time beneath the crowd. He was knocked to his knees, his arms holding onto the legs of people to boost himself up, the hard bony knees of the crowd banging into his shaken head. Someone fell on top of him, and Mickey fell completely down again, pinned flat on the sidewalk. His head slammed into the sidewalk again, and a foot kicked him in the head. A gash cut his forehead, bleeding into his eyes. Another pointed foot, the black high heeled pump of a woman kicked him in the ribs, and he felt pain like a lance shoot into his side. He was crushed beneath the crowd, the feet of the protesters were trampling him like a stampede of cattle. The pointed shoes of two other women were kicking him all over his body. Mickey was finally able to rise as far as his hands and knees, like a beaten dog, shaking his head to remove the blood from his eyes.

'Don't kill him!' a voice in the crowd called out. Helping hands reached down to drag him to his feet. Upright again, half blinded from the blood flowing down his forehead into his eyes, Mickey panicked, and desperately tried to fight his way out of the crowd to freedom. He had a plant to catch. He could not find one foot of ground to stand on anywhere in his own country anymore. Mickey looked upwards, trying to see above the surging crowd pushing around him, trying to see what the police were doing. He wiped the blood out of his eyes with the sleeve of his torn coat. He saw more police cars arriving, the officers setting up lines of yellow police tape to keep back the passing pedestrians, cordoning off the area all around Craigenback's, but some late arriving protesters slipped under the tape on their hands and knees to join the pushing crowd. Police snipers took their positions on the roofs of the houses across the street, including the roof of the Crisis Pregnancy Center, aiming their rifles at the pack of people struggling in front of the abortion clinic doors. No one was firing yet. He saw the clinic staff, with armbands over their ordinary street clothes proclaiming ESCORT and SECURITY shepherding the women who had come to the clinic that morning, guiding them behind the police lines to wait for their interrupted appointments.

Pro-life sidewalk counselors approached the women waiting behind the police barricades. Some of the women looked irritated, angry at the protesters blocking the way to the clinic. Others looked thoughtful, wondering why people would try so hard to stop them. Some of the women looked embarrassed, with scarves drawn up and hats pulled down to conceal their faces. Their privacy invaded, they did not want to be seen on the evening news. The news van from the television station had already arrived, the reporters setting up their cameras. Sincerity Burstall was speaking into a reporter's handheld microphone, giving an interview to the Daily Record. More police cars were arriving, the piercing screeching of their sirens filling the air. The opposing chants of the fighting crowd still sounded above the battle in the streets:

Women Must Decide Their Fate-
It's a Baby, It's a Baby.

Mickey saw it was hopeless, there was no way out, he was not going to get away. He was trapped. He would be arrested again, missing his plane flight to another country and freedom. Soon he would be dragged into court once more, have to face Judge Dockendorff yet again. But then the peace came. He stopped trying to get away. His fear was gone, a blessed relief. He calmly waited his coming arrest, his latest defeat. A tremendous power descended upon him. He turned to face the coming policemen. He prayed again:

Lord, not my will, but yours be done.

They had taken away his freedom, putting him in jail, taken away his legal rights to defend himself in court, taken away his rights of peaceful assembly with the buffer zone, and his freedom of speech to carry his signs with his own words, taken away his telephone and his house, taken away his reputation and disgraced him. They had destroyed his crisis pregnancy center, and he had lost his health through his dependence on painkiller drugs through all the stress. Today they had beaten him up. Most of all they had taken away his religious freedom to be a Christian who opposes abortion. He could only be pro-life if he did not interfere with abortion, which was not pro-life at all. They had him completely under their control.

66

*Not the Church, Not the State,
Women Must Decide Their Fate-
It's a Baby, It's a Baby*

He saw the police advancing closer in the swarming multitude. More reinforcements had arrived, and a phalanx of policemen was clearing a path to get to the pro-lifers blocking the abortion clinic doors. The police were not arresting the pro-abortion counter protesters, only clearing them out of the way to get to the pro-lifers, to get to Mickey Finnegan the leader. The police were dragging the pro-life demonstrators away and throwing them into the waiting police vans. Mickey saw Dennis Johnson dragged away, and Carol Conrad arrested. The police were dragging Dr. Lawrence to the vans, and then he saw Sgt. Ryan leading the policemen towards him. They were getting nearer and nearer, closing in on him. But now he did not want to get away. He wanted to stay and fight abortion. He had been on a false path to run away. Now he was on the true path. If he ran away abortion would win. He must do something, however small, even if he failed. Only if he quit would abortion triumph.

He saw two policemen carrying Dolores to one of the arrest vans. He was surprised she had gone limp in civil disobedience, forcing the police to physically remove her. He admired her new activism; she had always stuck with the counselling before. Something must have inspired her to want to do more even as she was leaving, even as he himself had changed in the morning's battle. The police were almost upon him. This was his moment of triumph, his victory over himself. He had been afraid of them, afraid of losing everything, losing the house, everything he had worked for his whole life. He was not afraid of them anymore. He felt new spiritual steel strengthen his soul. In a world worshipping only success, suffering would be his battle cry for the right to life.

The police were upon him now, encircling him, tightening the net. He turned to face Sgt. Ryan, ready to be arrested by the police. He hoped they would use the metal handcuffs. The plastic flex cuffs cut off the circulation in his wrists when they were tightly bound together. The plastic handcuffs hurt far worse than the metal ones. He hoped they would not handcuff his hands behind his back. He would not be able to wipe the blood out of his eyes. He saw David Ryan standing right in front of him, reaching out his hand to seize his arm and arrest him. Hell was reaching out for him, and would not let him go. He had a last moment to wipe his eyes. He took a deep breath. He said his last prayer:

Please God, do not leave me trapped here, with every way closed.

67

*Not the Church, Not the State,
Women must-*

An explosion from a bomb in a backpack left lying against the front doors of the Craigenback Abortion Clinic ripped through the rioting crowd. The blast blew the front doors off the hinges, leaving the gray steel twisted and crumpled, blackened from the heat. Shards of broken glass from the windows sprayed into the crowd, and the nails packed in the bomb wounded many more. Choking smoke and dust filled the air, coating the people. A huge cloud of debris and ash rose across the sky obscuring the morning sun. A smashed police car lay turned on its side, and the windows in the houses across the street, including the Crisis Pregnancy Center were blown apart. The sunny morning was turned upside down in darkness, full of smoke and noise, and dim shapes moving grimly in the shattered crowd.

People were lying everywhere, bleeding and moaning in pain, injured from the first blast of the bomb and from the scattered glass and shrapnel cutting the flesh of their bodies, pieces of glass and nails embedding themselves in many of the protesters on both sides. People from both sides of the struggle lay dead, their torn bodies bleeding on the cold cement of the sidewalk. Red flames of fire ate their way through the wooden frame of the house of Craigenback, while at the same moments a winter rain began, cold drizzle chilling the injured victims.

Sandy and Chrissie lay dead, their bodies twisted together in death lying on the ground. Charlie Kelly lay fallen beside them. Dennis Johnson was dazed, thrown out of the police van, wandering sightless through the crowd, his eardrums burst from the noise of the explosion, his eyes blinded by the dust. Carol Conrad lay groaning on the sidewalk, her left leg bent beneath her at an impossible angle, broken in three places. The police vans holding the pro-life prisoners lay tossed on their sides, twisted wrecks of metal, some of the prisoners like Dennis and Dolores thrown out of the vans, and some still trapped inside screaming for help.

Sgt. Ryan ran over to a woman lying on the sidewalk, people stepping on her in their panicked rush to get away. A sharp piece of glass was stuck in the woman's right eye. She was the one crawling over the heads of the massed crowd to get to the abortion clinic doors. He tried to comfort the woman, and shouted to one of his policemen: 'Radio for ambulances. Hurry.' News media cameramen scrambled to get pictures of the exciting surprise. Ryan shouted at them: 'Get away from her.' The bomb blast hit Mickey on his left side, knocking him to the ground. He struggled up, supporting himself on his right arm. His mangled left arm hung useless by his side, shredded by the blast, and his left leg was bleeding from a jagged wound in his thigh. He hobbled over to help David Ryan with the injured woman. She was bleeding from her entire face and eyes. Mickey wiped the blood out of her left eye with his good right hand, but he was afraid to touch her right eye with the piece of protruding glass. He held her hand as she gripped his right hand tightly, moaning: 'It hurts.'

'Hold on,' Mickey said. 'Help is coming.'

'Leave her alone,' Sincerity Burstall said, shoving Mickey out of the way, bending down to nurse the fallen woman herself. Mickey stood up, stepped back, and wiped the blood out of his own eyes. He had to use his right hand as he could not raise his left arm at all. He looked around at the carnage of the bleeding and moaning, screaming and frightened people. He was stunned. He had never believed the bomb threats were real. Who were these people? The one threatening phone call he received months ago from the Warriors of God was the only contact he ever had with them. Mickey was further saddened to see Ethel across the street, lying motionless on the ground in front of the Crisis Pregnancy Center, bleeding from beneath her orange coat, her ceaseless motion of her constant walking stopped at last. He saw Dolores lying unconscious on the sidewalk beside her, the police van which held her lying overturned on the road.

Then he heard the Evil One laugh.

68

Mickey felt on the raw skin of his bleeding face the healing touch of a warm wind rising in the cold winter air. He saw a shining light brightening the fringes of the gray rainclouds floating high above the battle in the city street below. The glowing winter sun broke through the clouds like a shaft of purity dancing in a patch of light blue, streaking white lightning flashed, a long low rumble of echoing thunder rocked his ears, and the earth quaked beneath his unsteady feet. Over his head he heard music in the air, the tolling of invisible great bells followed by the fanfare of trumpets. A multicolored rainbow arched above the sky, and the sweet scent of roses drifted across the smoke scorched air.

In the high firmament he saw the heavens were torn open, and the luminous form or a woman appeared. Her dress was dazzling white, with a blue mantle cloaking her long and golden hair. Her face was as radiant as the sun, She stood silent and still on the clouds, a foul black serpent twisting and turning trampled beneath her feet crushing its head, and she was bearing in her arms a wounded baby boy. The sad eyed woman gazed downward at the baby in her arms, all of her attention fastened on him, and she was weeping, her eyes full of tears falling, the baby lying so helpless and still, his wounded head fallen backwards on his partly severed neck.

The heavenly mother held the dying baby close to her breast

rocking him while the serpent thrashed beneath her feet, but she held on tight to the battered baby embraced close to her heart in death rocking him, and then she kissed him. His death was seen by her, buried in her arms, buried in her breast, buried in her heart, transfixed in her eyes weeping for him her arms rocking him. Mickey exclaimed: 'I love your tears,' and then, 'Mama Mary, Mama Mary, bring us peace.'

At the sight of the beautiful lady and the dying baby Mickey in the midst of hell felt a new and different kind of holy fear. He stood outside himself in a spiritual ecstasy. 'I'm sorry, I'm sorry,' he said, his heart full of sorrow yet exultant joy. His broken body still bleeding he fell to his knees, and bowed his head, kneeling in the bloodstained street at the abortion mill. He clasped his hands, and closed his eyes to pray, but moments later his body was roughly shaken. He opened his eyes, but the woman and baby were gone. A great gray cloud covered the sun, the sky was dark, hard rain drenched the earth, the wind was cold and wet, and the abortion clinic burned with fire red and black. Sgt. Ryan had grabbed his right arm, and was dragging him to his feet, arresting him.

69

'Mr. Finnegan, how do you plead?'

'Not guilty.'

They were the first words spoken by Mickey since his arrest. In his silence he refused to speak either to the police or the reporters, withdrawing into a private world far away. He heard all the talking around him, the processing policemen searching them, taking their information, taking their belts and shoelaces and watches, and marching them to the holding cell to await their arraignment, throwing the pro-lifers in with the general prison population. He heard the chatter among the prisoners, the exchanges between the prisoners and the guards on their rounds. He himself had said absolutely nothing. He was struck by all the words, everyone incessantly talking.

Words, words, words from everyone, a war of words, the war of tongues in the naked public square, God far removed. People were deaf and blind, not hearing or seeing the truth, not caring about it, but they were not mute. Everyone had an opinion or feeling or a need to be expressed in the speech of words. He longed for the peace of silence, but jail was not a place of silence or peace, the caged men in their unnatural loss of freedom all on edge, calling their bitter words down the concrete corridors from cell to cell.

The date was only December 29th, the day after the Feast

of the Holy Innocents. Still Christmas Day for Mickey as a Catholic, the Octave of Christmas, 8 days of joyful celebrations begun on Christmas Day.

'*Not guilty.*'

Mickey spoke out with a firm voice, not afraid or nervous anymore. He even felt an extraordinary happiness to be standing in front of Judge Dockendorff again, under armed guard, the policemen standing with their holstered guns around the walls of the courtroom, the reporters setting in the Press section, the public sitting on their benches behind the prisoners. He was glad he was here fighting for the right to life, instead of flying free on an airplane to somewhere else, running away. He would face things as they are, and stand up for the lives of the unborn children, and see it through to the end in his fallen country of Canada. Divine mysteries had been revealed to him. Would anyone understand his unexpected joy? He was in the thick of it now; he was all in. Standing beside him were other pro-lifers arrested the day before, also facing their arraignment.

The eleven defendants were dressed in the standard jail issue of orange jump suits, the burnt smell from the smoke of the bomb still on their bodies and hair, their feet chained together and hobbled by leg irons. Dolores was standing beside him. She had regained consciousness but was still shaken up by the force of the blast. She also pleaded Not Guilty. Sincerity Burstall sat in the front row of court benches behind the railing, her arm in a sling. Mickey stood with his left arm in a splint, with tension bandages wrapped around the thigh of his left leg, and around his waist under the jumpsuit. The bandage was damp and sticky with blood still seeping out of his side. The prison infirmary had treated his wounds, but had not given him any painkillers. His head and body ached, but he did not want the deadly pills anymore. He was exhausted, but his mind was clear, and how explain the peace in his soul? Sincerity glared at Mickey, back to playing his legal games. *How could he possibly plead Not Guilty she wondered.* Even Smiling Jake Corcoran in his press release said Mickey and the other protesters at Craigenback's were criminals who were not part of the Pro-life movement. Sincerity did not believe Smiling Jake's spin-doctoring and public relations distancing ploy, but his statement would be useful to convict Mickey as a criminal at last.

Jessica Sterne rose to speak. 'Your Honor, the facts in this case are indisputable. Despite your clear warning the last time we were all here before you in this very same courtroom, the defendant Mickey Finnegan and the other defendants returned to the Craigenback Abortion Clinic and blocked the doorways, interfering with the legal rights of access to health care for women. Dr. Craigenback has been murdered. The clinic is a bombed out shell. Innocent people have died. This pro-life terrorism must be stopped, and now these people who make a mockery of the rule of law want a trial and a platform to grandstand for the news media and preach their cause. I beg you do not let these fetus fanatics use the court.'

'I am well aware Mr. Finnegan is a powerless man who would unleash the power of the court if he could,' Judge Dockendorff said.

'But we have rights to defend ourselves,' Mickey said.

'Charges are not convictions, simply because we are accused. We have the right to present evidence we were not part of any violence towards the abortion mill. The woman who killed Dr. Craigenback was an unhappy former patient of his, a woman he harmed. She was not a member of the pro-life movement. Abortion is the real violence, the real terrorism against women and children. The woman Sadie Summers was destroyed by it. We want to present evidence on that. One has to be out of jail to investigate and collect evidence. The right to answer your accusers is fundamental in our society under the rule of law.'

Judge Dockendorff was not going to have Mickey Finnegan teach him the law again.

'Do not lecture me Mr. Finnegan. You were warned. The warning was deliberately ignored, with the most damaging insurrection hurting the good people and institutions of our society. You are all in very serious trouble. I suggest once again you get a lawyer. You are facing criminal charges this time.'

'We can't afford a lawyer, and no one will help us voluntarily. We have legal rights to defend ourselves. We need time to prepare our defense. A rush to judgment cannot be pushed through today. This is only the arraignment, not the trial.'

'You will have your trial Mr. Finnegan. But you will all be remanded into custody prior to the trial. You will not be let loose upon this community again. Your extremism has become extremely dangerous.'

Mickey stood his ground, his head held high, his shoulders back, his spine straight, his chest open and expanded outwards. Dockendorff could not know yet the changes within him.

'We are not extremists. You can't blame what happened on us. Our people were injured and killed too. I reiterate, it will be difficult to prepare for trial from a jail cell.'

'Then accept the court appointed lawyer. If you insist on defending yourselves, you must accept your limitations as prisoners.'

'Is there any answer we can make to the charges, or is your mind already made up?'

Dockendorff ignored the accusation of bias. 'I am not a lawyer, Mr. Finnegan. Don't ask me for legal advice.'

'I have always shown up for court hearings. And I have always spoken out against violence.'

'Not this time, Your Honor,' Jessica Sterne said. 'Nothing could be further from the truth. Mr. Finnegan is a flight risk. When he was arrested he was found to have an international airplane ticket and his passport in his pockets. His house was recently sold, and the money went missing. I might add the pro-life accusations of baby-killing, years of protests, and disruptive sit-ins at the abortion clinic trying to close it down are all evidences of shared responsibility for the eventual open violence. He should be denied bail. He is an extremist.'

'Your Honor-'

'I agree,' Judge Dockendorff said, cutting off Mickey. 'There will be no bail for you Mr. Finnegan. You ignored the rulings and warnings of this court and now you must face the consequences. These proceedings are adjourned, until the trial. Guards, take the prisoners back to their cells. Put Mr.

Finnegan in solitary, isolated from the others. Sedate him if necessary, and put him on suicide watch,' he ordered.

'I must insist we are not responsible for the violence,' Mickey said.

'There will be a day of reckoning for you Mr. Finnegan,' Judge Dockendorff said as he rose to leave the courtroom.

70

Only Sadie's divorced father and mother, and her twin brother Sean attended her rushed funeral at Sacred Heart Church. Her parents did not sit together. Sean also sat by himself. Her old boyfriend Rick was nowhere to be found. Mickey and Dolores were in jail, and Julie with baby Jeffrey had disappeared.

Sadie's closed casket was placed in the front of the church, before the altar, the simple coffin covered with a white cloth placed over it, the pall, symbolizing the innocence of her day of baptism. A small metal crucifix lay at the head of the coffin. A photograph of her from younger days when she was still pretty, encased in a wooden frame behind glass, was also placed at the head of her coffin. The flickering flames of the sanctuary candles gleamed on the burnished wood. The large Christ candle was lit, and two small bouquets of funeral flowers, red roses and white carnations, flanked the altar. The scent of the flowers mingled with the aroma of the burnt incense Fr. MacIntyre had used to bless the altar and her casket.

At the other end of town, Dr. Nathan Craigenback was buried in a magnificent High Mass at Saint Mary's Cathedral, attended by over 2,000 mourners packing the church, the funeral presided over by His Excellency Bishop Horace Blair, surrounded by several of the Calgary priests.

All the dignitaries of the city attended, including the Mayor Kathy Winters, the Honorable Judge Lester Dockendorff, and Jeremiah Patrick, Publisher of the Daily Record. Dr. Craigenback's wife, Christina Alice Craigenback, a Catholic journalist who wrote a weekly column for the Record, attended with her bodyguard. She had written her latest column on pro-life terrorism, how she and her family had suffered for years living in fear for their safety. Craigenback's mistress sat silent in the last pew in the back of the church. A large photograph of Dr. Craigenback graced the newspaper accounts of his assassination, and several reporters and photographers from both the print and television news media were present at the funeral. Banks of flowers surrounded Dr. Craigenback's ornate brass casket, an expensive one as befitting his prominent social status, while the Cathedral choir sang Mozart's Requiem to the accompaniment of a full chamber orchestra.

The Craigenback family had requested in the newspaper obituary that in lieu of flowers donations be made in Dr. Craigenback's memory to the Craigenback Fund for Common Ground, for the relief of poor women who could not afford abortions. The obituary notice was the only reference to abortion, which was not mentioned at all throughout the funeral. Dr. Craigenback's dedicated service to the community as a doctor who bravely stood for his principles throughout his distinguished career was eulogized by the speakers. Bishop Blair canonized Dr. Craigenback, encouraging his listeners this day there was surely more joy in heaven to welcome him home.

'The Church does not judge,' Bishop Blair had preached. 'We leave the judgment to God. Society is changing, and the understanding of the Church is changing. We must take the logs out of our own eyes before taking the grain of dust out of our neighbor's eyes.'

At Sadie's funeral, the white haired Catholic priest Fr. MacIntyre walked unsteadily to the pulpit beside her coffin, using a cane. His thin body was emaciated after years of ascetic self-denial, never eating after a light supper in the evening to the next morning's even lighter breakfast. He was retired, but the shortage of the priests in the city forced him to continue serving the people, whenever a need arose the younger priests could not or did not want to handle. Fr. MacIntyre wanted the funeral ritual of the Church to comfort the three mourners. He decided it was best not to preach a long homily in the empty cavern of the church. He did not know Sadie, and did not know what to say in the extraordinary circumstances of her suicide with the sin of murder on her soul. It was best to say nothing. When he reached the lectern, he paused for a moment. Then he said the same thing as Bishop Blair, speaking softly but firmly in his elderly voice.

> **'The Church does not judge. We leave the judgments to God. Sadie was first welcomed into the Church as an infant, when the waters of baptism plunged her soul into the death and resurrection of Christ, and wiped away her share in original sin. Now Sadie will be buried within the Church, in consecrated ground.**

That was his only oblique reference to the circumstances of Sadie's death. Her parents and her brother listened intently to Fr. MacIntyre's voice speaking just to them. Could they have done anything to prevent Sadie's suicide? How had they failed her? What signs had they missed? Truth was they had lost touch with her and never saw her for some time. Fr. MacIntyre continued his brief funeral sermon.

'We commend Sadie to the understanding and love and mercy of Almighty God. May she rest in peace. We will remember her in our prayers, and in our tears. The child of such tears can never be lost. Be consoled. Now we take our final farewell of Sadie, but you will see your daughter and sister again, in God's Kingdom to come.'

Pausing once more to look out at the congregation of three people, Fr. MacIntyre no longer knew what to say. He bowed his head, and closed his eyes in a moment of silent prayer. Then he lifted his head and looked at the people, and sighed. He was tired. Soon it would be his turn to meet the Lord. He half turned from the pulpit to face Sadie's coffin, raised his frail right hand, and silently made the sign of the cross over her. Then he turned to face the people, and raised his hand again, making the sign of the cross over them.

71

Mickey woke with his right wrist chained to the frame of the hard metal bed, and both his legs shackled with leg irons. The cell was shrouded in darkness, dim illumination penetrating from the light bulbs in the corridor outside. He swung his chained legs over the side of the bed, the only range of motion he could perform with his manacled and aching body, and sat on the edge of the thin mattress. His injured leg hurt, as did his shattered left arm, hanging useless by his wounded side stabbed by a spasm of pain. His temples throbbed with a new headache. He had been pushed beyond all possible endurance, beyond the last of his strength. He had reached his limits, with nothing left to give. He leaned his painful head in his chained right hand, supported by his elbow resting on his knee while he sat on the unforgiving bed of the silent jail cell. He closed his eyes again, withdrawing inward. All the recent events were too much to take in so quickly.

His thoughts turned to Dolores. In the silence he did not know she had been placed in the holding cell beside him. He had long known what solitary confinement was like; he had become a pariah even among the pro-lifers. Now he sat alone detained in a darkened cell, silent and invisible to the rest of the world, like a baby in the womb.

'Mickey, are you there?'

'Dolores, is that you?'

'I'm in the cell beside you. Mickey, I'm scared. What's going to happen to us now?'

'I don't know. I'm a little disoriented, trying to understand what's going on.'

'We never expected it would come to this.'

'Just a minute.'

He heard the unlikely sound of singing coming down the corridor outside his cell. Two guards were making their rounds, and they were intoxicated with the holiday partying, even on their shift at work. They were singing back and forth to each other in jolly good cheer.

'Jingle Bells, Jingle Bells, Jingle all the way,
Oh what fun it is to ride in a one horse open sleigh…'

one guard was singing, while the other guard answered him in a competing song:

'Here comes Santa Claus, Here comes Santa Claus,
Right down Santa Claus lane…'

The two guards laughed at their raucous mismatched singing, carefree in their happy holiday serenade. They stopped their walking and singing when they reached Mickey's cell, and he heard them whispering through the gaps between the bars. The guards kept a frequent watch on him, shining their flashlights into the darkened cell, writing down everything he did and said for their report to the court psychiatrist.

He did not have anything more to say to them, and there was nothing he could do chained to the bed, so there were not many observations in the notebooks kept by the guards. The guards were ordered not to speak to him, only observe him. He opened his eyes to look upward from where he was sitting towards the guards standing outside his cell. They were exchanging comments in low voices, and pointing and laughing at him. The guards broke the rules and spoke to him, their taunts scourging his spirit, whipping him with words.

'You made quite a show for a while Mickey, but look at you now. You anti-abortion fanatics are finished. You have failed. Finnegan, you're a failure.'

'Extremists,' the other guard said. 'We have you crazies under control now.'

'Loser,' the first guard said. 'Goof.'

'You've made no difference. Do you know that?' the other guard said.

The first guard thought that was hilarious, pitching forward in laughter, placing his hands on his knees.

Judge Dockendorff and the guards were right. He had failed. Nothing would change because of his life in pro-life. Mickey closed his eyes again. He thought once more of Dolores, worried about her. Best not to speak to her in front of the guards. He prayed the beautiful lady would come back to him. The mockery continued. 'Are you praying, Mickey?' the first guard said. 'Don't you know that's nothing? Nothing exists but here.'

'Yeah,' the second guard, a lapsed Catholic said. 'You're

praying to yourself. It's auto-suggestion. It's as crazy as kneeling and worshipping a piece of bread.'

Mickey kept on praying. He prayed, sinner that he was, that whenever death came it would find him in a state of grace. Then the beautiful lady appeared above him, smiling at him, extending her arms towards him, reaching out to him to come into her warm embrace. He smiled back at her.

'The end has come,' the first guard said, his eyes gleaming with hate. 'The end has come. He's ignoring us, won't even look at us. We'll show him who is boss. Back me up on this. The prisoner created a violent disturbance. He attacked us. Let's see if this gets his attention.'

'I don't know,' the other guard said. 'It looks suspicious. We will have some explaining to do.'

'We can say anything. They're prolifers"

The first guard pulled his gun out of his holster and fired once through the bars, shooting Mickey in the face. Mickey slumped and twisted sideways, his body crumpling to the hard stone floor of the prison cell, blood flowing down his cheeks, his shackled legs splayed beneath him, his outstretched arm chained to the metal bed, his arm bent behind him still pointing upwards in the air. In his last moments his mind took flight elsewhere. He saw himself as a younger man, full of life and energy and zeal, full of hope, buying tools in the hardware store to renovate the old house, and shopping for furniture and desks in the second hand store to begin a pro-life counselling center to help the unborn children and their mothers, and talking to people in his church, recruiting them to volunteer to help in the work. Then he breathed his last, and remembered no more.

'You got him,' the second guard said, nodding his satisfaction. 'He never made it.'

72

'What about the other one? She heard us, saw us.'

'You mean the brown mousey woman, the fat one arrested with him?'

'Yeah, she's a witness in her cell next door.'

'Mickey are you okay?' Dolores called out, 'I heard voices, and a gunshot, even here in the jail. Mickey?'

But there was no answer, only silence. The two guards whispered between them.

'What is she doing here? She belongs in a separate female jail. Not here with the men.'

'You're still new. These are the first holding cells for the prisoners when they are arrested, before being processed through the system.

'Why are only these two here. There were a lot more arrested at the demonstration.'

'I think they were identified as the ring leaders, put here for special treatment.'

'I'll take care of her.'

'What do we do now?'

'Special Treatment.'

'How explain that? A woman alone in a locked cell guarded by two men?'

'We could plant a gun on her, say she was attacking us, shooting at us?'

'That's improbable. They were all already searched at intake before they got this far. There are no visitors allowed here. Where would she get a gun? I don't like it.'

'You got any better ideas?'

The guard who shot Mickey walked over to the cell holding Dolores. He looked in at her. She cowered against the far wall of the cell, her fingers holding the medal of Mary on the chain around her neck. He unlocked the door and entered, her cell too as dark as a baby's womb. Dolores felt very afraid, but she knew there was nothing she could do. Then the other guard came into her cell.

'What did you do to Mickey?' she asked.

'Get down on your knees,' the first guard said.

'Why?'

'Just do what I say, do what you're told.'

Dolores obeyed him and knelt. She felt like it was the same position when she knelt for prayer in church. She felt for Mary on the chain about her neck.

The first guard took out his gun and placed it against Dolores' head at the back of her skull, pressing the gun into the top of her neck.

'They call this the coup de grace in war,' he said.

'The kill shot,' the first guard said.

'The mafia always like two shots in the head, just to make sure,'

Dolores was trembling in fear yet silently prayed to Our Lady to protect her, and she remained so worried about Mickey. *Why were they trying to terrify her? This was a cruel way to treat prisoners. They could get in trouble for this.*

'Mickey,' she cried out to him again, "Mickey.'

The guard pulled the trigger and shot Dolores who collapsed dead on the jail cell floor. Then the guard walked behind her fallen body and shot her a second time in the back of her head.

He smiled at the other guard.

"Just to make sure.'

'It's an execution,' the other guard said. 'We can never explain this, never come up with a story that will hold up and fit all the facts.'

'Not to worry,' the first guard said, stepping over the slumped body of Dolores, her limp fingers still touching the medallion of Mary.

'They're pro-lifers. You can say anything you want about them. They are nothing.'

'Watch your boots.' the other guard said. 'It's a messy pool of blood and brains there.'

73

Julie sat in the straight-backed chair in a cheap motel room, rocking baby Jeffrey in her arms. The room was cold, and although she had asked the manager to turn up the heat and he promised he would, she could feel no difference. She pulled the shawl she wore up over her head to keep in her body warmth. The wool shawl was one knitted by her mother and given to her at Christmas, navy blue in color, covering her head and shoulders, flowing over her white nightgown. As she rocked Jeffrey to sleep he yawned his little mouth, and screwed up his face and eyes. He stretched his arms and legs, wiggling the fingers and toes of his tiny hands and feet, arching his body into hers, burrowing close into the comforting presence of her breast. She sang to him to help him sleep:

> **Hush little baby, don't you cry,**
> **Momma's going to sing you a lullaby.**

She did not like the feeling of being on the run, but after Christmas at her parents, and seeing the news reports on television about Craigenback's, and hearing of the suspicious deaths of Mickey and Dolores in the jail, she did not want to return to Calgary. She felt more protected in the small town of Cochrane on the outskirts of the big city, and would soon make her way on the bus to the safety of a new life in Vancouver in British Columbia, just over the Rocky Mountains. She had cousins living there who would take her and Jeffrey in.

She did not know if anyone was even looking for her, but she did not want to be questioned about anything she might know. A lowly receptionist in the Crisis Pregnancy Center, she would be under the radar, except for crazy Dora and Sara who would be telling the authorities everything they knew about everyone, and making all their accusations. But Dora and Sara did not know about her contacts with the Warriors of God, and the Warriors did not know anymore where she was, or how to contact her since she had closed her email account.

Jeffrey was restless, unable to sleep, crying a little. He seemed to sense things were not right with his mother. He snuggled closer into her, closing his eyes, and sighed. Julie hoped for rest, and the happiness soon of a new life in the future, but dreaded the worst from her past, and all the fallout from the insanity of the abortion war. As she waited for the bus departure tomorrow morning, she continued softly singing lullabies, rocking Jeffrey in her arms, the blue shawl about her head and shoulders covering the both of them, the twilight darkening outside the motel window, the dim bulb under the lampshade casting a warm light in the room:

> *Rock-a-bye baby, in the treetop*
> *When the wind blows, the cradle will rock*
> *When the bough breaks, the cradle will fall*
> *And down will come baby, cradle and all.*

74

Marie's contractions were coming more quickly, her pains overwhelming. She cried out, squeezing her husband's hand as she lay on the gurney in the hospital corridor, waiting to be wheeled into the delivery room. He squeezed her hand back, and wiped the sweat from her brow, murmuring tender words of support and encouragement. Labor had come on her so suddenly they were not prepared, the ambulance coming in response to the late night call to take her to the hospital. She remembered the ambulance paramedic softly singing Away In A Manger, and commenting on the pretty lights decorating the houses they passed to distract her and keep her calm. The lights were shining everywhere in the darkness of the cold winter night as the ambulance raced through the deserted city streets.

'The doctor is hurrying, it won't be long now,' John said.

Another contraction came, and she screamed again.

'I can't bear it anymore,' she said. 'I'm going to die.'

'No, no. You will soon be fine, happy with our first born child.'

'Don't leave me John.'

'I'm here.'

'John, if I die and you're left alone, I know what name I want for our baby.'

'You never told me that before.'

She panted, gasping for breath: 'I never told you many things.'

'Try to rest now.'

'I must tell you in case I don't make it. It bothers me. I never told you but when I first missed my period I went to this place I found in the phone book. I was thinking of an abortion. You were out of work, and the time didn't seem right to have a baby.'

'Some place in the phone book?'

'Yeah, I just went there. I didn't want to call first. It was a Saturday afternoon and it was closed. It was in a house and a man came to the front door, holding a book under his arm he was reading.'

She moaned as a sudden contraction bent her body. Breathing hard, she wanted to keep talking to John.

'It was a big, fat, hard covered book, colored red. I asked him what he was reading, and he said it was a law book. I asked him why he was reading it, and he said he was going to sue the newspaper for libel.'

'I never heard of the case.'

'There wasn't much news about it. He lost.'

'That's enough talk for now.'

'I want to tell you this. The man said he would help me, even though none of the women counselors were there. He gave me a pregnancy test, and I watched a video, and then we talked.'

'You never told me any of this.'

'I was too ashamed I ever considered abortion. I learned so much from the man, and I changed my mind. So I never told you about it.'

'You showed me the pregnancy test. You seemed so happy when you told me, and I got a job later. It all worked out.'

'John, I learned some other things about the man. He was never married, had no kids of his own, but he worked all the time so other people could have children.'

'Sounds like a good man.'

'I thought then, and I know it now. I wanted to name our child after him. There was something about him. I didn't meet him for long, but I always remembered him.'

'We could use his name, maybe. We don't know yet if it is a boy or a girl.'

'The name would fit both.'

The doctor was running down the hallway, the nurse behind him. The orderlies began to wheel her into the operating room, John still holding her hand, keeping pace with the gurney.

'Marie, what's the name?' John asked at the last moment. 'What is the name of our child?'

Marie smiled at him through her pain and labored breathing, panting and gasping for breath.

'Mickey.'

75

Later that same morning a child was playing. His name was Scotty, his mother Linda, the first client of the Crisis Pregnancy Center who changed her mind so long ago, the one who showed Mickey it was worth advertising in the phone book to have the chance to talk to people who thought they wanted an abortion. Dolores was the counsellor that day who reached her. She had always felt Scotty was her boy too in a way.

Now Linda sat in the chilly air in the seats at the ice rink, watching the early morning hockey game twelve years later. Scotty wobbled on his skates, but it didn't matter to Linda rooting for him. Scotty looked up at the stands to see his mother when he heard her encouragement. She smiled proudly at her son in the bulky hockey uniform fully encasing his child's body. He wanted to impress his Mom.

Scotty took a pass from another player, the black puck banging against the blade of his hockey stick. Skating unsurely, he felt like he was racing towards the other team's goal, a winger with a deadly slap shot. Another boy bumped into him, checking him, and Scotty went down, sprawling on the ice, his rush down the ice to score blocked, Scotty losing the puck to the other player. He scrambled to his feet, and chased the other team the other way back down the ice. Scotty caught up with the other player and stick handled the puck away from him.

The other boy then fell on the ice too. Scotty turned and skated down the ice alone towards the other team's goalie who awaited his breakaway rush. No one could catch him, as all the young boys were just learning to skate, but Scotty as unsteady as he was felt like he was just too fast for the rest of the players chasing him. He saw himself as the most dangerous shooter in the league as he bore down shakily on the opposing team's goal at the far end of the ice rink. Linda along with the other parents in the stands all jumped to their feet to cheer him on:

Hurray! Hurray!

www.ingramcontent.com/pod-product-compliance
Lightning Source LLC
Chambersburg PA
CBHW031400290426
44110CB00011B/220